Gilbert Szlumper and Leo Amery of the Southern Railway

John King

PEN & SWORD TRANSPORT

AN IMPRINT OF PEN & SWORD BOOKS LTD.
YORKSHIRE – PHILADELPHIA

First published in Great Britain in 2018 by
Pen & Sword TRANSPORT
An imprint of
Pen & Sword Books Ltd
Yorkshire - Philadelphia

ISBN 9781473835276

A CIP catalogue record for this book is
available from the British Library.

Printed and bound by Replika Press Pvt. Ltd.

Pen & Sword Books Ltd incorporates the Imprints of
Pen & Sword Archaeology, Atlas, Aviation, Battleground, Discovery, Family
History, History, Maritime, Military, Naval, Politics, Railways, Select,
Transport, True Crime, Fiction, Frontline Books, Leo Cooper, Praetorian
Press, Seaforth Publishing, Wharncliffe and White Owl.

For a complete list of Pen & Sword titles please contact
PEN & SWORD BOOKS LIMITED
47 Church Street, Barnsley, South Yorkshire, S70 2AS, England
E-mail: enquiries@pen-and-sword.co.uk
Website: www.pen-and-sword.co.uk

Contents

Acknowledgements

The work for this publication has been greatly facilitated by a number of people, most of them being the staff of various archives and libraries. They include Churchill College at Cambridge where Amery's diaries are held and the Imperial War Museum in London which holds Szlumper's diaries. I am also grateful to the staff of the Library at the National Railway Museum and of Southampton Local Studies & Maritime Library for assistance with photographs and other records. Other institutions include Dover Museum, Dover Library, the National Archives at Kew, the libraries of the Institute of Civil Engineers and of the London School of Economics.

Many others have helped including Gilbert Kendzior (Gilbert Szlumper's grandson) in North Carolina, the Old Southeronians' Association, the LMS Society, the Railway & Canal Historical Society and Dover Ferry Photos. Last but not least, John Scott-Morgan of the publisher must not be forgotten for his patience and encouragement.

I have attempted to detail the copyright holder of photographs but in some cases I have been unable to discover the identity.

Introduction

The diaries of leading railway managers and directors can be very interesting if they reveal the workings of the company, the character of its people and its internal politics, especially when many primary records have not survived as in the case of the Southern Railway. Unfortunately few diaries appear to have been kept by such people and even fewer have survived to enter the public domain. In the case of Leopold Amery who was a director of the Southern Railway from 1932, his diaries have not only survived but have been published at length. Unfortunately the publisher limited them to Amery's political life with the result that the entries on the railway and other business activities were largely omitted. This was unfortunate as Amery was usually at meetings at the Waterloo headquarters at least twice a week until 1940. The entries themselves are, however, a little disappointing as they were brief and rarely revealed any insight into developments and people. Nevertheless they do add some relevant information that is not available elsewhere. Amery's autobiography was also disappointing and contained little on the Southern Railway and other directorships, all of which he took very seriously.

By contrast, the diary entries of Gilbert Szlumper who was General Manager of the Southern Railway from 1937, were very rich in comments on developments and people but unfortunately only started in 1936 and initially were very uneven with many gaps. It is not known whether Gilbert kept diaries in his early years but he sometimes made no entries in the mid-1930s for weeks at a time. Szlumper's diaries were, however, very revealing in their portrayal of relationships in the head office at Waterloo. Previous histories of the Southern have tended to portray the railway as a very happy family. These diaries have revealed this to be somewhat of an exaggeration. His diaries were also interesting where they revealed his anguish in his relations with the General Manager, Sir Herbert Walker, to whom he was deputy for several years. Later they revealed his greater anguish over his inability to get back to the position at Waterloo that he vacated temporarily at the beginning of the war. It is surprising that his diaries have not been published before. There is some evidence that they have been examined by historians and others but they have been little mentioned and never quoted.

The unevenness of the 1930 entries is, in part, compensated by the war years, although Gilbert was no longer working for the railway. But he was still involved in transport and made some very detailed and interesting entries. His comments on the military world, the social scene in the war and the workings of Whitehall where in effect he was working as an unpaid civil servant, were also important.

A shrewd judge of character, his opinions of people were always interesting. In most cases, it has been easy to identify nearly all the people as so many of them were amongst the great and good in transport, the Civil Service and politics. In addition, Szlumper often explained who people were and even recorded times of meetings and trains. It is interesting just how many people the two diarists knew.

It has not been practical to detail every entry of the two while several entries have been edited. In many cases, the actual words have been reproduced but in several cases a narrative style has been adopted in the interest of the flow of words and brevity. Amery's railway entries ceased in 1940 when he returned to government service and resigned his directorships but Szlumper's diary continued until 1945.

In an ideal world, records of many railway policy meetings and correspondence would have survived but in the case of the Southern Railway, many were destroyed by enemy action on Waterloo or were later disposed of without authority while others never came into the public domain and disappeared. The diaries are therefore very important in that they contain details of meetings, conversations and sentiments that the historian would not otherwise discover.

John King,
Grove Park, London SE12

Chapter One

❧❧

Setting the Scene

Leopold Amery and Gilbert Szlumper were born within twelve years of one another in the nineteenth century. They had some points in common but in many ways were very different. They were both very conscientious, hard working and professional. They both went to primary schools in Brighton and then to schools of note; and they both went to university colleges. Involvement in the Southern Railway was of course something else they had in common, Amery as a director and Szlumper as an employee. They both kept diaries but that broadly was the extent of their commonality.

Leopold Charles Maurice Stennett Amery was born on 22 November 1873. He never appeared to have an interest in railways until 1932 when he became a director of the Southern Railway which was largely the result of the need to improve his finances by company directorships. He was essentially a journalist, historian and politician but with the reputation of a statesman. His primary education was at small schools in Brighton, Cologne and Folkestone. At Harrow School, he excelled and this continued at Balliol College at Oxford. His early career was academic as a fellow at All Saints College in Oxford, although this was mixed with journalism from 1899 when he also joined the staff of *The Times* newspaper. With a great intellect, he had a capacity and appetite for work. According to the Dictionary of National Biography (DNB), he acquired a reputation for rejecting prevailing philosophical and economic orthodoxies. In 1908 he turned down the editorship of *The Times* for politics; and in 1912 he turned down the editorship of *The Observer*. He kept a diary from 1910 which was the year that he married Florence Greenwood. The following year he was elected as Conservative Member of Parliament for South Birmingham, later Sparkbrook, which seat he held until 1945.

In the First World War, he served as an intelligence officer in various theatres. In 1916 he was appointed Assistant Secretary to Maurice Hankey at the War Cabinet Secretariat. In 1919 he progressed to Parliamentary Under-Secretary of State at the Colonial Office. Two years later he was Parliamentary & Financial Secretary to the Admiralty and in October 1922, he rose to be First Lord of the Admiralty. From 1924 Amery was Secretary of State for the Colonies, a post which he had coveted. From 1925 he was at the same time Secretary of State

Amery poses for the camera.

for the Dominions. He held the posts until the change of government in 1929. It was during his office that there were some real achievements in the policy of colonial development. The DNB entry noted that few in the cabinet had his versatility and breadth of experience of the world but at the same time he did not command commensurate influence. Contemporaries maintained that he was ineffective in discussion, spoke too often and for too long. But he never bore grudges and easily shrugged off disappointments.

Gilbert Savil Szlumper was born on 18 April 1884 at Kew. He was one of a family of distinguished railway civil engineers who had descended from Albert Szlumper, an immigrant from Poland. Albert's first son, James, was involved as a civil engineer in the construction of railways in Wales and England. It was from Albert's second marriage that Alfred was born in 1858. Articled to his brother James, Alfred was also involved in railway construction work in Wales. After serving as Engineering Assistant of the South Eastern Railway in 1880, Alfred was Resident Engineer on a railway in India until 1883 when he returned to England to join the London & South Western Railway where he became involved in widening works and bridge reconstructions. In 1914 he became Chief Engineer of the railway and in 1923 was appointed to the same post upon the formation of the Southern Railway.

Alfred's son, Gilbert, attended schools in Brighton and Putney. In 1898 he went to King's College School at Wimbledon but was only there for two years. Little is known about his days at this prestigious school but he did become a cadet in the London Rifle Brigade, setting a course for a long involvement in volunteer army life. He continued his education in 1900 at the university of King's College, London. For reasons unknown, he did not appear to take his studies to degree level, leaving after two years. In 1902 he joined the London & South Western Railway as a cadet in his father's department. This gave him varied indoor and outdoor experience, going through the drawing offices of the engineering department. In 1904, he was resident engineer in charge of building the light railway from

Bentley to Bordon in Hampshire. In 1905 he undertook the examination of the strength of cast-iron bridges to ascertain their ability to take the load of increasing road transport. From 1908 he was involved in alignment improvements and for the three succeeding years was Chief Assistant in the railway's Eastleigh District. From May 1913 to February 1914, he was in charge of trackwork and cable-laying for the suburban electrification.

It was towards the end of the year of joining the railway that Gilbert became a rifleman in the 16th, London Queen's Westminster Volunteers. When the Volunteer Force was re-organised in 1908, merging with the Yeomanry to become the Territorial Force, Gilbert transferred to the Kent (Fortress) Engineers of the Royal Engineers at Chatham, rising to lieutenant in 1910. Transferring to Work Companies Hants (Fortress) Royal Engineers, he subsequently took command of the Eastleigh Company. During this period he studied to qualify as a civil engineer. In 1913 he married Jessie Salter.

In 1914 Gilbert moved to management when on 13 February he became Assistant to the General Manager, the then Herbert Walker, a man he would work closely with for much of the ensuing twenty-three years. Walker had just become Acting Chairman of the shadow Railway Executive Committee [REC] which would co-ordinate the work of the railways in the event of war. Walker subsequently asked Gilbert to be Secretary of the REC which he did. When only a few months later planning became reality, Szlumper acquired a more or less full-time job for the duration of the war. During this period, he became Captain in the Engineer & Railway Staff Corps and Major in 1916.

Gilbert Szlumper returned to the railway at the end of 1919 to become the Deputy Docks & Marine Manager at Southampton, and the following year the Docks & Marine Manager. This coincided with the railway's plans to expand the port of Southampton and he became very involved with the project which would involve the reclamation of a large area of mud land. With the grouping of the railways on 1 January 1923, Szlumper became Docks & Marine Manager of the Southern Railway, thus becoming responsible for several ports in the south of England and the railway's fifty-two ships. The ships were based at Southampton, Dover, Folkestone, Newhaven and Portsmouth, although only Southampton, Folkestone and Newhaven were owned and managed by the railway. The railway also provided services across the Solent between Portsmouth and Ryde and between Lymington and Yarmouth.

The developments at Southampton culminated at the end of June 1924 in the opening of the largest floating dock in the world. Nearly a year later, Szlumper returned to Waterloo to the new post of Assistant General Manager. The Southern Railway's staff magazine of May 1925 announced his appointment with acclaim:

Szlumper in his Southampton office in 1923. (*Southampton Local Studies Library*)

> He has proved himself a man of outstanding ability, allied with
> amazing energy, a sympathetic temperament and a persuasiveness that
> is irresistible. He has not only commanded the esteem and affection
> of his own staff but throughout the Southern Railway his unique and
> charming personality has left its impression, and with all grades the
> news of his appointment has been received with the utmost satisfaction.

In the meantime, more plans to continue the expansion of Southampton were
evolving. In 1928 Gilbert was raised to the rank of Lieutenant-Colonel in the
Territorial Army.

It was legislation in 1928 that enabled the railways to operate bus and
road haulage services. The main line railways subsequently acquired controlling
interests in several bus operators. The action of the railways was protracted and
generally concerted, although there were deviations. In the case of the Southern,
the first development was in conjunction with the National Omnibus & Transport
Company. This led to the formation of the Southern National Omnibus Company
in Dorset and adjoining counties at the beginning of 1929, the Southern holding
half of the shares while Szlumper became the railway's director on the bus
company's board. It was followed by the railway acquiring an interest in the Vectis
Bus Service in the Isle of Wight. At the end of August 1929, a new company
was formed, Southern Vectis Omnibus Co Ltd, with fifty per cent of the shares
held by the railway which accordingly nominated fifty per cent of the directors.

Szlumper became the chairman of the new company with a registered office at Waterloo. Meanwhile, negotiations at a higher and national level continued between the railways and the holding company, Tilling & British Automobile Traction Ltd. When agreement was reached, the Southern became part owner of several bus companies at the beginning of 1930. Thus it was that Szlumper became nominee director on the boards of another six bus companies but not chairman. Very little is known about the part he played in the subsequent deliberations of the bus companies, the minutes of the companies being rather uninformative while he would rarely mention them in his diaries. Involvement by the railways in road haulage companies would come later.

It was during Szlumper's years as Assistant General Manager that the Southern's development continued with electrification of suburban lines over a wide area with the resultant subsequent increase in passenger journeys, the introduction of new ships and the expansion of facilities at Southampton. During this period, Szlumper gave a number of addresses to a variety of organisations which included the Institute of Transport and the Railway Students Association – he had been a founding member of the former in 1920. In his talks, he demonstrated a clear thinking and an ability to challenge the conventional wisdom. He was often outspoken.

Chapter Two

❧❧❧

The Amery Diaries, 1932-35

The exact circumstances of how L.S. Amery came to join the board of the Southern Railway are not clear, but it was most likely that an approach came from a director, probably the railway's Chairman, Everard Baring, if he knew that Amery was seeking directorships which he needed to sustain his lifestyle. What is clear is that at the railway's board meeting on 26 November 1931, it was recorded that the Member of Parliament, Hilton Young, the later Lord Kennett, had resigned from the board as he had just joined the government and that upon the motion of the chairman, Amery was co-opted to fill the vacancy. Thus on 6 January 1932, Amery attended meetings of two committees of the board, Stores and Finance. He noted his attendance in his diary but otherwise made no comment. He attended the same committees exactly a week later after which he went on the 16.45 train from Waterloo with General Manager, Sir Herbert Walker, and Assistant General Manager, Gilbert Szlumper, to Southampton. They dined in the city where they were joined by G.R. Newcombe, the railway's Docks & Marine Manager and later by director, Lord Ebbisham. The purpose of the visit was to inspect the new graving dock the following day. Describing the development as gigantic – it would be the biggest graving dock in the world, Amery reflected in his diary that it 'ought to play no small part in emphasising a shift of industry from North to South.'

At the same time as the railway directorship was developing, Amery received another invitation to become a director. It was from the Iraq Currency Board following the resignation of Hilton Young. He quickly accepted it but his offer to be a director of the National Provincial Bank was not taken up as he was regarded in the City as too much of a politician rather than a businessman.

20 January 1932
Amery was at Waterloo in the morning when after discussion with the chairman and Robert Holland-Martin, he decided to join the board of the Gloucester Railway Carriage & Wagon Company which he had just been invited to become a member of. Three days later, Sir Leslie Boyce, Chairman of the Gloucester Railway Carriage & Wagon Company and the Gloucester Member of Parliament, wrote to Amery that he was pleased that he had accepted the invitation to join the board.

27 January 1932

Amery attended the Stores and Finance Committee meetings at Waterloo. After lunch, he was at a meeting of the Docks Committee but recorded no details of discussions of these meetings. Later that day he was at a function at the Royal United Services Institute.

30 January 1932

Much about Szlumper's railway life at this time is known as his movements were often reported in the railway press. Thus it was noted in the railway's staff magazine that he was the guest of honour at the sixth annual dinner of the Southern Railway Regular Army Supplementary Reservists at the Duke of York's barracks in Chelsea when he proposed the toast of the Railway Training Centre at Longmoor. As this book is focused on diaries which in Szlumper's case did not begin until 1936, his activities are not detailed in this chapter except in the case of significant events.

3 February 1932

Amery's diaries record that he had several meetings at Waterloo in February but on this day no subject was detailed. On 5 February he was with some Southern Railway directors and auditors but again no reason was given. On 8 February, Amery recorded his attendance at a special board meeting to discuss the annual accounts and dividend, noting that it was decided there would be a final distribution of two-and-a-half per cent on the preferred stock. It was that same day that a meeting in London of the Gloucester Railway Carriage & Wagon Company formally appointed him to be a director. The following day this appointment was described in the press as being of the greatest importance to the company as in the past a large number of orders had come from the Dominions and Crown Colonies; and it was stressed that his position as an Empire Statesman was unrivalled. He was at Waterloo on 10 February, and on 17 February he was at meetings of the Stores and Finance Committees. He was at Waterloo again on 24 February.

It was a meeting of the railway's board on 18 February that decided that in view of the number of road companies in which the company was involved, it was desirable that Szlumper as nominee director on the bus companies should be relieved of some of the work. This was not in any way a demotion for the Assistant General Manager but was a very sensible action to relieve him of the considerable amount of time that he was spending at board meetings of bus companies which were sometimes away from London. Consequently a new post was created, Road Transport Liaison Officer, with as its first holder H.A. Short, who was already dealing with road services in the General Manager's office. Thus Szlumper would relinquish his position on the boards of Hants & Dorset Motor Services and Wilts & Dorset Motor Services, Short taking over his directorships.

29 February 1932

Amery attended the railway's Annual General Meeting for his formal election to the board. It did not, however, go as smoothly as he and his colleagues might have expected. According to his diary, an 'ill-conditioned fellow protested at my election onto the board as I was not a technical railwayman.' *The Times* and other newspapers noted that a George Ellison objected to giving the 'politically unemployed a pensioner's seat', suggesting that with his committee work as an MP, his correspondence, political clubs, journalism and other directorships, he would not have to earn the £1,000 which the railway was going to pay him. According to Amery, the critic was supported by a Charles Nordon who, he thought, made trouble at other meetings. Nordon declared that politics and business did not mix and proposed that Amery's name should not be accepted. Another shareholder said no director should be appointed unless he had knowledge of railway and road transport. When another shareholder protested at the personal attack, there was uproar. Nevertheless, Amery was elected, although there were cries of dissent which continued during the transaction of other business. Amery considered that the discussion was absurd as very few of the critics had any idea of what they were talking about.

The meeting was chaired by the Deputy Chairman, Gerald Loder, as the chairman was ill. Detailing changes on the board, Loder said that the company could congratulate itself on securing the services of Amery. 'With his wide experience, he will be of great assistance to us in the direction of the company's affairs.' At the meeting, Loder announced that the number of passenger journeys had fallen from 330,000,000 in 1930 to 324,000,000 in 1931 while there had been a decline in passenger revenue of £900,000. Loder complained that while railways had to provide and maintain their own permanent way and signalling and also had to pay rates, practically the whole capital cost of roadways had been provided by the public.

2 March 1932

Amery attended Stores and Finance committee meetings. Often Amery's diary entries were brief and uninformative on railway matters and would, with a few exceptions, always be so. Consequently many of his diary entries are not detailed hereafter.

17 March 1932

Amery was at the board meeting when he noted that the chairman 'turned up looking terribly frail and wasted.' Brigadier General the Hon. Everard Baring had been a director of the South Eastern Railway before the First World War and upon the formation of the Southern Railway in 1923, had become a Deputy Chairman and Chairman the following year.

Szlumper's wife presents the railway's first aid award to the Waterloo A team at Southern House, Cannon Street, 15 April 1932. (*Southampton Local Studies Library*)

4 May 1932
Amery recorded that he had heard that the Southern Railway chairman was not likely to live many days. He would die three days later.

5 May 1932
One of the duties of a director was to join inspections of particular areas or developments. With his many commitments, Amery would not have had time to partake in many of the visits but on this day he joined fellow directors and senior managers in an inspection of the Brighton line which was in the course of being electrified. Travelling in a special train, they visited the Electricity Control Room at Three Bridges which he thought was most impressive, 'the whole thing being a most interesting combination of modern electrification equipment and appropriate architecture.' They continued to Brighton where they inspected two short branch lines – Kemp Town which was to close for passengers the following year and Devil's Dyke which would survive until 1938. Amery was in no doubt about the reality of their economics and considered there was no point in competing with buses on either line.

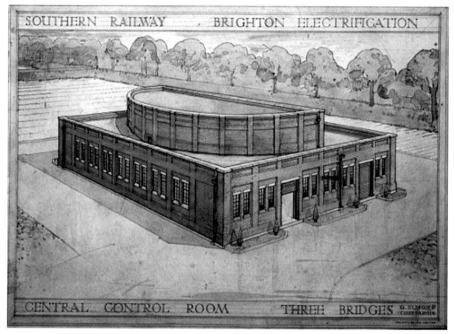

The Electrical Control Room at Three Bridges. (*Railway Gazette*)

6 May 1932

Amery was a conscientious director in all the companies in which he was involved. In the case of the Southern, this extended to making himself available to monitor railway discussions in Parliament. Thus he attended the House of Commons for a few minutes to observe the progress of the railway's annual Bill. Three days later he was in the House of Commons for the third reading of the Bill which 'slipped through without objections.'

10 May 1932

The funeral of Baring took place at Tandridge in Surrey. The General Manager was unable to be there as he was already committed to appear before a committee in the House of Commons. Nor was Gilbert Szlumper there but his father and Amery were.

11 May 1932

Amery attended a meeting at Waterloo about the railway's chairmanship. He noted that Loder was willing to continue for two or three years, although some directors favoured Holland-Martin as he was younger and more able and who otherwise was the chairman of the London board of Martins Bank.

26 May 1932
Amery was at the board meeting when it was decided that Loder would be Chairman with Holland-Martin the Deputy Chairman.

28 May 1932
Amery recorded taking the train to Haywards Heath for a weekend at the new chairman's sixteenth-century house at Wakehurst Place near Ardingly in Sussex.

5 June 1932
Amery went for lunch and tennis to Fairmile Hatch, near Cobham in Surrey, the large and rather grand house of fellow director, Lord Ebbisham.

9 June 1932
Amery was unable to be on the directors' visit to Southampton Docks as he was already committed to a meeting of the Sugar Federation of the British Empire. Ebbisham and Holland-Martin were, however, in the group of twenty-seven as was Gilbert Szlumper.

22 June 1932
Amery attended several committee meetings at Waterloo and a special board meeting to consider the advisability of raising fresh capital. That day Szlumper hosted a visit to Southampton Docks of the Retired Railways Officers' Society which included his father.

30 June 1932
Amery lunched with his fellow directors at Waterloo to consider the issue of new debentures. It was noted that one of the directors 'had created no small amount of difficulty by going to his own brokers independently of Holland-Martin and Gore-Browne and getting a better quote but based on much less knowledge of the facts.' That director was Dudley Docker, who had been with the Southern from its beginning. He was a most powerful businessman and exercised considerable influence on the railway but he was secretive and sometimes controversial. According to Amery, all the directors supported the chairman which caused Docker to threaten to resign 'which no doubt he will forget.'

July 1932
It was during this month that Amery acquired another directorship. The shipbuilding industry had been badly affected by the depression with the consequent reduction in orders for new ships. One company, Cammell Laird & Co of Birkenhead, submitted a scheme of capital re-organisation in an attempt to improve its finances. This was approved of but it required the appointment of three new directors.

21 September 1932

Amery was at the Finance Committee when the General Manager 'mentioned that travel agent George Lunn was getting into a serious position and suggested a small sub-committee be formed to consider if he should be bolstered up further or bought out.' The company's problems were the result of Britain coming off the gold standard, the government's request to people not to travel abroad and the depression. Walker reported that George's brother, Sir Henry Lunn, thought he would be able to pull through. Five days later the special committee met at Waterloo to consider whether 'to guarantee another £25,000 to see them through.' Amery agreed with Walker 'that it would be good business for the Southern to spend that amount on keeping alive an organisation which brought at least £10,000 per annum pure profit.' Another director and former general manager of the South Eastern & Chatham Railway, Sir Francis Dent, endorsed this view but Holland-Martin and Sir Charles Morgan did not support it. Amery, himself a skilled skier and mountaineer, knew all the Lunns personally. George Lunn had been taking passengers to Oberammergau from as early as 1900 and had formed George Lunn's Tours in 1912 while Sir Henry headed a successful travel agency in his own name.

5 October 1932

Amery was at the Finance Committee which decided to wind up George Lunn but he and the General Manager were still not convinced that this was the best action. There was also some discussion at the meeting about the train ferry proposal which Amery described as confused: 'To me and Walker it is clear that unless we start the ferry, we shall be out of it but most of the board were only concerned to avoid expenditure.' The project for a train ferry between Dover and a French port had been under consideration since 1930 after Parliament had rejected a Channel Tunnel.

13 October 1932

Amery attended a meeting in London of the Gloucester Railway Carriage & Wagon Company. He went home for lunch, then to Waterloo for a board meeting which decided there would be no more credit for George Lunn. Amery correctly interpreted this to mean that the company would be wound up as it owed the railway £15,000.

19 October 1932

Amery was at a special committee of the board to discuss the train ferry proposal. He wrote that it was clear from figures that unless the company built the train ferry, the Southern would lose very heavily to the Harwich/Zeebrugge service. Amery recorded that he spoke very strongly in favour and that most members agreed except Charles Sheath, the former Secretary of the South & Eastern Chatham Railway, who protested vehemently. As for the Southern chairman, he 'looked with suspicion on the whole matter and would have preferred some kind of danegeld being paid to the LNER.' It was a complex issue but in the event, it was agreed to establish a train ferry service to France.

26 October 1932

Amery attended committee meetings at Waterloo. From one of the meetings, he learnt that in the rush of the recent debenture issue, several mistakes had been made in the prospectus sent to the press, the railway finding itself committed to 750,000 more debentures than it had. Consequently Holland-Martin and Gore-Browne who was a Managing Partner of the bank Glynn, Mills & Co, had to 'go round to the brokers and get them to induce those who had taken up allocations, to scale them down.'

24 November 1932

Amery attended the railway's board meeting when the General Manager reported on meetings about the train ferry project with the Nord Railway of France, the Angleterre Lorraine Alsace Societé Anonyme de Navigation and the French government. It was stated the idea of using Calais or Boulogne had been abandoned, especially as the former was tidal. But Dunkirk had excellent accommodation; and there would be no cost to the Southern there while there would be lower port dues, although the sea route would be longer. Walker also reported he had met Sir Ralph Wedgwood, the Chief General Manager of the London & North Eastern Railway (LNER), about a pool but this had proved unworkable. The discussion ended with the decision to issue tenders for three train ferries. Amery made no mention of the meeting in his diary. The decision was reported in the press which stressed that the ships would be primarily for merchandise while a limited number of passengers would be carried and that it should, therefore, be possible to run through sleeping cars from London to Paris and elsewhere.

27 January 1933

In the absence of archives, the extent of Szlumper's involvement in the train ferry project is not obvious but as Assistant General Manager with a background in both civil engineering and shipping, he would have been aware of the challenges. It was at the annual dinner of Dover's Chamber of Commerce at the railway's Lord Warden Hotel that he outlined the proposal and the difficulties. The cost would be considerable which was largely because of the tide at Dover. It was not easy, he explained, to cater for a vessel, the deck of which had to register with a fixed rail level on the quay. It was a physical impossibility to make a bridge long enough to cater for that difference in levels

Szlumper with a group of mayors at Worthing at the opening of the electrified services, 30 December 1932. (*Southampton Local Studies Library*)

and yet not be too steep for the vehicles that would pass over it. So the railway was going to make it virtually a dry dock, at any rate closely fitting the ship and in which the water would be impounded in order to bring the ship up to the level corresponding with the quay. He claimed that where train ferries had been introduced all over the world, there had been a remarkable and in many cases unexpected increase in traffic.

26 April 1933

Amery was at the Docks Committee in the afternoon and then went to the House of Commons. In the evening he dined with his fellow directors at Charing Cross 'where we got the question of aviation taken more seriously than hitherto.' The board meeting duly took place the following day when it was decided at the suggestion of the Chairman to form a committee to consider with the General Manager, the company's attitude towards air transport.

The context of the aviation issue was that two weeks earlier the Great Western Railway had inaugurated an experimental air service between Cardiff and Plymouth with an aircraft chartered from Imperial Airways. The railway was able to do this as the four main line railways had together obtained air powers from Parliament in 1929 but hitherto had not used them, although the Southern still owned a large block of shares in Imperial Airways from when it had attempted to gain control of the airline. Moreover, it was public knowledge that a number of internal air services were being planned by various interests that year. The four railways were themselves considering joint action in conjunction with Imperial Airways.

14 June 1933
Amery attended Stores and Finance meetings and an Emergency Board meeting to consider the report of the naval architect Sir Westcott Abell and the decision to give the contract for three train ferries to Swan, Hunter & Wigham Richardson. Two weeks later the railway would place the order for three train ferries.

29 June 1933
Amery made no comment about the board meeting which received the report from its Aviation Committee. This had recommended that the consultants Norman, Muntz & Dawbarn, be authorised to 'investigate the influence of aviation development upon the policy and business of the Southern Railway.'

26 July 1933
The railway's directors were at Southampton for the opening of the new King George V Graving Dock. Amery noted that it was 'beautifully done, a real triumph of organisation. Loder was running about, perspiring but did everything admirably including his address.' The opening was by the King who expressed his admiration for the enterprise displayed by the board of the railway in undertaking the work in difficult times. Szlumper who a few days earlier had been admitted to the Freedom and Livery of the city livery company, the Worshipful Company of Shipwrights, took some cine film of the celebrations.

11 January 1934
Another of Amery's directorships was with the Fanti Consolidated Investment Company, a finance company with mining interests in Africa. At the annual meeting at Southern House, Cannon Street, he took the chair in the absence of the chairman who was ill. Southern House had been a railway hotel until 1931, subsequently becoming offices with rooms available for hire.

20 April 1934
Szlumper's involvement in bus companies may have been reduced but he was quite involved in the railways' entry into air transport and attended a meeting of the railway airline, Railway Air Services Ltd, as the Southern's nominee. The airline which had just been formed, was jointly owned by the four main line railways together with Imperial Airways. The railway involvement in air transport would, however, be somewhat controversial with its constant threat of its booking ban

Walker, Szlumper, Missenden and Biddle on the deck of one of the railway's ships at Southampton before a luncheon, 6 September 1933. (*Southampton Local Studies Library*)

to withhold the franchise of travel agents which sold tickets for non-approved airlines.

26 April 1934

Amery was at a lunch at Waterloo followed by a board meeting 'at which our aviation business went through very smoothly.' It was at this meeting that the General Manager submitted the Memorandum of Association and Articles of Incorporation of Railway Air Services Ltd. The record of the meeting also referred to the Aviation Committee and the decision to co-operate with Spartan Air Lines in a joint service from Croydon to the Isle of Wight from 1 May.

It was the April board meeting that added Amery and Henry Mansbridge to membership of the Aviation Committee, the latter being chairman of the railway-owned Hay's Wharf Cartage Company and a director of its subsidiary, Pickfords Ltd. The day after the meeting, Szlumper wrote to the Secretary of

Railway Air Services at the Imperial Airways head office at Victoria to advise that the Southern did not want to be tied to the co-operation agreement with Imperial Airways. Three days later, the board of the railway airline met and recorded its criticism of the Southern, its Chairman Sir Harold Hartley writing to Szlumper to deprecate its action in associating with Spartan Air Lines which was contrary to the spirit of the understanding between the four railways. Hartley, the nominee of the London, Midland & Scottish Railway [LMS] on the airline's board, was also a Vice President of that railway which would be the main sponsor of air services.

10 May 1934

In the morning Amery was with his board colleagues on an inspection to the riverside wharf and yard at Nine Elms in Battersea where there was a rebuilding proposal. The following day was fully occupied by another inspection visit of which the first point of call was Angerstein Wharf near Charlton. The special train proceeded to Gravesend and Allhallows-on-Sea. Amery noted that the Chairman was keen to develop the Allhallows site as a resort to be 'the Blackpool for South London'. Amery seemed to share his enthusiasm, recording that he believed that a rival to Southend could be established. Nearly two miles long from a junction on the Hundred of Hoo line to Port Victoria and Grain on the Medway estuary, the line had been opened in 1932 but had not been an immediate success.

This view of Allhallows-on-Sea station captures the bleakness of the location. (*Rob Poole collection*)

Szlumper and Walker at the new bowling green at Waddon, 26 May 1934.
(*Southampton Local Studies Library*)

30 May 1934

Amery attended his first meeting of the railway's Aviation Committee when it was agreed that the shipbuilder, Sir John Thornycroft, would be the chairman. With regard to Imperial Airways, it was stated that the draft agreement was unacceptable and it was recommended that notice be given to terminate the existing agreement.

The new bowling green at Waddon, 26 May 1934. (*Southampton Local Studies Library***)**

Szlumper with Lord Mottistone at the opening of the new Southern Vectis bus garage at Newport, 20 June 1934. (*Southampton Local Studies Library***)**

Interior of new Southern Vectis bus garage at Newport, 20 June 1934.
(*Southampton Local Studies Library*)

Southern Vectis drivers and conductors at the new bus garage at Newport, 20 June
1934. (*Southampton Local Studies Library*)

2 July 1934

Amery, Szlumper with other directors, managers and their wives travelled in the morning by train to Dover where they boarded the railway's SS *Isle of Sark* which took them to Dunkirk to see the train ferry equipment under construction. They sailed on to Calais the following day and then to Boulogne. Dieppe was reached on 4 July. On 5 July they were at Le Havre, on 6 July Cherbourg, on 7 July Jersey and St Malo on 8 July, returning to England the following day. Apart from detailing the dates and ports, Amery made no other comment in his diary but he mentioned the journey in his autobiography. Contacts, he wrote, were made everywhere over endless *vins d'honneur* at mayoral receptions.

25 July 1934

Amery was at Waterloo in the morning, afterwards lunching at the Savoy but not on railway business. This was followed by a Docks Committee at Waterloo, then the House of Commons. In the evening he was at a Southern dinner where he was seated next to Sir William Whitelaw, Chairman of the LNER. They discussed the demand for increased wages by railwaymen.

1 August 1934

Amery's entry revealed that his services were also in demand in the Middle East when Pinhas Rutenberg of the Palestine Electric Company came to him with a suggestion that he should act as chairman of a new airline to be started with Imperial Airways. In the event, the airline would be incorporated as Palestine

Inspection by directors and officers at Calais, 3 July 1934. This is one of the few railway photographs of both Szlumper and Amery. The then Assistant General Manager is on the far left while Amery in the front row is dwarfed by Walker. (*Southampton Local Studies Library*)

Airways Ltd in December but would not begin operations for three years. Amery would be a director but not chairman.

17 October 1934

Before committee meetings at Waterloo, Amery had 'an informal preliminary talk with Holland-Martin, Gore-Browne and Thornycroft.' This was in preparation for a meeting later with the Imperial Airways Managing Director, Woods Humphery. It was agreed that Amery, a keen supporter of civil aviation, would take the lead in the discussion. The committee meetings duly took place after which they met the airline's Managing Director. They were joined by Walker, Southern Solicitor Wil Bishop, and Szlumper. According to Woods Humphery's record of the meeting, Amery stated the case for arriving at a mutual understanding, particularly about the Paris route, before going into the details of the agreement. The Southern's concern was explained – it did not like being tied to Imperial Airways in a way that would prevent the railway taking an interest in other airlines. The railway thought it possible that several airlines could be successfully operating services across the Channel to France as well as Imperial Airways and the Southern might like to co-operate by supplying the necessary railway connections. More than that, the railway thought it might be worthwhile paying a small subsidy to such airlines in view of the traffic that might be brought to the connecting railway services. With regard to the Paris service, Amery said that there was no getting away from it that Imperial Airways had taken away from the Southern tens of thousands passengers a year. Quite apart from the large investment it still had in the airline, it wanted to consider the possibility of being more closely identified with the Paris service and he asked Woods Humphery if the airline would entertain some arrangement that would permit that. This annoyed Woods Humphery who pointed out that the airline had negotiated with Walker on lines which at that time met with the approval of the railway's board. Having agreed the draft of an agreement, Imperial Airways then proceeded to invest money in Railway Air Services, lending aircraft, pilots, personnel, trained railway staff and in effect managed the airline for the railways. Six months later the Southern's board seemed to change its mind on fundamental points. He felt that the Southern ought to ratify the agreement before further discussions; and it should not expect to get all the advantages but be relieved of all the disadvantages. The airline would not object to the Southern supplying services to other airlines but it would object very strongly to any suggestion of subsidising such airlines, either directly with cash or indirectly by supplying railway services at prices below those charged to the general public. His airline would also object to the railways taking a capital interest in such concerns. Shorn of the protection given to Imperial against the possibility of the Southern bolstering other airlines, the agreement would have no attraction left to it.

It was Gore-Browne who said the railway did not like the virtual monopoly which the agreement bestowed upon Imperial Airways. Woods Humphery challenged the suggestion that the agreement would give the airline a monopoly and said he did not think that there was the slightest chance that his board would agree to any arrangement which left the railway free to bolster little airlines so as to make them a bigger nuisance value than they were already. The airline foresaw that the proposed agreement would mean sacrifices by all the partners, Imperial giving up its freedom to operate internal services while the railways would also have sacrifices to make. Paris had not been discussed by the airline's board but he thought that it would be prepared to consider a scheme whereby the Southern could have a more direct interest in the route. But he did not think his board would consider an arrangement in respect of the Paris route alone, leaving Imperial with the less attractive Cologne and Swiss routes. If the board agreed, it would also be necessary to obtain the approval of the Air Ministry where there was a big fear that the entry of the railways would slow up the development of air transport. Amery recorded in his diary that he thought the airline was bluffing in suggesting that it might go back on the mutual agreement which had never been signed. Woods Humphery agreed however to discuss with his colleagues the possibility of a joint SR/IAL scheme which would cover all new Continental traffic.

31 October 1934
Amery was at a Stores Committee after which Loder, who in the summer had been ennobled as Lord Wakehurst of Ardingly, asked him to his room to discuss his resignation and who should be Deputy Chairman in the event of Holland-Martin succeeding him as Chairman. 'Holland-Martin favours Gore-Browne whom everybody likes but many people think unsuitable as there would be two city finance people as Chairman and Deputy.' Loder said the other candidate was Sir George Courthope, but he had too many directorships and was also a Member of Parliament. He then asked Amery if he would be Chairman. Amery recorded his reaction as one of surprise. In the event, the chairmanship did not materialise. Two days later, Amery had another, and long, talk with Loder about the Deputy Chairman position. 'Most favoured Gore-Browne over Courthope. I favour Gore-Browne.'

7 November 1934
Amery was at the railway's board meeting when it was decided that Gore-Browne would be the Deputy Chairman. He described the deliberations as comic. 'Holland-Martin had persuaded Loder that he must retire in the autumn. But at the last informal meeting, one or two of the older boys had suggested that it was better to

Szlumper presents a model of the Schools class locomotive, *King's Wimbledon*, to the headmaster of King's College School at the station on 15 February 1935 while pupils admire the locomotive. (*Southampton Local Studies Library*)

postpone retirement until the next annual meeting. Loder who was hoping to stay, encouraged a debate. Most preferred that he go. Loder feels he is being badly hustled by Holland-Martin which is true but desirable. He is a pretty poor chairman, deaf and inaudible, discursive and generally not too clear about railway affairs.'

23 January 1935

Amery was at a meeting of the Docks Committee at Waterloo. This was followed by a long Aviation Committee at which he suggested the railway agree to amend the agreement with Imperial Airways subject to an accompanying letter in which certain points would be emphasised. The meeting noted the Southern's continued involvement in the Isle of Wight service of Spartan Air Lines and the Nottingham to Shoreham service operated by the state-sponsored airline; and the intention to acquire a shareholding together with the Great Western in Jersey Airways. It was also recorded that a letter had been received from a company to be formed, Airports Ltd, about co-operation over a station to be built for Gatwick Airport.

30 January 1935

Amery recorded that after the Finance Committee, he, together with Holland-Martin and Gore-Browne had 'a little conference with the chairman of Railway Air Services, Sir Harold Hartley, with a view to making Imperial Airways understand our real objections to the agreement and seeing if we could arrive at something more attractive.' A week later, Hartley saw the Imperial Airways's chairman, Sir Eric Geddes, and told him that in railway circles there was great dissatisfaction as to the way Railway Air Services was working out and that they felt they had got to extend it or give it up.

28 March 1935

Amery attended the railway's Aviation Committee. In the evening, he was at the directors' dinner when he sat between the Secretary, Frank Willis and Gore-Browne, the latter asking him if he was still open to directorships and how far he was still committed to politics.

19 June 1935

Amery attended the Aviation Committee. 'My original idea of Imperial Airways surrendering Continental traffic to a new joint company at last taking shape and likely to come to something.'

24 July 1935

Amery attended the Aviation Committee which again discussed Continental air services but it was not the only meeting at Waterloo relating to civil aviation. The other meeting was between Walker, Szlumper and the aviation pioneer, Sir Alan

Cobham who at this stage was concentrating on airport consultancy. A record of the meeting does not appear to have survived and how it came about is not clear but from later correspondence, it appeared that both the General Manager and the Chairman were keen on developing the potential airport site which Cobham had just discovered and which could displace Croydon as the country's main airport. At that stage Cobham did not disclose the location which was at Lullingstone near Eynsford in Kent.

Cobham was invited to Waterloo to see Walker the following day but this clashed with an appointment he had at the Air Ministry. Nevertheless Cobham did have a long meeting that day with Szlumper. Again, no record of the meeting appears to have survived but in a letter the following day to the airline, Cobham claimed the railway wanted him to get an option on the site. He had told Szlumper that it was impossible as he had already contracted to purchase it. Szlumper suggested that the best thing they could do was to have a site visit the following week.

30 July 1935

At the end of July, another directorship appeared for Amery in the form of the toothpaste manufacturer Macleans. Amery was invited to meet the directors of the company which he did on 30 July when he was also invited to be the chairman.

5 October 1935

Szlumper and his wife took a holiday for a month to South America. The circumstances are not clear but it was a real holiday in that Szlumper did no work during the course of their break. They travelled on the boat train to Southampton where they boarded Royal Mail's RMS *Asturias*.

9 October 1935

Amery recorded attending the Aviation Committee when it was reported that there was no more progress with Imperial Airways. But there was an announcement by the General Manager – that certain land at Lullingstone was suitable for an airport. The issue was referred to the board which met the following day when it was resolved that it was desirable to acquire the land with a view to developing it as an airport if it could be bought for a reasonable price.

14 November 1935

This was an important day for Szlumper as it was the occasion of his presidential address to the Railway Students Association [RSA]. It is detailed here as it revealed much about his thought processes and his forward-thinking. It is also very important as an insight into to the state of the railway at the time; and it is an interesting piece of self-criticism. It was at the association's traditional meeting place, the London School of Economics (LSE), and was chaired by Sir William Beveridge who was the Director of the LSE and President of the RSA in the previous session. Essentially, it was a wide-ranging critical view of the way that the Southern treated its passengers. He told his audience that he hoped his paper would whet the appetite of the audience by suggesting some of the problems, leaving it to the individual to ponder over them and hopefully find the correct solution.

He then described what he imagined an average passenger experienced on trying to make a rail journey from London. He began by challenging the need to purchase a timetable in order to fully appreciate the range of times – how many firms could afford to charge a potential customer for a catalogue of its goods, he asked; and then one needed a magnifying glass to read the microscopic print. He then presented himself at a well-known London station with time in hand which he spent in looking around but without any resultant pleasure as the dirt of ages was on every ledge.

As for the train itself, it seemed to have lacked recent attention, no brush having sullied its upholstery for some time. He wondered if the railway had found the ideal internal and external finishes, and the ideal means of cleaning them without prohibitive cost. He was also critical of the train's toilets, refreshments, speed and comfort. As for the locomotive, he learnt its efficiency could be as low as 7%. He hoped that someday some unorthodox locomotive engineer would be born who would set to work to design afresh his steam locomotive and arrive at a machine with a more creditable figure of efficiency and find some means of treating the feed water so as to obviate laying his expensive engine off for one day a fortnight to clean out its boiler. He hoped that by the time the locomotive engineer had improved his machine, the civil engineer would have found some way of protecting his roadbed and strengthening his bridges at a reasonable cost while the traffic and signal departments would have put their heads together and re-signalled the line with some modern system and with revised sections so that the speed of trains would be increased appreciably.

As for expenditure, he acknowledged that no one knew better than he did the necessity for keeping a check on it, but he believed that many amenities could be introduced into rail travel without any loss of net revenue. The leisurely pace of the journey galled him exceedingly as he remembered the craze for speed and the way in which travellers were willing to pay high prices for air travel when it was quicker than surface travel. On the loss of traffic on cross-country lines and between stations of minor importance, he wondered if the stopping places of passenger trains should be revised with calls at only the more important towns some 25 miles apart. At the same time, arrangements could be made with the associated bus companies to serve the intervening country and villages. He suggested that perhaps the railway had made false god of the length and weight of a train that a locomotive could haul. Did customers want a tremendous train at infrequent intervals or prefer a short one at frequent intervals? Certainly the Southern's experience on electrification had supplied an unmistakeable answer to the question – frequency and regular intervals were assets that were difficult to overvalue. On the branch line problem, he wondered if traffic could be resuscitated by a lower tariff through simplification of working methods. Could the driver or guard carry a key with which they could operate the signals of the section ahead and the section just left?

On internal air services, he claimed the time factor would not give the railways any trouble for some time to come because of the distance from the cities of the airports. But the railways would have to see how far it would be wise to counter the increase in air speed by improving train equipment and increasing frequency and expediting schedules. If the railways did not become interested in air services to Europe, the question would be to what extent the railways should foster competition by providing train services to rail-connected airports. He believed that air traffic was bound to reach large dimensions on such routes and that rather than lose all the revenue from passengers who elected to use air services, he would prefer to make it attractive for him to perform some part of the journey by rail. Thus the railway was co-operating with the owner of Gatwick Airport by providing it with a station.

With regard to shipping, he stressed that the railway's problem was that it was not practical to increase the speed of the cross-Channel vessels as the railway had already gone beyond the speed suited to the dimensions of its vessels. Greater speed would only mean discomfort and disproportionate expense. But he wondered if the irritating delays at ports could be reduced and if better transfer arrangements from train to boat could be obtained. He asked if the railway had devised the best method of relieving passengers from the worry of looking after their luggage.

He acknowledged that he had only touched the fringe of the relationship with customers but he hoped that the questions he had asked would cause some of the members to apply themselves to the task of finding a satisfactory answer and also to setting their minds working along the same theme. Was it too much, he asked, to hope that some of them at least would put themselves in the position of a member of the public who wanted to travel or despatch goods? We are, he said, still apt to feel that we are very fine fellows, brought up in a great tradition, carrying on as our fathers did before us. He concluded that the problem was to find out what the purchaser of rail transport wanted and then how to hand it out to him at a price that would attract him and leave the railway in profit. He acknowledged his words had been unorthodox but that was because he believed that unorthodox minds and methods were the only way to meet the vagaries of current demands.

Who of the railway's hierarchy was in the audience was not recorded. Was Walker there? Had he seen Szlumper's paper before it was delivered and just what did he think of it? Why Szlumper's speech was not reported in the national press is a mystery. It was similarly ignored by the railway press with the exception of the *Railway Gazette* which detailed it almost word for word, although there was no editorial comment. The Southern Railway magazine made no mention of it.

20 November 1935

Amery was at the Aviation Committee when it was reported that negotiations with Imperial Airways about air services had been abandoned but negotiations were proceeding for the purchase of farmland at Lullingstone.

3 January 1936

Amery and Paul Lindenberg, who was chairman of the Industrial & Finance Investment Corporation, went to Claridge's for the lunch of the Trust & Loan Company of Canada together with Simon Marks and Israel Sieff who were Joint Managing Directors of Marks & Spencer. Amery who was also a director of both Lindenberg's company and the Canadian company, noted in his diary that Lindenberg had told him some months previously that Marks & Spencer wanted to improve its board and would like Amery to consider joining it. Five days later, the board approved of his membership.

Chapter Three

છ૰ન્

The Szlumper and Amery Diaries, 1936-39

9 January 1936

This date is significant as it was the first entry in Szlumper's diaries. Still Assistant General Manager at Waterloo, he recorded taking the chair at the Southern Railway's Lecture & Debating Society at Southwark Cathedral's Chapter House. The meeting was addressed by Col Tyrrell, the Assistant Director of Transportation at the War Office, on the subject of the Construction and Wartime Operation of the Palestine Railways. Szlumper described the meeting as full and the talk quite good, being an account of railway construction in wartime. Two days later he travelled on the Great Western to Exeter where he had dinner at Loco Hall, noting that this was given by serving grades to retired staff.

17 January 1936

As the Southern Railway's nominee director, Szlumper attended a board meeting of the railway airline, Railway Air Services Ltd, at the Imperial Airways offices at Victoria but he did not record it in his diary. In fact, he would rarely mention attending the airline's board meetings.

18 January 1936

Szlumper noted it was first announced that King George V was ill while later that day there was a moving announcement that his life was moving peacefully towards its end. Two days later, Amery returned from Austria after his annual holiday. Arriving at Dover, he heard of the King's grave illness and of the death of the celebrated writer Kipling.

21 January 1936

Amery awoke to funeral bells for the King. In the afternoon he went to St James's Palace with other privy councillors for the proclamation of the accession of Edward VIII.

23 January 1936

Szlumper recorded that with Holland-Martin, Walker, and a number of officers, they inspected 'the long overdue reconstruction at Woking and also the electrification preparations.' The station was being reconstructed in the art deco style which was then the chosen style for such work on the Southern. He noted that he had been unable to find out why the substation buildings for the electrification extensions had been finished in bastard cement while most buildings were in brickwork which looked more elegant. The group proceeded by special train to Aldershot and Alton to which point it had been decided to electrify, and then to Winchester from where they returned to London. Apart from the chairman, there were no directors in the group, Amery being at Kipling's funeral in Westminster Abbey.

In the evening, Szlumper was at Waterloo to chair the RSA debate on his presidential address. He recorded he was very disappointed at the 'lack of constructive suggestions.' He noted that most of those present endorsed his grumbles or added a little to them but with notably few bits of advice on how to get matters rectified.

24 January 1936

Rutenberg went to lunch at Amery's flat in Eaton Square. There was some discussion about the airline proposal as Amery noted that 'Palestine Airways may come to life after all as HMG is now anxious to see an air service between Haifa and Cyprus.' Civil aviation was also a focus that day for Szlumper when he went to the Air Ministry to discuss the Lullingstone airport proposal with Deputy Secretary, J.G. Gibson, and Ivor McClure, the Chief Operational Adviser to the Director-General of Civil Aviation. McClure said he thought that the railway had taken on a project of huge financial dimensions. Certainly the Air Ministry was pleased that the railway was prepared to develop the site at Lullingstone at its own expense. Szlumper recorded that he appreciated that it would be a big project but if the railway committed itself to develop and finalise the whole area right away, he could see no reason that it should not develop and expand according to requirements from time to time and at reasonable costs.

29 January 1936

Amery attended railway committees at Waterloo. After lunch he was at the Docks Committee. He later met Rutenberg and Burchall, General Manager of Imperial Airways, to discuss the possibilities of a Cyprus to Palestine air service. It was agreed that he should see Viscount Swinton, the Secretary of State for Air. Later Amery attended the directors' railway dinner at Charing Cross where he was seated between Mansbridge and Szlumper. The latter described it as all very affable, noting that Walker gave a splendid and clear discourse on the railway rating decision. This was a reference to the House of Lords legal decision five days earlier which had involved the Southern Railway, the Railway Assessment Authority and the London County Council over the net annual value of the company for rating purposes.

10 February 1936

Amery was at a meeting at Waterloo about the annual accounts which would be presented to the public at the end of the month. 'Thanks to the success of the rating appeal, we were able to decide on a full 5% for the preferred shares.' In the evening, Szlumper was at an open meeting of the Institute of Transport when the General Manager of the Port of London Authority, Sir David Owen, 'was bleating rather pathetically on grouping of ports. He hates anyone spending a penny on competition with the Port of London Authority. I gave my views.'

12 February 1936

Szlumper was at lunch at Euston with Keith Grand, the Commercial & Advertising Agent of the Great Western, and Sir Harold Hartley. The subject of discussion was the railway airline on which Grand was also a nominee director. It was 'to try and paint a picture of Railway Air Services as it ought to be.' Exactly what he meant is not clear but he was probably referring to the intense competition from a number of small domestic airlines, to which the railways had responded by increasing their services or forming joint airline companies with their competitors when the latter did not disappear. There was no prospect of any of the airlines breaking even. Hartley was originally a scientist and had come to the railway in 1930 but it was interesting that Szlumper described him as indecisive and not of the business world. In the evening, Szlumper went to Southern House for a concert for the railway orphanage. Walker was in the chair and the hall was full but he described the acoustics as 'damned bad'.

14 February 1936

Szlumper went to the Admiralty for a meeting with the Director of Dockyards, Sir Percy Addison, 'to find out anything about the suggested removal of Chatham Dockyard to Milford Haven in South Wales.' Addison told him there was no likelihood of such action as Chatham had just been given three years' work. Szlumper recorded that he tried to trade the surplus floating dock at Southampton on the grounds that such a large proportion of the British fleet was at Alexandria on account of Mussolini's activities in Abbysinia but Addison's response was negative. Later Szlumper chaired a meeting at Waterloo of the Southern Vectis board. While he made no reference to this, he did note that Sir William Forbes, the former General Manager of the London, Brighton & South Coast Railway, had died at eighty-one. Szlumper described him as 'a good companion and universally liked.'

18 February 1936

Another of Amery's directorships in this period was with the Australian Youanmi Gold Mining Ltd. After attending a meeting of the company, he 'looked up Sir Eric Geddes at his office at Victoria to agree the text of a letter by Palestine Airways to the Air Ministry. We had a general talk about his aviation schemes.' Szlumper that day had lunch at Euston with R.C. Irwin, the former Secretary of both the Lancashire & Yorkshire Railway and the LMS. 'He begins to fail a little.'

21 February 1936

Szlumper was at St John's Gate with his daughter, Cynthia, for his investiture as Commander of the Venerable Order of the Hospital of St John of Jerusalem. He described it as quite a nice ceremony in a very historic place. In the evening he chaired the Supervisors' Association dinner at Lyons Corner House next to Charing Cross. 'As usual, an enthusiastic group, 370 strong. Would have liked when talking of economics to have remarked on the distastefulness it must be for a man of sixty-eight to have to put to pension so many excellent men of sixty but as Cox was sitting next to me, I refrained.' Cox, the Traffic Manager, was sixty-eight and had himself yet to declare when he would retire.

24 February 1936

Szlumper had lunch with his friend, Norman Hulbert 'who wants us to be the first company to show television to the public. He knows the BBC man who will look after it. I find later that Cuthbert Grasemann [the railway's Public Relations & Advertising Officer] also knows him and it is difficult to see how Hulbert can come into the picture.' Hulbert, Member of Parliament for Stockport, was also the chairman and managing director of Capital News Theatres Ltd.

25 February 1936

Szlumper had lunch with Group Captain W.H. Primrose who was about to retire from the Post Office as its Air Mail Adviser. He told Szlumper that he would be setting up his own consultancy. He was quite blunt when he said he had no use for Railway Air Services and little for Imperial Airways. He believed the Southern would be best advised to join forces with British Airways Ltd which had been formed the previous year and which, with the encouragement of the government, was expanding its services to Europe. In the evening, Walker and Szlumper visited the British Industries Fair at Olympia, Szlumper describing it as a very fine display of what Britain could produce.

27 February 1936

Both Amery and Szlumper attended the railway's Annual General Meeting at Southern House. Amery described it as a very friendly affair. 'Holland-Martin's speech was interesting and encouraging and there was practically no criticism.' Szlumper described the meeting as 'a very tame affair as we are paying the full 5% on the preferred ordinary shares.' Both men went to meetings afterwards, Amery going to the House of Commons with fellow director and MP, Sir John Thornycroft, while Szlumper went to Euston for a meeting of the Railway Air Services board which he also described as a very tame affair.

28 February 1936

Szlumper received for lunch at Waterloo the Director-General of Civil Aviation at the Air Ministry, Sir Francis Shelmerdine, for a general discussion. According to Szlumper, Shelmerdine said he wanted to help the railways 'so long as they play their part.'

29 February 1936

In the evening Szlumper and his wife were at Waddon, the location of one of the railway's sports centres, for a dinner and dance. The chairman and his wife were also present. Szlumper commented, 'one might have thought the occasion too small for their weight but they seemed to enjoy it well enough.'

1 March 1936

Szlumper noted that Percy Montague Brooke-Hitching and wife came to tea at his Surbiton home. 'Tells of approaches to Holland-Martin, of a split on the board and how some think too many ex-railwaymen on it already.' Brooke-Hitching was a man of inherited wealth with an obsession for railway timetables. He had no official business connection with railways but was accepted in the railway family, often attending semi-public railway meetings.

3 March 1936

Szlumper attended the Retired Railway Officers' Society luncheon at the Abercorn Rooms in the Great Eastern Hotel at Liverpool Street. 'Tried to enliven them with some respectable cheerinesss. A very good old crowd who rather jumped at the idea of coming again to Southampton for the summer outing and seeing the *Queen Mary*.' Cunard's new flagship for the Atlantic crossing was due to arrive from her builders on the Clyde later in the month and would be going to the new graving dock for cleaning, surveying and painting.

4 March 1936

Szlumper's diary entry for that day was most interesting for what it revealed of the human qualities of the Chief Engineer, George Ellson who had held the post since 1927 after the retirement of Szlumper's father. By invitation Szlumper had lunch with the Assistant Engineer, New Works & Bridges, Conrad Gribble, and the Assistant Engineer, Signals & Telegraphs, G.L. Hall. 'There was nothing they wanted me to do or nothing they thought I could do but they wished to inform me of the feelings of the staff of the Engineer's Department that was engendered by Ellson. The lower ranks are in fear – they instanced Curtis, the Chief Clerk, being one recent day in a state of collapse as a result of being bullied by Ellson. Both Hall and Gribble gave instances of apparently uncontrollable temper that Ellson had visited on them. Hall and Gribble said that they would resign today if they at their age could find any other sort of job. They did not mind being complained at if there was any justification but Ellson continuously raves at them and treats them like dirt in a most ungentlemanly manner. They said he takes care to secure what credit there might be without ever passing any on to anyone else and that he takes care that no one shall ever be in the picture. The consequence was that the whole of his staff feared to do a thing and spent their time trying to avoid trouble instead of getting on with their jobs to the best of their ability. There was in the department a state of nervous tension which would have some serious outcome some day. Hall and Gribble are not singled out for this treatment. Ellson visits everyone in turn with his displeasure, violently and rudely expressed. He treats everyone as a bloody fool and a rogue.'

Szlumper wrote that he did his best to mollify them and told them that Walker knew their ability and appreciated it as did others. He also acknowledged that he had heard similarly from many quarters in the Engineer's Department. He begged them to be patient and ride out the storm for the sake of the company. They all agreed that the course was to grin and bear it.

5 March 1936

Walker and Szlumper were together on an inspection, first to Portsmouth and then to Southampton. They travelled back together from Southampton. On their return, they discussed staff arrangements. Walker told Szlumper that the company secretary, Frank Willis, was in high dudgeon over his retirement, 'an attitude not helped by him having been informed by the Chairman or Deputy Chairman that he was to be succeeded by someone outside the railway service. Willis says Walker has let him down after promising that when Sire [Chief Commercial Manager until 1930] went and Willis was made secretary, he should not suffer thereby. He now compares himself to the other chief officers and says he is only getting £2,600 salary instead of £3,500 to £4,500.' Szlumper suggested a solution in his pension but Walker replied that it had been agreed to. Certainly Willis had not been happy as Secretary and considered that the post had been gradually marginalised since he had taken it on. Walker said he had done nothing further about a successor to the

Chief Mechanical Engineer [CME], Richard Maunsell, as he had been away sick. Szlumper suggested it might be a good thing to send H.A. Short (Road Transport Liaison Officer) to Southampton as number two if Biddle, Assistant to the Docks & Marine Manager, succeeded Missenden.

12 March 1936
W.G. Pape, the railway's Indoor Assistant, took Szlumper to lunch to meet Lawson Billinton as a possible successor to Maunsell. 'He seems a decent sort of fellow but with an inclination towards laziness, also without polish. I would not fancy him as Locomotive Engineer somehow.' Billinton had been the CME of the London, Brighton & South Coast Railway until 1923 but he had not been taken into the Southern.

20 March 1936
Szlumper was in the inspection group that visited Raynes Park, the others including Walker, Cox and Ellson. He did not comment on the visit as such but he did record that Cox told him that he would be retiring at the end of September after his medical adviser had told him he would not be responsible for him on account of his low blood pressure. Cox said to Szlumper, 'One cannot stay forever, can one?' Szlumper wrote that he was not sure as he had had a good try but somehow this time it seemed to be genuine as later in the day Walker mentioned the question of contingent changes in the docks with Missenden coming up to succeed Cox who had started with the South Eastern & Chatham Railway in 1883. In the event, Cox would live to the ripe age of ninety-one.

24 March 1936
Szlumper lunched at the American Club with Alfred Ball of the Pennsylvania Railroad and its London representative. The Pennsylvania was the largest railway by traffic and revenue in North America and also the largest employer in the USA. 'Alfred is as cheerful as ever and says the Pennsylvania is doing pretty well but things are pretty bad with most of the American railroads.'

25 March 1936
Amery was at Waterloo in the morning. This was followed by a meeting of the Iraq Currency Board. He was back at Waterloo in the afternoon for the Aviation Committee when the meeting was advised that negotiations to purchase land at Lullingstone for an airport were continuing. Amery then went to the House of Commons but was back at Waterloo in the evening for a dinner when the election of a new director in place of Wakehurst (the former Gerald Loder) who had had a stroke, was discussed. 'I should have liked to get back Hilton Young but Holland-Martin wants Clive Pearson of Whitehall Securities and no doubt he might bring

more business.' They also discussed Walker's successor. 'I stood up strongly for not rejecting Szlumper without some trial of him in spite of his lack of manners. This found general approval and it was left that the Chairman should suggest to Herbert Walker to go round the empire to sell Southampton, giving Szlumper the chance to show his quality when on his own.'

26 March 1936
Szlumper recorded that he had learnt with great pleasure that Wakehurst would be retiring from the board and that his place would be filled by Clive Pearson. He described Pearson as a charming and able man in contrast to Wakehurst whom he described as a brainless bore.

27 March 1936
Szlumper went with others to Southampton where from the deck of the railway's SS *Twickenham Ferry*, they viewed the 'much-vaunted and much-advertised arrival of Cunard's RMS *Queen Mary* at Southampton.' He noted the ship arrived thirty minutes late in squally weather but was manoeuvred into the King George V graving dock without difficulty. 'She looks a fine vessel and equally fine internally as we saw from a very brief inspection – particularly good wide alleyways but for my taste far too much gaudiness in the way of pictures and carvings and decorations. True, most of them as individual pieces are agreeable enough but I do not agree in turning a ship into a somewhat crowded art gallery.' He described the day as very successful.

28 March 1936
Szlumper was at the Bray parish church near Maidenhead for the wedding of Elisabeth Garcke. He noted that it was most lavishly and hospitably done and that all the bus world was there. Elizabeth's father, Sidney Garcke, who had played an important role in the establishment of the bus industry in England, was chairman of the holding company, Tilling & British Automobile Traction and a director of British Electric Traction (BET). With the railways, BET and Thomas Tilling still effectively controlled the bus industry. The wedding was very much a society affair, the local press listing the wedding gifts in great detail – the Szlumpers' present was a coffee set. The bridegroom, John Spencer Wills, was involved in the management of some of BET's bus companies.

30 March 1936
Amery was in the House of Commons in the afternoon when Cole-Deacon, the Secretary of the Railway Companies' Association (RCA), asked him to make some 'unwise suggestions on the Air Navigation Bill which I refused to do.' The association existed to protect the railways and their shareholders from parliamentary interference.

'The Bill did not come on until 19.00 and I hung about the House of Commons reading monthly magazines and generally wasting time. Sir Philip Sassoon [Under-Secretary of State for Air] introduced it rather tamely but things evidently got lively afterwards as when I came back from dinner, the atmosphere was rather excited and got more so when Sassoon in a rather hurried reply did not acknowledge some of the arguments and charges raised. The House got rather out of hand and Baldwin's intervention was required to secure the vote of second reading at 01.00. The fact is that Sassoon is not of sufficient weight to face a restless House and the Air Minister ought to be in the House.' During the debate there was considerable criticism of government civil aviation policy and of Imperial Airways.

31 March 1936
Szlumper travelled to Southampton with Traffic Manager, Eustace Missenden. With Maurice and Jack Denny, they went out on the SS *Isle of Sark* to try out the

Visitors queue to see the RMS *Queen Mary*. (*Southampton Local Studies Library*)

special stabiliser which had been fitted to it. 'Unfortunately it was a very smooth day but by hand operation we worked up a twelve degree roll which was completely damped out in 1½ rolls when the stabiliser was put in operation. All agreed that the apparatus looked very promising.' Denny Brothers of Dumbarton had delivered the ship to the railway in 1932 as the first vessel in a modernisation programme. Meanwhile Amery was being offered another directorship when he met Major Hemming, 'the Air Survey man who is trying to amalgamate the various air survey companies and wished me to become chairman.' Amery declined.

24 April 1936

Szlumper and Walker visited the Docks at Southampton. Szlumper noted that the *Queen Mary* had attracted 80,000 sightseers which had brought revenue to the railway of £6,400. On their return they again discussed retirements and successors. On the Docks & Marine Manager position, Szlumper told Walker that he thought it would be difficult not giving it to Biddle as he had the ability and knowledge to do the job, but he wished his personality was a bit different. They agreed it might work well to send Short down to Southampton as his assistant. Szlumper believed they could profitably transfer all Short's work to the Traffic Department, combining it with the licensing side and the goods haulage side. He said he would also like to see the repair side coming under the control of the man operating the transport. He considered the work to be unsuitable for a steam engineer and he was sure it was costing a good deal more than it ought. He recorded that he held a very poor opinion of the ability and energy of J.W. Wild, the Road Maintenance Engineer at Bricklayers Arms under whom it came. Walker was not averse to the idea but doubted if Missenden would require an assistant to replace Elliot to come to the General Manager's office. 'Walker thought with me that Elliot, if made Assistant General Manager, should not be hindered by bus directorships and I said I thought it would be useful to have a sort of printer's devil in the office, a gentleman and a presentable man who could be seen anywhere and do anything and who could be on all the bus boards. The man who came to mind was Chambers, the solicitor who has been doing all the road legal work and therefore au fait with a good deal on the bus side of things. He says Wil Bishop will go anytime in the autumn but the CME, Richard Maunsell, wants to stay in post until the Portsmouth electrification is finished next year. I expect it would get on just as well without him. It would have to if he stepped on a banana skin and broke his neck.'

30 April 1936

Amery spent the morning at home before having lunch at Waterloo which was followed by a board meeting, then one at Marks & Spencer. Finally he went to the

RMS *Queen Mary* leaving Southampton on 27 May 1936 for Cherbourg and the inaugural sailing to New York. (*Southampton Local Studies Library*)

The officers' team at Waddon before the bowls match against the club, 23 May 1936. (*Southampton Local Studies Library*)

House of Commons, afterwards taking the night train to Liverpool for a Cammell & Laird board meeting the following day. He commented that the new LMS sleeping cars were admirable.

20 May 1936

Amery attended committee meetings at Waterloo before proceeding with his fellow directors to Weymouth for an inspection tour. The following day they were in Southampton where they spent some time in the docks. After lunch Amery noted that he took Major Dawes, the railway's Secretary-designate, over the *Queen Mary*.

6 June 1936

Szlumper did not record it but, according to the press, he was at Gatwick for the airport's official re-opening. The airport had started as a grass aerodrome for private flying in 1930. It had just been re-developed by its third owner into a London airport with its own railway station, a revolutionary terminal and the services of British Airways Ltd to Paris, Germany, Scandinavia and the Isle of Wight. The formal opening by the Secretary of State for Air, Viscount Swinton, was celebrated with an air show.

19 June 1936

Szlumper visited Templecombe on the main line to Exeter. It was at Salisbury on his return that Southern director, the Earl of Radnor, got into his compartment. Szlumper told Radnor, a landowner and farmer near Salisbury, that the air was thick with rumours about the future management structure shape of the railway which could include an executive type as practiced by the LMS but which he considered as 'practically unbreathable.' Radnor replied that if it was so, some decisions would be required and that rumours were very unsettling for everybody.

22 June 1936

It was this diary entry that revealed most dramatically Szlumper's frustration with Walker, and perhaps the General Manager's failure to take his deputy fully into his confidence. Thus he wrote that at last he had got Walker to agree on Short going to Southampton as Biddle's assistant when Missenden took on Cox's job. He had detailed these changes on the staff list and had taken it in to Walker to sign. 'I said I had been waiting for over a week for the opportunity to have a chat with him as I felt I ought to tell him that I was now making a determined effort to find outside employment and leave the railway. He asked why on earth did I want to do that? I replied that it was because the more time went on, the less clear did the future become. He asked me in what way. I said that the air was surcharged with rumours, some vague and from unreliable sources, others from undoubtedly authoritative sources – rumours which had become most general, some of them being put to me by grades as low as platform foremen. One very prevalent rumour being that when he retired, there is to be no General Manager but an organisation like the LMS with a President of the Executive and Vice Presidents – he replied he had never heard of any such suggestion and would not give any credence to it. He said surely the chairman at his age could not contemplate shouldering such a burden as this would mean. I told him that a rumour which came from well-informed quarters in the city was to the effect that the chairman had decided to soon retire as he did not believe in staying on beyond the age of sixty-five – Holland-Martin is now sixty-three. I said it was rumoured an outsider would be brought in as General Manager upon his retirement. He said that there was not the least likelihood of this; he was not in the confidence of the directors in the matter but it never entered his mind that anyone other than I would succeed him. He was sure I need have no apprehensions at all. I reminded him that an army man – a grand little fellow, Major Dawes – had just been brought in as Secretary and therefore there would be nothing extraordinary about say a banker being brought in as General Manager. He agreed a bad precedent had been set but again tried to re-assure me that there was no question but that I would succeed him. Anyway, I did not feel justified waiting one, two, three or more years. Finding myself much older, perhaps to be told I was too old to be appointed, finding perhaps that I had also become too old to jump to the outside world, I feel I ought to jump now. Indeed, I would have jumped three years ago had I known then that this would be my position at the age of fifty-two. Walker then said that he would be going before the end of next year. The directors wanted him to put into force the changes (retirements of Cox, Bishop and Maunsell) and to stop for six months to see the new appointments settle down, so that he would be going sometime in 1937, probably in the late autumn. I said that did not clear the position for me. I might then learn that an Executive was to be formed. I had no intention of holding a pistol at his head or of the directors. Much as I disliked the idea of throwing up a thirty-five years railway career, I felt my only course in view of the uncertainty was to secure outside employment and then come to ask to be relieved of my railway duties. I had thought it proper to come and advise him of this while the other changes were in contemplation. He then went on to advise me to think well over my project, not to jump from the frying pan into the fire, not to worsen my position or my cash situation. Told him the sort of things I had in mind included becoming a MP and told him had already thrown out feelers to three undertakings which had been very agreeably received. Had quite a nice chat on the pros and cons. Told him had not given a hint of my feelings to any of the directors but added that on 19 June had learnt from Radnor that Sir Francis Dent wished to resign. He was surprised and would have a chat with him on the general subject of our interview. I said that before Dent went to Australia, he said something to me which confirmed my suspicions as to the future policy of the board but I would be very glad if he would have a talk with Dent and advise me of the result. Our talk was perfectly friendly and pleasant – as between brothers.'

24 June 1936

Amery was not at the Aviation Committee as he was at two non-railway meetings that day. It was at the railway meeting that Clive Pearson joined the committee. Amery was, however, at the customary dinner of directors and officers that preceded the board meeting the following day. Szlumper was not there but according to his diary of the following day, Walker took the opportunity at the dinner of sounding out two or three directors on the subject of organisation; and it was at this dinner that Gore-Browne asked Walker what he thought of the Executive idea. Walker replied that it had brought the LMS to a very sorry state. 'In the USA where conditions were vaster and one General Manager could not possibly keep control of a great system, it worked because the President of the Executive was a technical railwayman – virtually a General Manager – and his Vice Presidents were technical men (engineer, motive power etc) and they really acted as an Executive Committee of the board. But the organisation really took practically all the power out of the board's hands, especially where the President of the Executive was also chairman of the board. If Mr A as President of the Executive authorised or recommended a thing, it was unlikely that Mr A as chairman of the board would turn it down when it came up for board confirmation.'

25 June 1936

Amery was not at the Southern's board meeting as he was at the speech day of his old school, Harrow. But Szlumper was there and after the meeting, Walker told him that he was quite sure the idea of a LMS-type Executive on the Southern was dead, although he acknowledged that 'it had been on the tapis at one time to a small extent.'

26 June 1936

This was the last board meeting for the Southern's Secretary, Frank Willis. Szlumper noted that at the end of the meeting the Chairman just said, 'Well, Gentlemen, that concludes the business,' and the meeting just dissolved. 'Not one word of good wishes or thanks to Willis, very pointed.' The reasons for this is not obvious but it may have been related to a strain in relations with the chairman about the financial details of retirement which had been mentioned in Szlumper's diary in March. It was interesting that as Willis retired, he gave an interview to the *Evening News* as to how he saw the future of the British railway system – an amalgamation of the four main line railways and control by the railways of all transport outside the London area.

30 June 1936
Szlumper made no mention of the annual summer outing of the Retired Railway Officers' Society to Southampton, although he acted as the host. Over a hundred participated in a tour of the docks before inspecting the RMS *Queen Mary*.

5 August 1936
In July Major Dawes had moved into the post of Secretary that had been vacated by Willis. A career army officer with a background in military engineering both at home and overseas, Dawes had latterly been a General Staff Officer at the War Office. In April he had been offered the post of Secretary. It was at an unrecorded date in July that Szlumper had a heart-to-heart meeting with Dawes when he explained that he was considering leaving the railway. No diary record was made of the conversation but a later entry is a clear indicator of what was said. On this day of

Szlumper was president of the Railway Students Association when the annual convention was held at Highfield Hall, Southampton, 17 July 1936. (*Southampton Local Studies Library*)

5 August, the Deputy Chairman asked Szlumper to have a word with him. 'After a brief chat about the week's traffic, he said that what he really wanted to talk to me about was my own position. Dawes had passed on to him my conversation to the effect that I was seeking to go outside and he imagined I had wished Dawes to do so. But above all he wanted me to look upon him as my friend in the matter. I told him I did not want Dawes to pass it on to him but I told Dawes that our chat was not confidential and he could do what he thought right about it. I made it quite clear I was not trying to hold a pistol at anyone's head. As I told Dawes, my intention was to secure my outside job first and then go to Walker and say I wished to be released from the railway – it would be irrevocable. Gore-Browne said he perfectly understood that – did I want to leave the railway?'

Szlumper replied that it was very difficult to speak frankly as it would obviously implicate Walker who was not present. Szlumper told him that he had had a talk a week before the last board with Walker and also with Bishop who thought he should open his mind to Gore-Browne. He had replied to Bishop that he would not do so for fear of being thought to be holding a pistol, either for action or for information. 'However, it was in consequence of these talks that I did not prohibit Dawes from telling Gore-Browne. Gore-Browne asked what was my trouble, was it lack of promotion? I replied "partly". He said he could wholeheartedly sympathise with me because for years he had suffered under a benevolent despot and had often been thoroughly down about it and he could believe I was similarly suffering. I said that I could sum up my feelings in three sentences but would first say that the air at Waterloo was so thick with rumours as to be practically unbreathable. My three sentences were: For years I have been living in a state of expectation; now owing to rumours I felt I was living in a state of uncertainty; and promotion was very slow. Gore-Browne said he could entirely see my point of view and entirely sympathised with it. As to rumours, he could say that there was nothing agreed. I gathered that he had been somewhat taken by the LMS organisation but had personally dropped it but it was still lingering in the minds of some of the directors – anyway, nothing was settled. As to promotion, he said I would no doubt see their difficulty – with a man of such conspicuous ability as Walker, and a man for whom he and I had such admiration, the directors could not put a pistol to his head and say, "when are you going?" I agreed and said it was my constant care to do nothing that would expedite his departure. No one knows better than me the loss to the company it would be when he did go. Gore-Browne did not think Walker had discussed the question with the chairman but he had said to Gore-Browne that he was going when the Portsmouth electrification was finished – when would that be, October? I said, no – June 1937. Gore-Browne said perhaps Walker meant Portsmouth No. 2 scheme. I said that when I spoke to Walker in the middle of last month, Walker had said to me "Well, Gilbert, I am going next June when the Portsmouth electrification is finished." But I said I have heard "next year" repeated so often that it is one of the causes of my unsettlement – when Walker returned to work in 1928 after his duodenal trouble, he told me he would not be stopping much longer. Szlumper explained that each year from 1933, Walker had told him he would be retiring but it never happened.

'Gore-Browne said he thoroughly agreed with me and knew exactly how I felt, having experienced the same sort of thing himself. I said I did really feel rather straining at the bit while I had sufficient years of energy left to do something. Gore-Browne asked me of my intentions. I said intended to try and secure a bread-and-butter job which would enable me to live and pay my £1,200 annual insurance premiums but a job which would leave me enough spare time to take on other jobs when and if I had earned what I considered enough to "move" upon. I was going to Walker and saying, "I am definitely going to leave the railway. Will you please say when I may go." Gore-Browne then repeated that he wanted me to look upon him as my friend in the matter. Did I really want to leave the railway? Replied, obviously did not, I had been born and bred on the railway and did not want to throw away my thirty-five years service. But I felt at the moment that I would be doing myself less than justice if I did not make a change. He was very nice and said that though entitled is perhaps a strong word, I was entitled to know something more definite about my future – did I mind having a talk with the Chairman? Might he act as an intermediary and speak to the Chairman first and then get the Chairman to see me? No objection, always on the understanding that it was clear I was not trying to hold a pistol to their heads – I had no intention of coming and saying I have the offer of these jobs and will you make it worth my while to stay? He said that was quite clear and he was entirely with me.

'He then asked if the matter pressed – all the directors were away until October – could I wait until then for some further news? He repeated there was nothing settled. He did not know if the organisation would change. Various directors were thinking in various directions. Did I feel I had to take definite steps before October? Replied that unless some unexpected and most attractive offer were made to me and requiring an immediate decision, I thought I would wait – I did not want to incommode them and my position at the moment was that I had only mentioned my desires to three outside people – one quite casually and he had bitten hard on it and had asked me twice when I was coming to see him. One friend had put to me a tentative offer saying he would put it to his board if he could know I would be willing to accept – I had not yet done this. So many people were away this holiday season that I probably could not do much if I did press and anyway I could not actually commit myself without first letting him know.

'He asked how old I was – about his age of fifty? Said no, fifty-two and I feel I must move before I am too old. I may stop on one, two or three years and find things mature in a way that does not suit me and also find I am too old to move. As I told Walker the other day, if I had known in 1934 when I had a strong offer made to me to go outside, that in 1936 my feelings would be what they now are, I should certainly have gone then – I had kicked myself for not going and in another two or three years I did not want to be kicking myself again. He said he perfectly understood my feelings, the state and the rumours must be very unsettling. I replied that they were to everybody and all sorts of railwaymen had come to me to find out if there was any truth in this and that – there was a great deal of unsettlement. I felt it was now or never as my experience could be of great value to some firms. And I still had plenty of energy to throw into a new job and make a success of it. He agreed that I had and must get through a terrific lot of work daily. He was exceedingly nice and sympathetic and it was left he would have a talk with the Chairman and get him talk to me.'

23 September 1936

Dawes asked Szlumper how his affairs were progressing and if the Chairman had had a talk with him. He had not 'because after I had had a chat with the Deputy Chairman, I had played unintentional box and cox with the Chairman – when he was here, I was on holiday, now I am here and he is on holiday. Dawes said the Chairman was anxious to have a talk with me. I told Dawes a few hints as how things stood with me and what I thought were the disadvantages of an Executive with a President. Dawes said Walker was definitely going in October of next year and had so informed the Chairman. I said that Walker had apparently projected the date by another six months and would presumably go on doing so.'

6 October 1936

W.J. Hatcher, Assistant Secretary, told Szlumper that Dawes would not let him teach him his business. He also told him that the question of a President and Executive was very much to the fore and that he had been asked to provide particulars of all sorts of our men who might be considered as Vice Presidents. Szlumper noted that Holland-Martin and Gore-Browne had returned to duty after their vacations and he hoped they would like the alterations and decorations that had been effected in their absence: 'the old luncheon room turned into an Engineering Committee Room while the old Engineering Committee Room had been turned into a more capacious luncheon room to be equipped with small tables, the intention being to invite thereto several of the assistants and junior officers.'

Szlumper noted that the first train ferry arrived that day safely at Dover and Dunkirk respectively. 'I wonder if any except a very few of us realise the mountain of work and worry the damned thing has meant.'

The deck of one of the train ferries in 1936 before entering service.
(*Dover Ferry Photos*)

7 October 1936
Amery was at Docks and Aviation Committee meetings. At the latter, it was reported that the railway would purchase 800 acres of land at £80 per acre from the Kemp Town Brewery for the proposed Lullingstone airport.

12 October 1936
Szlumper travelled on the 08.45 special train with a party from Victoria to Dover and then on to Paris to officially inaugurate the train ferry service. They arrived in Paris at 17.20 and motored to Eugene Massett's office for an Extraordinary General Meeting to wind up the old Société Anonyme de Navigation Alsace Lorraine Angleterre [ALA]. Masset was the head of Société Anonyme de Gérance et d'Armement [SAGA] which had owned ALA until the Southern had purchased it in 1933, although he was still director of ALA which operated the train ferries. This was followed by a board meeting of the new ALA company with Walker and Szlumper as directors. They then motored to the George V Hotel to unpack, 'dress in war paint' and repack to arrive at the banquet in the hotel by 20.00. 'A good job and much back scratching, a Commander of Legion d'Honneur for Walker (the highest French honour).' They then went to the Nord station, leaving it at 23.20 in sleeping cars to Dunkirk.

Loading trials of the Night Ferry coaches at Dunkirk. (*Dover Ferry Photos*)

The Inaugural Night Ferry at Dover. (*Dover Ferry Photos*)

These two official 1936 photographs of the Night Ferry were captioned 'supervised loading'. (*Dover Ferry Photos*)

'Quite a successful trip except some damned fool of a Frenchman against printed instructions placed a scotch in some unseeable position in front of the wheels of one coach which derailed as the train was being pulled off at Dover.' Unfortunately the carriage was carrying Szlumper, Walker and the Home Secretary, Sir John Simon. He noted they were thirty minutes late arriving in London with several frayed tempers but on the whole he felt it was a very successful trip except for the pitifully long time schedule which he considered had somehow to be expedited. Two days later the through sleeping car services started for the public between London and Paris, leaving Victoria at 22.00 while in the other direction a train left Paris at 21.50.

15 October 1936

This entry in Szlumper's diary again reveals something of his relationship with the General Manager when he recorded Sir Maurice Denny visiting him at Waterloo. When he took him to Walker to shake hands, Denny said to Walker that he understood he was going away on a trip to South Africa. Walker replied that he would be away seven weeks, a business trip. This was news to Szlumper and when Denny had departed, he immediately went back to Walker. 'You just said to Denny something that has been worrying me for some time.' Asking what it was, Szlumper replied 'You are going to South Africa and I am wondering why you have been bottling the fact up.' Walker responded that surely he knew all about it.

Szlumper acknowledged that he had heard a rumour that he was going but there were so many rumours that he could not spare time to listen to them all. Walker apologised and said he thought everyone knew and that there had never been an intention of keeping it from him. He insisted the omission was entirely unintended and he thought Szlumper knew all about it. Moreover he had not made up his mind about going until two weeks previously. Szlumper declared he still was pressing ahead with seeking employment outside the railway because of the uncertainty with the rumours of an executive which again were very strong. Walker's response was that he had had several talks with the Chairman and Deputy Chairman and the idea of an Executive Committee with the chairman as President of the Executive had been dropped. Moreover there was no question of Szlumper not succeeding him and he had never talked with the Chairman along other lines. 'Who else could succeed him? I said they might find someone from the army, navy, air force or the banking world. He said that was unthinkable but I replied I was glad to hear it so far but it did not seem very definite to me. He asked me what my outside world ideas were. I said to collect directorships enough to bring me in a good income without so much work as at present. He begged me not to do anything hastily. He was sure I had no grounds for worry on the question.'

Walker said he was sure Szlumper was the only person in mind to succeed him. Szlumper said he was still uncertain and did not want to turn down outside offers only to find in a few months that the directors had made another appointment. Walker asked him to be patient as it would be discussed by the directors at the dinner before the 19 November board. Szlumper said he was still unsettled, although he did not want to throw away thirty-five years of railway work. Walker said that he had such a thorough grasp of all the details of railway working and was sure there was no question about his appointment as General Manager; and he could think of no one else who could succeed him. Walker's journey to South Africa would be for the Empire Exhibition in Johannesburg and he, his wife and director Sir George Courthope would leave England on 23 October.

25 October 1936

The Chairman and Deputy asked Szlumper to see them at 16.15. Holland-Martin said he and his colleagues had been giving much thought to the future and felt there should be a closer liaison between the board and the officers – not only the chief officers but also their assistants, and they thought the best way to achieve this would be to have some form of committee, for instance the Chairman, Deputy, General Manager and some others who would need to be very carefully selected with the Secretary in attendance. Their idea was that such a committee would not supplant the General Manager but help to take the load off him and give him time for thinking. They felt it very desirable that the Chairman should be in possession of some of the arguments for and against every scheme. Thus on an engineering matter, they would have not only Walker's summary of the case but also Ellson's, Hall's and Scott's (the architect) and they would wish the various officers to voice their opinions freely. It would enable the Chairman to fully support the scheme at the board and know all about it when it was discussed. Walker was such a big man and such a wonderful railwayman and could grasp a thing so completely that he was prone to put it before the board as a fait accompli and rather expect the board to accept it without question but the board sometimes felt they were being rushed without a real opportunity to consider the matter. A committee such as suggested would remove this feeling, the board would know that the chairman had, as it were, grown up with the facts and were in sympathy with the scheme put before them. The chairman instanced the new Portsmouth boat which had been thrust before an inappropriate finance committee at very short notice. But if he and the Deputy Chairman had known all the detailed arguments, they could have seen that the other interested parties were informed of the proposals and the reasons for them. Such a committee might meet, say, once a week but the question of the composition of the committee would need very careful thought. The General Manager would be the most important member of it and would in every way be General Manager but he should be able to share his very great load with the committee and should have more time for thinking and for inspection and supervision. Further, it would give the Chairman and Deputy more opportunity to know the junior officers – suppose the General Manager or one of the chief officers collapsed, the Chairman would find it very difficult to know who to promote.

Holland-Martin also said there was some positive information about Walker retiring upon the opening of Portsmouth No.1 Electrification and that the board had decided to offer Szlumper the position of General Manager. 'They were most anxious to promote someone on the railway and not go outside, and they had in mind my many years of excellent service and those of my father as well. I was known to such a great number of the staff who looked up to me and esteemed me and would work wholeheartedly with me, that they the directors looked to me to keep them together and to maintain the family spirit. I said I much appreciated what they said and did not see why the idea of a properly selected committee should not work but I felt unable to discuss what they had outlined in the absence of the General Manager as by doing so I might seem to be casting reflections on his conduct of affairs. I doubted if the committee idea would appeal to a man of his ability and at his stage and I hoped therefore they had not in mind to put it into force until he had retired. The Chairman said they had not. I told them I was glad to know of their ideas because I had felt an unsettlement about the future and the Deputy said he quite understood and sympathised and had put this point to the directors and had told them how much he appreciated that I had not put a pistol at his head. They both congratulated me and said they looked forward to many years of happy and successful co-operation and with me.'

18 November 1936

After attending committee meetings at Waterloo, Amery was at a railway dinner in the evening. It was most revealing in that there was a discussion on the proposal of Gore-Browne that the railway change its organisation to LMS-type in spite of what had been said previously. Amery wrote that his underlying idea was sound but was not clearly worked out and was mixed up with his anxiety that if Szlumper became General Manager, he could be the autocrat that Walker had been. Amery suggested a modification – that there should be a standing executive committee or council on which besides the Chairman and Deputy Chairman, the heads of the main branches of the services should sit as equals with full power of limitation. 'This commended itself to everybody and was finally adopted together with the decision that Szlumper should be told that he is going to succeed.'

17 February 1937

Amery was at committee meetings at Waterloo in the morning. They included aviation but he made no comment – the minutes recorded that powers would be sought from Parliament to build a short line off the railway near Eynsford into the proposed airport at Lullingstone. In the afternoon, he attended the Docks Committee. Szlumper that day was at the Senate of London University for election as a Fellow of King's College.

11 May 1937

Szlumper did not mention it in his diary but according to Sean Day-Lewis, the official biographer of the celebrated locomotive engineer Oliver Bulleid, the Assistant General Manager played an important role in identifying and recommending Bulleid for the post of the Chief Mechanical Engineer. Thus it was that Bulleid attended Waterloo on Walker's invitation to be told to apply for the job. Bulleid had been the Assistant to the LNER CME, Sir Nigel Gresley, at King's Cross for over ten years.

26 May 1937

Szlumper recorded that after the Chairman's Committee, Holland-Martin asked him to his room. Gore-Browne was also there. The chairman said they had been having a chat with their colleagues and were looking forward to appointing him as General Manager at the board meeting the following day. The question was when the appointment would date from as Walker wanted to pilot some of his schemes through and it would not seem very friendly if he were just allowed to melt away after the July board when people were scattering for holidays and he would not have much of a send off.

'Would I object if the change-over took place at the following board as that would give them the chance of entertaining him and all the chief officers at the directors' dinner the night before and the opportunity of saying goodbye officially at the board on 14 October? I would take over the next day.' Szlumper replied that he would not have the least objection, his only anxiety being not when the change would be and when Sir Herbert would retire but what would happen when he did go. He was in no desperate hurry and he said he thought his patience had shown that. It was Gore-Browne who said that he and the chairman varied in their outlook on the subject of salary. The Chairman was inclined to pay a larger commencing salary whereas he, Gore-Browne, believed in giving a man an incentive to work for. He would prefer to start on the more modest side and give handsome increases at not far distant dates. The salary proposed was £6,000 to start with. Would it be acceptable? Szlumper replied in a non-enthusiastic way that it would. He noted they were both very agreeable and reiterated their pleasure at the appointment and that they looked forward to a happy and prosperous association with him. The board meeting duly took place the following day, Holland-Martin stating that Walker would retire on 14 October when Szlumper would become General Manager.

27 May 1937

After 26 May Szlumper made no diary entries until 19 July. But in his diary he filed a hand-written copy of a letter to the Chairman. I cannot allow the day to pass, he wrote, without recording to you my sincere thanks for having commended me to your colleagues as a successor to Sir Herbert Walker and for having appointed me to that very responsible office. 'Yours truly said that Sir Herbert is leaving behind him a brilliant example and I know therefore that you realise it is a most difficult example to follow. To the extent that I may fall short, I look to your forbearance, and I for my part will exert my utmost effort to make the deficit as small as possible. In this and in every other way I will show, better than I can express in words, my keen appreciation of the confidence you are placing in me.'

Szlumper also wrote to the Deputy Chairman. I know, he wrote, that much of the onus of today's board decisions is upon you. 'Before leaving the office, I do wish to express to you my heartfelt thanks, not only for your share in the decisions but also for the friendly support you have given my flagging spirits in the matter. Had it not been for you last November, I firmly believe I should not now be in the railway service. As it is, I will have added zest in endeavouring to repay your kindness and your help by wholehearted effort and devoted service to the concern on which I was born and bred and to those who direct its services. It is with real pleasure that I look forward to some years of happy association with you and the opportunity to justify your confidence in me.'

28 May 1937

Gore-Browne's reply to Szlumper was also filed in the diary. The Deputy Chairman declared that he much appreciated his letter. 'You have had my heartfelt sympathy during the last few months, and I quite realise that on occasions your heart must have felt very sick with hope deferred. However, all that is now over, and I am very glad that you have been appointed to this great position. I am quite sure you will do the work most admirably. You will realise that the Chairman and I are only out to help and not to interfere. We have given you our confidence, and I am sure you will give us yours. If there is anything that I can do to help – and sometimes an outside mind is helpful, even though completely ignorant of railway working, please do not hesitate to let me know. I feel that your first problem is a difficult one, and it is vitally important for you to have working under you young men of great ability who will be of real assistance to you so that you can be out and about the line, and not chained to your office stool. I much look forward to a talk with you at an early date, and you will please not hesitate to let me know when your views have matured. Our ambition is to go to the board next month with concrete proposals as to your immediate subordinates.

The bowls, tennis and cricket teams of the officers and the Club at Waddon, 12 June 1937. (*Southampton Local Studies Library*)

I look forward to many years of close co-operation with you in the service of the great company to which you have devoted so much of your life and to which I hope I may be able to devote a good deal of mine.'

23 June 1937
A busy day for Amery started with committee meetings at Waterloo followed by his first meeting at yet another company that he had become a director of – the Goodyear Tyre & Rubber Company, an American company of international repute that was a market leader. He was back to Waterloo for a Docks Committee, then the House of Commons. Dinner was taken with his fellow railway directors when they discussed insurance and electrification. He returned to the House of Commons for a division.

30 June 1937
Amery was at Waterloo for committee meetings. An inspection followed of the Portsmouth line electrification. Dinner was later taken at the Queens Hotel in Southsea where Amery was seated between Bulleid and timetable specialist, Toby Wheeler. Amery noted that he talked largely on his war experience with Bulleid whom he described as a pleasant and intelligent fellow.

Szlumper and the Dover mayor, on an 1898 Benz car, inaugurate the new arrangements for loading of cars onto the train ferries by driving onto the ramp to access *Shepperton Ferry*, 28 June 1937. (*Dover Ferry Photos*)

1 July 1937

Amery continued the tour with his fellow directors to Havant and Fratton. At Portsmouth there was an official reception with the Lord Mayor, the Portsmouth MPs and the General Manager. Walker proposed the toast of the Lord Mayor who in reply said the City of Portsmouth proposed to build an empire air base in Langstone Harbour; and he hoped that when the airport was established, the railway would back the city and provide a good train service into the base.

15 July 1937

Amery attended in the morning a meeting at the Gloucester Railway Carriage & Wagon Company. At some stage that day, Sir Christopher Bullock asked Amery if he would keep him in mind for a directorship. Bullock told Amery that Swinton was 'a pretty mean creature.' Bullock had been the Permanent Secretary at the Air Ministry until he was sacked in 1936 by the Air Minister for an indiscretion about a possible involvement in Imperial Airways after his retirement.

19 July 1937

Szlumper noted that Gore-Browne came to discuss suggested staff appointments. Szlumper suggested Elliot, the Assistant Traffic Manager, to Assistant General

Szlumper with a group at Southampton, before a flight over Southampton in empire flying boat *Canopus*, 29 November 1937. The 'C' Class flying-boat *Canopus* begins its departure. (*Southampton Local Studies Library*)

Manager, R.M.T Richards, the Development Officer, to Assistant Traffic Manager and E.F.E. Livesey, Deputy Continental Assistant, to Development Officer. Gore-Browne said he was whole-heartedly in favour of them but thought he would have trouble with Dent who did not believe in having an Assistant General Manager. 'We discussed the question and decided that the size of the Southern as compared with any of its pre-war precedents warranted an assistant to enable the work to be covered.' Gore-Browne then asked Szlumper if he was satisfied with the salary the directors had settled for him. Szlumper replied he was not as by the time the added surtax and income tax were deducted from it, he would only receive some £800 or £900 more for all the responsibility of being General Manager. The Deputy Chairman felt this could not be the fact but Szlumper assured him it was. Gore-Browne then asked Szlumper to remind him later in the year. Szlumper said he would not do so as he had brought the fact to his attention and that was all he proposed to do, the rest being up to him. After the discussion, Szlumper travelled with Holland-Martin to Southampton for a luncheon on the Canadian Pacific Steamship Company's RMS *Empress of Britain* for the opening of a Canadian government-sponsored campaign to increase trade between Southampton and Canada.

14 October 1937
After the first board meeting that Szlumper attended as General Manager, Amery recorded that he had helped to prevent what he considered a rather unceremonious and wounding treatment of Walker about his joining the board after a short interval. It was this meeting that also relieved Szlumper of some more of his directorships. Consequently Elliot became the nominee director on Railway Air Services Ltd and on the Devon General, Southern National and Southern Vectis bus companies while J.C. Chambers took Aldershot & District, Maidstone & District and Southdown Motor Services.

20 October 1937
After attending committee meetings at Waterloo, Amery spoke briefly to Paul Lindenberg of the Industrial Finance & Investment Corporation about the scheme of Frank Bustard to introduce cheaper and less ostentatious Transatlantic travel. Bustard, a former White Star Line manager, had formed the Atlantic Steam Navigation Company in 1934 but his scheme had been blocked by the government. The company would however figure in Szlumper's post-war career.

26 October 1937
For reasons unknown, Szlumper made no diary entries between August and December. This day was his first public appearance as General Manager. The occasion was the annual dinner of the Southern Railway Supervisors' Association.

It was at Lyons' Corner House in Coventry Street before a gathering of over 200 railwaymen. According to the Southern Railway Magazine, Missenden paid a stirring tribute to the qualities of the new General Manager. In a long reply, Szlumper said that as an eleven-day old infant, he felt a certain amount of bashfulness in speaking but was very proud to have been appointed to the executive hub of the great railway.

November 1937
The Southern Railway magazine described the career of the new General Manager. Paying tribute to his predecessor, Szlumper wrote that he wondered if sometimes sight was lost of the objects of daily work which was to run the railway so efficiently that it could pay for employment and pay a reasonable return to the railway's partners, the stockholders. To enable that to be done, everyone had to work for the marketing of the commodity of transport. It had to be remembered that they were the servants of the public and had to provide them with efficient, reliable and safe transport.

9 November 1937
With his new position, Szlumper joined his fellow General Managers as a director of Carter Paterson and the Hay's Wharf Cartage Company, the latter company controlling the removals company, Pickfords Ltd and some road hauliers. Carter Paterson and Hay's Wharf had been acquired by the railways in 1933.

24 November 1937
Amery dined at Waterloo with his fellow directors. He noted that Szlumper put forward some projects for competition among stations and for increasing the number of canvassing staff. He also reported a big development to the dockside at Southampton, a six-acre shed for General Motors to assemble American and German cars.

29 November 1937
Holland-Martin and Szlumper visited Southampton Docks with a group from Waterloo. They travelled in a special Pullman car attached to the 08.30 train. At Southampton the coach was detached and taken to no.9 berth from which they were taken in launches to the Imperial Airways empire flying boat 'Canopus' at Hythe. The group included the Deputy Chairman and other directors, Bishop, Bulleid, Biddle, Woods Humphery and the Chief Inspecting Officer of Railways, Alan Mount. They were flown over the docks to see the temporary facilities for the airline's empire air base.

1 December 1937

After attending meetings at Waterloo, Amery lunched alone with the wife of the Marquess of Willingdon who had just become Lord Warden of the Cinque Ports. She and her husband had recently returned from India where he had been Viceroy. Amery told her there was little chance of Freeman getting a directorship with the railway as Walker would be taking the vacancy.

10 December 1937

This was the first entry in Szlumper's diary since July and he noted that after discussing with Holland-Martin merit increases of £1,000 for officers, the chairman said that he thought that they should tell him that they did not intend to do anything about his salary at that stage as he had only been in the saddle a short time 'but we are all very pleased with the way you are doing and I think I can promise you something by next midsummer.'

16 December 1937

After the board meeting, Szlumper went to Holland-Martin in his office. At the end of their discussion, Szlumper stated that he had survived two board meetings and asked if there was anything he would like altered. 'Did I speak too much, or too little, or with too much levity? I had adopted my own style and had not tried to ape Walker; but if there was anything he would like adjusted, it would be much easier to do it now than let it grow into a habit?' The Chairman replied that he was doing excellently and everyone was delighted at the way he was doing things.

19 January 1938

It is perhaps surprising that hitherto and given the enormity of the airport proposal, Szlumper had made only a few references to Lullingstone. With the New Year there was an opportunity for review, the task being given to the young Leslie Harrington who had been very much involved with the Southern's air activities from the beginning in 1934. His report detailed the known costs and revenues at Croydon airport, noting that in no year had receipts at Croydon reached the figure of annual expenditure. It was difficult, he explained, to make projections for revenue because government policy was not clear. If Lullingstone was to be built, what would happen to Croydon, he asked. Would most traffic be concentrated at Lullingstone or would it be divided between other airports such as Heston which the government had not long acquired with a view to its ultimate expansion and development into a first class airport? There was also Gatwick which had lost its passenger services in 1937 but its owner, Airports Ltd, had just submitted plans to the Air Ministry for its re-development. Finally, Harrington wrote, there was Fairlop in Essex which the Corporation of the City of London was proposing to develop as an airport. If it developed in a big way, the passenger traffic at

Lullingstone could be considerable but it would not be profitable. The result of Harrington's memorandum was quite dramatic – the Southern would no longer be prepared to buy the land at Lullingstone and build the airport.

26 January 1938

After attending Stores and Finance Committee meetings at Waterloo, Amery was at a board meeting at Goodyear. After taking lunch at home, he returned to Waterloo for Docks and Aviation committee meetings. Amery did not comment on the latter when the Lullingstone airport project was again discussed, the General Manager being instructed to use Harrington's report as basis for communicating the railway's change of policy to the Air Ministry. Amery then went to a meeting at the Iraq Currency Board. Finally he was at a Southern Railway dinner 'to bid farewell to Bishop who made a rambling speech about his parentage and youth.'

27 January 1938

Amery lunched at Waterloo before the board meeting when Szlumper made a presentation to Bishop on his retirement. It was also the first board meeting that Walker attended as a co-opted director.

2 February 1938

Szlumper recorded that the Deputy Chairman came to his room to tell him that the directors wanted to adopt a little different procedure at the special board meeting for the annual accounts that year. He explained that Walker had always given the whole story, telling the board what they could pay but the previous year Sheath had suggested that this was a wrong procedure and the Chairman was the proper person to undertake that. Sheath's view, he said, had commended itself to several of his colleagues, and the intention was that the Chairman should get up and say briefly what the increases and decreases in expenditure were and then call on Szlumper to supplement it with any detail he thought wise. Gore-Browne concluded by asking what he thought about it. Szlumper replied that he considered it was the directors' decision and that was all there was to it but he had always regarded it as an account of the General Manager's stewardship. Gore-Browne agreed but said that it would still be left to the General Manager with the Chairman only giving outline figures. This was the last entry in Szlumper's diaries until 25 August 1939.

10 February 1938

Szlumper explained the change on the railway's Lullingstone policy to Shelmerdine at the Air Ministry. He was quite frank when he said that the railway felt it was more of a national venture than one for private enterprise. Nevertheless, the Southern was still enthusiastic about Lullingstone which it considered had many advantages and was prepared at its own expense to construct a branch line direct into the terminal buildings to give the fullest access between London and the airport.

17 February 1938
Amery was at the Southern board when it was stated that Dudley Docker was not seeking re-election, Walker offering to fill the vacancy.

24 February 1938
Both Szlumper and Amery were at the annual meeting of the railway. Amery described it as a very happy affair. Theodore Instone said the shareholders welcomed Szlumper as the General Manager and were convinced he would be a worthy successor to Sir Herbert Walker. The chairman spoke of the continued growth of Continental traffic including that on the train ferries. Holland-Martin also said the company had decided to curtail its airline operations. With regard to Lullingstone, he said the Southern did not feel it was for the company as a railway to develop the site as an airport. He was of the opinion that an airport of international importance so close to the capital of the Empire was not a matter for private enterprise.

4 March 1938
Until this time, it was Cobham who had been pursuing and pushing the various parties involved in the Lullingstone proposals and it was Cobham who had had all the anxiety but it was now the turn of the officers of the Air Ministry. As a result of Holland-Martin's statement at the railway's annual meeting, Szlumper was summoned to a meeting at the Air Ministry. He was told by the civil servants that the Secretary of State for Air was concerned at the announcement that the development of the airport would not be proceeded with; and he was anxious to know whether the decision was final and the position of the option for the purchase of the land.

While there is no diary record of Szlumper's sentiments on Lullingstone, the Air Ministry file has survived. According to this, he told the meeting that the idea of abandoning the scheme had been in the chairman's mind for some time. It was the size of the estimated capital and maintenance costs which had led the railway to decide that it would not be financially to its advantage to proceed with the development. Discussion followed about the option the Southern had had since 1936 to buy the land. Szlumper expressed the opinion that the option would still be exercised even if his company or the government did not intend to develop the land as an airport as it was cheap and the area was good for housing development. On the assumption that there were no legal difficulties, he said that he envisaged the railway buying the land and holding it until the time was ripe for its sale. Szlumper assured the officials that if a first class airport should be built at Lullingstone, the railway could be relied upon

Szlumper and Bulleid at Ashford, 8 March 1938. (*Southampton Local Studies Library*)

to provide ample rail facilities including the building of the spur line into the airport at its own expense.

1 April 1938
Szlumper inspected the first Air Raid Precautions class at the railway's Brunswick House near Vauxhall where he put on a gas mask. The following day *The Times*

Szlumper trys on a gas mask at first ARP class, Nine Elms 1 April 38.

Szlumper inspects the ARP class. (*Southampton Local Studies Library*)

reported that the Southern had enrolled over 10,000 Air Raid Precautions volunteers from its staff.

11 April 1938

The issue of the railway booking ban again entered the correspondence columns of *The Times* in the April of 1938. Although there had been less criticism of the railways for threatening to withdraw the franchise of travel agents which sold tickets for non-approved airlines, the controversy had not gone away. The Southern was no longer directly involved in Railway Air Services but it was Szlumper who responded to the newspaper as he was the chairman of the Railway Companies' Association for the year. In his letter, he defended the railways' action on the grounds that it was reasonable that the railways' travel agents should restrict their activities to selling rail travel; and he asserted that the suggestion by a Member of Parliament that railway Bills might be blocked would be against the public interest and might cause the postponement of railway works.

29 June 1938

Amery was at a railway dinner when it was decided to raise the salary of the General Manager. Amery noted there was discussion about a coat of arms and that Holland-Martin got quite excited about it while everyone else seemed to think it a little absurd.

4 August 1938

Amery was on the 11.00 *Golden Arrow* train from Victoria to Dover, crossed the Channel and on to Paris from where a train was taken to Horfluh in Switzerland. This was to be his last great mountaineering holiday which would focus on Davos and Zermatt.

10 October 1938

Szlumper gave his presidential address to the Institute of Transport. On road transport, he said it was difficult to foresee a halt to its progress but with a large mileage of main road coming under the jurisdiction of the Ministry of Transport, there was an expectation of a uniform policy being applied, covering questions of layout, width, curvature, surface, etc. The organisation to look after 250,000 miles of roads compared ill with that found necessary to attend to about one-tenth of that length comprised in the railways. There was a need for a comprehensive and statesmanlike road policy. He emphasised that he was not one of those who would abolish road transport by a stroke of the pen. The fact that the mileage of roads was roughly ten times that of railways and that roads served every village and homestead made it obvious that a vast amount of traffic had to be carried on the roads.

On railways, he reminded his audience that in the war, they had fulfilled the many demands that were made of them. The limiting factors in railway

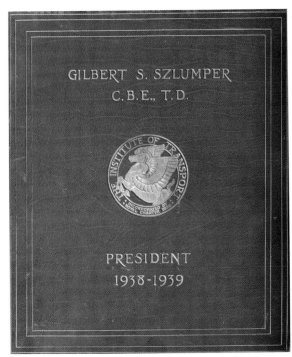

A founder member of the Institute of Transport, Szlumper was always a keen supporter. In the 1938-9 session, he was its president.

development were the loading gauge and the strength of underbridges and permanent way. It was no light matter to increase the strength of the underbridges or the permanent way to accommodate perhaps a new heavier type of locomotive to meet the incessant demand for speed and for more luxurious and heavier trains. It was rarely that the strengthening cost could be spread over more than very few trains. When the full costs of each form of transport including capital charges, operating costs and renewal provisions formed a major component of the price charged to the users, it would be found that the railways could comfortably hold their own against all comers, having regard to speed and the ability to handle large masses of traffic conveniently.

23 October 1938
Szlumper was in a deputation to the Minister of Transport seeking changes to the way by which the railways were regulated. Known as the Square Deal campaign, the deputation also included Holland-Martin and Stamp.

25 November 1938
As the year was approaching its end, the dilemma for the Air Ministry was whether to allow the option to buy the land at Lullingstone to expire or to ask the

Holland-Martin at the unveiling of a commemorative column for the centenary of Southampton Docks, 12 October 1938. Szlumper and guests listen to the words of the chairman. (*Southampton Local Studies Library*)

Southern to buy it and subsequently resell it. Having taken legal advice, Szlumper
wrote to Shelmerdine at the Air Ministry to tell him that he was quite willing to
recommend to his directors that the railway should buy the land but he would
require a letter from the Air Ministry undertaking to purchase the land from the
railway within a specified period of time at the price the Southern had paid plus
any out of pocket expenses.

16 December 1938

Shelmerdine saw Szlumper in the afternoon to explain the latest situation about
Lullingstone. According to the civil servant, they had a friendly chat, Szlumper
making light of the loss which the railway would incur over the option and
saying he was really only concerned with the legal position with the Kemp Town
Brewery. He admitted that the agreement with the brewery was drafted like so
many that no one understood exactly what it meant. Shelmerdine emphasised that
it was a matter of regret that it was not possible to proceed with the arrangement
previously envisaged.

6 February 1939

Amery attended a Finance Committee at Waterloo and a special board meeting
to review the year and decide the dividend. In spite of his earlier reservation

Szlumper presenting staff suggestions awards, 1 February 1939.
(*Southampton Local Studies Library*)

about Szlumper, Amery was full of praise for him. It was, he wrote, thanks to the admirable work of the General Manager and the staff that the final drop for the year was just over £600,000, which was almost directly due to extra wages and cost of materials. The ordinary preference shares would be paid in full with £94,000 to be carried forward; and the result should have a remarkable effect on the City and should contribute to a most successful annual meeting.

23 February 1939
At the annual meeting, the Chairman emphasised the railway had not felt the international storms unduly which was in great measure due to the General Manager. Szlumper, he said, had thoroughly justified the company's choice to succeed Walker. In the electrified area, there had been an increase of £180,000. Alone of the four main line railways, gross passengers receipts showed a slight increase.

2 March 1939
Szlumper wrote to Shelmerdine to confirm that the railway would be willing to hand over all the information on Lullingstone to enable the Air Ministry to take over where the Southern had left off. But Szlumper did feel that, in return, it was

only right that the company should be recompensed in some way for the work done and the expenditure incurred.

7 March 1939

Continuing to advance the railways' Square Deal campaign, Szlumper was was quite outspoken in a speech to the Portsmouth Chamber of Commerce. If steps were not taken to quickly implement the agreement between the two sides, he said there could be drastic reductions in railway services and facilities throughout the country. He also asserted that the whole economic and social structure of Britain was inescapably bound up with the railways. A collapse of the railway system would almost certainly mean the collapse of social and industrial life. The railways, he claimed, were on the brink of economic disaster which could only be averted by giving them freedom from out-of-date statutes. The alternative to the Square Deal was that the railways would close some of their unremunerative services while there would be a reduction in capital expenditure on new works.

3 May 1939

Shelmerdine replied to Szlumper about his offer and request for reimbursement over Lullingstone. The Director-General of Civil Aviation advised that the Air Ministry already had sufficient information for a decision as to the exact area needed and also had a provisional layout.

5 June 1939

Szlumper attended the annual dinner of Engineer & Railway Staff Corps – he had been promoted to Colonel in 1937. Stamp, who the previous year had been enno-bled, presided as Colonel while others present were Milne and Wedgwood who were also Colonels while Gresley, Elliot and Maunsell were Lieutenant Colonels.

14 June 1939

June must have been particularly demanding on Szlumper's time with the annual congress of the Institute of Transport at Southampton. Originally programmed to be in Northern Germany, it was switched to home waters with the deteriorating political situation in Europe. Being president, he opened the congress at the South Western Hotel.

25 and 26 August 1939

It was from this time that Szlumper's diary resumed in earnest and would continue throughout the war – and with entries at greater length. Thus he noted that meetings of the Railway Companies' Association in connection with the suspended strike of the Associated Society of Locomotive Steam Enginemen & Firemen [ASLEF] had left it that 'we were free to tell all the unions that if we

Szlumper is presented to the king and queen upon arriving back at Southampton from North America, 22 June 1939. (*Southampton Local Studies Library*)

could find a settlement of the demands of all of them that would be acceptable to all, we would recommend such a settlement to the RCA.'

He recorded that on the first day, the four general managers and staff assistants were at the Ministry of Labour from 15.00 to 23.25 and the following day from 16.00 until 23.15, holding meetings with ASLEF while Leggett, the Permanent Under-Secretary at the Ministry of Labour, acted when necessary as intermediary. The meetings culminated in agreement on the Saturday, laying down that any claim of any union for any grade should be given equal consideration on its merits with any other claim. This would enable ASLEF to come back with the machinery and to agree to put its claim to the tribunal. There would be a meeting of all unions on 28 August to discuss with the general managers a settlement satisfactory to all.

28 August 1939
Szlumper recorded that Col. J.P.S. Greig, the Assistant Director of Transportation in the Quartermaster-General's office at the War Office, telephoned at 12.30.

He said he knew that the arrangement with the railway was that A.B. Chester, the Divisional Engineer at Eastleigh and a captain in the Territorial Army, could not be spared; but he was getting very anxious about the stores job as he had ordered £500,000 worth that day. He wanted to know if Chester could be spared as he had considerable experience. 'Discussed this with Ellson, and he agreeing, I rang Greig at 13.00 and told him in the special circumstances I would be prepared to let him have Chester on condition that if we wanted him later, he would be returned to us. I said we could probably let him be with the army for six or even twelve months.'

29 August 1939

Szlumper noted that it was a placid day, 'so much so that Ellson, Missenden and I caught the 12.18 to Horsham (lunch on the train) and looked round the station alterations and back to Redhill to see the Battle Headquarters.' He recorded that the latter was proceeding well, was habitable and usable in twelve hours time or less but in some discomfort due to lack of chairs which could probably be purchased locally from church halls for cash. They returned to London by the 14.59 train, listening in on a Beethoven portable radio to the BBC commentary on proceedings in Parliament and, despite blank spots in tunnels and high cuttings, managed to take in most of the Prime Minister's speech.

'Nothing doing at Waterloo on our return. Got Chairman to agree renaming our City station as Bank. As things so slack, I caught 16.27 home and with Jessie and Cynthia motored to Deepdene. A lot of work remains to be done but the telephones seem adequate, which is the most important thing. Seats and sleeping accommodation short but interim arrangements made with Star & Garter Hotel at Dorking North station. Lavatory also very behind but some temporary latrines rigged in garden. Have already asked Missenden to arrange radiograms at GHQ and the various BHQs to keep the staff happy.' Once a country house and later a hotel near the Dorking station on the Redhill/Guildford line, Deepdene had been taken over by the railway for offices and control centre in the war.

30 August 1939

Szlumper attended the Chairman's Committee 'but there was nothing to do except dissuade the chairman from instituting a pigeon post. So Missenden, Ellson and I by the 11.00 to Brighton to look over all the non-essential staff quarters to accommodate 770. Work proceeding apace but it will not be finished until about Monday next week. Desks about 37% done, lighting 25% but no seating in the offices. Lavatories about 50% done but very short in numbers, some being five minutes distant for staff who will be working at the north end of the premises. Instructed to provide some Elsan mobile toilets for the emergency use of those people who cannot wait five minutes – there is no drainage at the north end of the premises. Inspected BHQ – everything first rate and ready. We caught 13.25 up but meantime Missenden had been called urgently to the phone soon after 12.00 to be informed that the Ministry of Transport had instructed the civilian evacuation scheme to be put into effect. About thirty minutes later he was again called to the telephone to hear the order was cancelled. On reaching London, I learned that at 12.00 Reginald Hill [Assistant Secretary] at the Ministry of Transport had ordered the scheme to be operated, it is said on an order signed by the Prime Minister himself. At 12.25 T.E. Thomas (General Manager, Operation, LPTB) had confirmed the order. At 12.35 Hill cancelled the order – again, it is said by Cole-Deacon, on the Prime Minister's written order and at 12.40 Thomas confirmed the cancellation. Missenden advised me that Pick and Thomas were trying to make themselves the channel of communication and had written to Smart accordingly. Smart, the Assistant for Train Services, had refused to accept this. I wrote Cole-Deacon a precise letter, sent by hand, that I would recognise only the REC in this and all matters of orders to any railway.' Cole-Deacon had been seconded in 1938 to the Railway Executive Committee [REC] which had been formed by the railways to facilitate government-control in the event of hostilities.

31 August 1939
Szlumper noted that Cole-Deacon acknowledged his letter to him at 11.16 when he advised that evacuation would take place the following day everywhere. 'It is a Cabinet decision, no nonsense this time, he has the order in his possession.' At 11.22 Szlumper transmitted the order by phone to Missenden. At 15.15 a note from Cole-Deacon arrived enclosing one from Hill saying that M day for the move had been fixed but without saying when it would be. At 17.00 on Missenden's recommendation, Szlumper instructed Staff Assistant, Cromwell, to tell all departments that any non-essential staff that were not absolutely required for work on Saturday, might be permitted to remain at home – to ease the Saturday midday load during the evacuation.

1 September 1939
The Minister of Transport issued the Emergency (Railway Control) Order 1939 which turned the REC from an advisory body into the Minister's executive agent for giving directions under the order. At the same time, Szlumper became a member of the REC, the other members being Wedgwood, Milne, Newton, Wood and Frank Pick who was Vice Chairman and Chief Executive of the London Passenger Transport Board [LPTB]. Szlumper recorded that at 10.00 the evacuation was proceeding smoothly everywhere and at 10.30 he went around the station to see the 10.40 and 10.45 evacuation trains loading. 'Everyone's

The general managers of the LNER and GWR remained at their posts at the beginning of the war. Szlumper had a lot of contact with them, as at times they were all on the Railway Executive Committee. Wedgwood (left) and Milne (right). (*Railway Gazette*)

organisation including the London County Council seems very good. Loading is very light, every train going out with many empty seats. A London County Council marshal thought many children were being held back so as to accompany their mothers tomorrow and Sunday. 11.00 Railway Clearing House enquired if we were moving out to war stations. Replied, "Not yet.'"

On the movement out of London of railway offices, he noted the LMS had gone while the LNER was completing its move that day; but the GWR was not ready. At 11.27 Wedgwood phoned for an informal meeting of the REC at 14.30 at Fielden House. At 11.35 there was a message from Cole-Deacon – the railways were taken over by warrant with control vested in the REC. He informed the chairman at 11.45. At 11.52 Szlumper instructed Elliot to send to Deepdene any impedimenta that could go on beforehand but personnel were not to move. At 12.15 he agreed with Elliot that the Savings Bank should move at once to Brighton while the Pension Department was to be considered for early removal. Other people should stand fast until the course of events could be seen.

'14.20 Over to Fielden House for REC meeting. On finding out from others that they had ordered train-lighting restrictions, I telephoned Elliot at 14.35 to do the same. At REC discussed various points, especially compensation; and taking over private owners' wagons which we think should be done at once. The Minister of Transport, Euan Wallace, and the Permanent Secretary at the Ministry, Sir Leonard Browett, came during our session. Very affable and admits we can do the job better than he can. He undertook to get compensation considered early and try to issue order at once taking over private owners' wagons. Wallace said Chamberlain might form a war cabinet; and he might be out of a job. 15.45 Ministry of Transport telephoned that tonight there is to be restricted lighting where it exists and a blackout elsewhere. REC to meet daily at 14.30 at Down Street [the disused Underground station on the Piccadilly Line between Hyde Park and Green Park.] Back to Waterloo about 16.45. Bulleid asked should he stop or proceed with building of the new express passenger engines [the Merchant Navy class]. I said proceed – we may be very glad of them or our allies may. Found the orders about tonight's blackout had not percolated from the REC. So gave instructions. Some doubt as to result of code order "Cover up" but we cleared this up and the order was issued at 17.15. Discussed with Missenden, Elliot, Davidson and R.M.T. Richards the question of moving out. We listened to the 18.00 bulletin from which it looked like things might get sticky any time. It seems wrong to have a safe place and not to use it. Accountants and cashier, especially paybill section, can only move at the end of a week. All agree it is better to move in conditions of comfort than when bombs may be dropping. So at 19.05, I issued the code word SHIFT to be given at 08.00 tomorrow and discussed full arrangements with the others. Evacuation on SR has gone well and so as far as I can hear no hitch of any sort.'

2 September 1939

When he got to Waterloo, Szlumper noted that the evacuation was working very well, the ordinary services also and with no hitches of any sort. He took the 11.27 train back to Surbiton from where he motored to Deepdene to find the move going smoothly and to plan but with much still to be done. 'Motored back to Surbiton and 12.38 to Waterloo. Quick lunch in office and taxi to Fielden House for REC meeting lasting until 17.30. Rather tedious with Wedgwood's slow care of detail. Many decisions taken about availability of tickets, daily reports, green arrow transits etc. Back to Waterloo to find everything gone very well – so well that we have taken on the evacuation of Croydon (23,000) and other areas on Monday. 18.27 home. At 21.12 old friend, Justice of Board of Trade [BoT], phoned saying Admiralty wanted *Maid of Kent* at Southampton as soon as possible to fit as a hospital carrier. Ministry of Transport has agreed. I agreed and after much trouble got through to Dorking.'

3 September 1939

Szlumper noted Britain's two hours ultimatum to Germany expired at 11.00 and that at 11.15 Chamberlain made a fine broadcast on 'why we were at war.' An air raid warning was heard and he bustled the family and servants into the cellar, putting on gas masks for practice. After about ten minutes, the 'all clear' was sounded. He noted it was a false alarm caused by a friendly aircraft approaching England. At 12.00 he took a train to Waterloo where he found 'everything going on splendidly. They got all the people about the station into air raid cover in four minutes with fifteen cases of fainting.' He found with difficulty a taxi which took him to Down Street for the REC meeting at 14.30. He described it as very noisy because of the men still working there and that there was an enormous amount of accommodation. At 16.45 he took a taxi to Waterloo and the 17.27 train to Surbiton. But it was not the end of his working day as he then motored to Deepdene, 'taking Jessie and Cynthia for a blow of air.' He noted everyone was settling in well and that telephones were better but very overloaded. W.G. Pape was very excited about everything but Elliot and everyone else were first rate. 'Jennery of the Board of Trade, someone not officially recognised, wants the TSS *Paris* for the Board of Trade. I said, No, must come through MoT and REC. I will not otherwise consider it.' He also spoke to Biddle who was 'cheerful and cool, masses of difficulties but ploughing through them. Several ships including meatships diverted to Southampton causing berthing difficulties and shed congestion but Biddle is arranging accommodation for the British Expeditionary Force moves. *Maid of Kent* arrived Southampton at dawn today. Biddle sailed *Isle of Jersey* which is now a hospital ship, with scratch stewards, our men having boggled about terms and maintaining messing differential – told him to sack our men.'

4 September 1939

At 09.00 Szlumper went by car with Elliot and the Assistant Traffic Manager, Richards, to Deepdene where they made a tour of the rooms and found everyone was settling in well. He sent out a circular to all the Southern staff 'to cheer them on.' At this moment of stress, he wrote, he was proud to be their leader, proud at the magnificent way they had carried out the evacuation and ARP schemes. 'I know I shall be proud of the way you will carry out the many and important duties that lie before each and every one of you on the successful performance of which much of the welfare of our country will depend. Keep stout hearts and cheerful faces, keep as fit and well-nourished as you can, obtain all the rest you can, and so let the Southern family play its part in helping this grand free country sweep the oppressor from the earth. I and my officers wish you and your families good luck in all you do.'

With the chairman, he went by the 11.55 train to Waterloo where he noted everything was 'quiet and working well.' He was at the REC at 14.30 and back to Waterloo at 17.00. At 17.30 Jennery at the BoT advised him he had been nominated as a liaison officer and wanted the SS *Maid of Orleans* sent with bunkers full to Southampton, sailing in hours of darkness and arriving by 06.00 on 6 September. He told Elliot to arrange it with Biddle. He subsequently rang Cole-Deacon to tell him that he had no knowledge that Jennery had been appointed a liaison and asked him to get the MoT to officially advise him.

5 September 1939
Szlumper with Richards went by SR car to Deepdene where an officers' meeting was held at 10.30 when a variety of minor points were settled. Afterwards Szlumper took the 12.18 train to Waterloo. With Holland-Martin and Sir Francis Dent, he went to Martin's Bank for lunch, thence by SR car on to Down Street for a 14.30 REC meeting, returning to Waterloo at 17.00. He telephoned Elliot about the REC's decisions and then Biddle at Southampton. 'Things seem OK there – timber under load is worst problem but told him to dump it on open ground if necessary. He must keep clear of congestion the next few days – he says it is being cleared but slowly. No one seems to know anything about boat moves but he knows what will be required of him in other directions and is keeping ready. Told him to father any other railway's boats arriving there – pay wages if necessary, provision and fuel them.'

6 September 1939
'The car managed to get here at 08.45, thanks to the Railways Official Car labels on it. Raid turns out to be a high altitude one over the East Coast, no bombs dropped but gunfire at various places, especially Chatham and Gillingham. Most trains running at 15mph as ordered but Control supervisor cut down current from various places – Raworth [Chief Electrical Engineer] to find out why. Also, some officious wardens preventing trains such as at Tattenham Corner from starting.'

With Richards he went by car to Deepdene, leaving home as the all clear sounded. He noted all was going well at GHQ but the Chairman wanted to know the movements of officers. He would be told it could not be done as they moved at short notice and could not share movements or information as they were under Official Secrets Act. He proceeded to Waterloo by the 11.55 train with A.A. Mertz of the Belgian Railways. Mertz told him, 'Belgium must come in soon, it is the only way to Germany.' He noted there was nothing doing at Waterloo and went to the Park Lane Hotel for lunch and the REC meeting at 14.30. 'Various questions of pay to staff unable reach work to time owing to air raid warning; also, workmen unable to get workmen's tickets in time.' He informed the MoT that orders should be issued that the railway was not to be interfered with.

7 September 1939

Szlumper left home at 09.00 to Deepdene. At 11.55 he went to Waterloo and then the War Office where he spoke to Greig about the transfer of the train ferries. Later he went to the REC before returning to Waterloo.

8 September 1939

Szlumper left home by car at 09.00 to Deepdene. He noted that Ellson had been awkward the previous day about the appointment of the Transport & Billeting Officer. Szlumper recorded that he 'put him right' but he was again awkward about petrol rationing arrangements and car apportionment at Deepdene, wanting his car tank kept full with thirty gallons and kept at home; and he wanted to use his own car and not a staff car. 'Sat on him. Beginning to tire of his nonsense.' Szlumper told Elliot to enquire as to where they might move the train ferries and suggested Fawley. He told R.G. Davidson [SR Accountant] to render account to the Admiralty for £125,000 for the redundant floating dock at Southampton that would be going to Portsmouth – this was the one that Szlumper had endeavoured to sell to the Admiralty in 1936.

'11.18 train to Waterloo. Chairman still busy visiting BHQs – told him I had studiously avoided doing so, so as not to be a nuisance to the Divisional Officers. REC at 14.30. Nothing special. Back to Waterloo 17.15. Arranged with Biddle to send SS *Normania* to Folkestone to help out with service to Boulogne, our usual boats having all been taken up. However, one of the SAGA captains thought he might venture out on the Channel again – first time since Sunday. This has eased the situation. Also, decided that where our boats work to and from strange ports for our own or Admiralty purposes, the deck and engine room crews should be victualled free by us – the stewards already are. If they do not like the new arrangement or want some differential, they can lump it or be sacked if they give trouble.'

9 September 1939

At 09.00 Szlumper went by car to Deepdene. 'Inspected the premises – getting much straighter but toilets proceeding very slowly. Annexe proceeding, several rooms ready but more still to do. Meeting at 10.30, no big matters but Cobb [Loco Running Supt] tells of one Bricklayers Arms driver who refused to run with his firebox glare curtains in place. He is having the foreman warn him today and suggests suspending him if still recalcitrant. I ordered to hand him over to the civil police as breaking the defence regulations. Cobb then informs me he is always a man looking for trouble – he can have all he wants this time. 11.55 to Waterloo where traffic fairly brisk but office very quiet. To Park Lane Hotel with T.E. Thomas and W. Gray to talk over Institute of Transport matters. At 14.30 to

REC. W.V. Wood still full of blaa about his Irish service troubles. Suggested he borrow some boats from the Swiss navy – this did not please him.'

10 September 1939

'Motored to Southampton to see Biddle by 11.00 and found everything going well as far as SR concerned but some stupid things in connection with our boats, eg the Board of Trade has allocated 1,710 men to be carried on the SS *Maid of Orleans* whose ticket is only 1,227. Apparently the BoT uses some calculation for putting men "under cover" irrespective of the actual carrying capacity of the boat or of the life-saving appliances.'

Later Szlumper received the Port Admiral, Rear Admiral Tillard, Commodore of Ocean Convoys, to lunch. 'A nice, quiet and efficient man. After lunch went with Biddle round the docks and saw the loading. Met Sir Walter Venning, Quartermaster-General [QMG], and the Embarkation Commandant.' Noting that Venning was concerned at the slow loading of some ships, it was found that this was because drivers brought vehicles to the docks and deposited them there, and then went to rest camps on Southampton Common. Fatigue parties from the rest camp were supposed to be at the docks to de-petrol the lorries and move them to the cranes for shipment but they were coming to the docks at about 05.00 without food or relief. The consequence was that they knocked off work when their energy gave out and went back to the rest camp.

According to the diary, Venning spoke to Szlumper about the Director-General of Transportation post and salary questions – this was the first mention in his diary that a position with the military was on the horizon. 'Sad to see the *Worthing* and others of our ships painted battleship grey from head to foot. Biddle tells me our crews are in many cases supplemented in chartered ships by naval ratings – if the latter are killed, their widows get a decent pension. Our fellows feel they should be similarly treated and I think they are right, when they are on government service.'

11 September 1939

'The Chairman rang me early that he had something important to say. Fixed him to arrive at Dorking North at 11.15.' Szlumper, Elliot and Richards left together for Deepdene at 09.30. Holland-Martin duly arrived at 11.15 to advise that Walker had seen Hore-Belisha, the Secretary of State for War, on Saturday and they wanted Szlumper to be Director-General of Transportation. 'Discussed various questions and we both went to Waterloo together and across to Martin's Bank for lunch. Walker was there and I pressed him to take on the post. No, he thought he would be unable to stand any prolonged strain and the job would certainly be a strain. I suggested Wedgwood but Walker said his health was not good enough and all including the QMG had agreed I was the man for the job. I said if that was the current feeling, I would take it on. Both Walker and the chairman were painfully complimentary.' After lunch Szlumper went to the REC where he warned Wedgwood prior to the meeting that something was afoot about the Director-General of Transportation and that Walker would be coming to see him. Walker arrived at 16.00 and had a discussion with Wedgwood. At the end of the meeting, Wedgwood announced that the REC would be losing Szlumper.

A handwritten page in Szlumper's diary detailed the new post. It was clearly related to any movement of the army into Europe, the prime duty being the general supervision and co-ordination of railway, inland waterway and dock requirements overseas and policy in regard thereto in all theatres of war. This included the provision of railway plant, materials, rolling stock and waterway, port and dock plant and material and the necessary personnel. There was also the exercise of War Office control at ports and of movements in Great Britain and by sea. Liaison would be required with the Ministry of Transport and the BoT in regard to facilities for movement by land and sea. The note also detailed a number of requirements. They included the need to ensure that every possible measure was taken to strengthen the machinery of the War Office to deal with movement and transportation; and to undertake long term planning to meet the expected shortage of shipping. The planning required an organisation with a man at its head with experience of railways, docks and, if possible, light railways and inland waterways in all their aspects. As the productive capacity of Britain, both of material and personnel, would be insufficient to meet transportation demands, the resources of the Empire and the USA may have to be tapped. This could more easily be effected by a man at the head of affairs in the War Office with personal contacts overseas and whose name carried weight. The document concluded that probably no one man existed who possessed all the qualifications required for the post but that only a general manager of one of the main line railways could possess the experience required. It was not surprising that Szlumper was the choice.

After the REC meeting, Szlumper collected Walker from the Devonshire Club to go to Waterloo. Walker told Szlumper that Venning was delighted. 'I should have to think over the military rank question but I said I did not want it. He said you will have to assume it in order to draw the pay, £2,500 – the most they could give. I said I wanted neither the rank nor the pay. Walker said that although the railway would continue my pay, I ought to take the £2,500 from the War Office to compensate me for the additional burden I would have to carry – and it would be a tremendous burden. I said, no, I would rather remain independent and be able to snap my fingers at anyone.'

At Waterloo they saw the Chairman. Szlumper recorded that he was like a schoolboy with a new toy. 'So glad they had chosen me for the job, a feather in the cap of the Southern, no one could do it so well as me, I had got the SR in such a wonderful shape that it would carry on alright. Walker also very nice.' At 18.00 Szlumper went to the War Office to see Venning who gave him a hearty welcome and said some of the names that had been suggested to him had made him quake but when he was told that he would take it on, he said would that night have a heavy sound sleep. They discussed the post with General Riddell-Webster, Deputy Quartermaster-General and Brigadier Holmes, the Director of Movements. Venning said he would pretty well be able to pick his own people for the sub-directorates but he would insist that the Director of Movements should always be a soldier, acknowledging they would probably have many fights about that. Left them all in good form and seeming to welcome me. Phoned Greig [Brigadier and Director of Transportation] who said he was over-joyed at the news.'

When he arrived home, he found Cole-Deacon was there. 'He was on the verge of a breakdown and so stale that he had to get away from Down Street. So I had invited him down for a change. Elliot also there as I had told him I wanted to see him. Told him the state of things, that personalities away from consideration, my view was that the railway was now shorn of all ordinary work and was primarily an operating organisation. Missenden was the operating man and had also had docks experience and some thirty-seven years railway experience and I thought the proper thing to do was to make Missenden Traffic Manager and Acting General Manager. It was no reflection on Elliot who had done his peacetime job first rate and his war time job splendidly. He accepted this absolutely without question and said if he were in my position, he would have been bound to come immediately to the same decision. The only thing was that he did not want his staff or friends to say "Hello, what has the Assistant General Manager done that he should not be made Acting General Manager." I quite agreed it was necessary to keep this absolutely right and that in any announcement to the staff and public, it would be made plain that Missenden's appointment was due to his seniority, his operating knowledge and his docks knowledge. After a talk, Elliot suggested that his position would be strengthened if he was promoted to Deputy General Manager during my absence. I agreed and promised to plead it with the Chairman. Elliot was altogether most helpful. He said that he was more delighted than he could say that I should have been appointed and at the same time heart-broken that I would be leaving the Southern as all Southernites would be. I said I had suggested to Walker that the above arrangements should operate and that to save Missenden running backwards and forwards between Dorking and London, that he – Walker – should act as the Southern representative on the REC. Elliot did not think this would work – Walker would be out of touch with the railway and would not be able to help interfering, however unwittingly. Missenden ought to be in touch with the REC and it was due to his position that he should be the SR representative on it. I agreed this seemed right and that I would rectify it, perhaps suggesting that Walker might be appointed an extra member of the REC so that Wedgwood would have his support and help.

'Later in the evening, I rang up the Chairman and put to him both points. He concurred and authorised me to tell the news at my officers' meeting at 10.30 tomorrow. Cole-Deacon was dejected about various things and very unhappy domestically. Delighted at my appointment but said Wedgwood was nearly in tears after the REC. He said I was the only sane and helpful one there and he was definitely of the opinion I ought to understudy him so as to become chairman of the REC if anything happened to him. Cole-Deacon gave Wedgwood three months before he crocked up.'

12 September 1939

When Szlumper reached Deepdene, he was telephoned by the Chairman – he had seen Wedgwood who was in agreement about Missenden on the REC and Walker becoming a supernumerary on it. But when he had gone to the Ministry of Transport, the Minister's Private Secretary, D.E. O'Neil, told him the railway was going much too fast with appointments. The Minister had not agreed to Szlumper's release and was consulting with the War Office; also, the Minister made all appointments to the REC. 'I therefore did not mention it at our meeting at Deepdene. Meanwhile I told Missenden who was thrilled both with my appointment and his. Chairman arrived 11.15, very impatient with the hitch – why was it? I was the most suitable man in England. Greig phoned and said the QMG wanted me or the Chairman to do anything we could to move the MoT from our end. Chairman rang O'Neil later to see if the thing was settled but Browett said, no, still a standstill. Chairman and Elliot caught 12.58 to London. I stayed on and mopped up. One of our BEF trains seventeen minutes late at the docks today owing to clerical muddle in ordering the loco for the empties, put right now to counterbalance all other trains well before time. I caught the 14.58 to Waterloo. Elliot came back from REC at 17.15. He regards Down Street as a madhouse, both as to accommodation and personnel – I quite agree. Elliot reported that there was a good old muddle this morning – when our newspaper trains were loaded, police came to unload the *Daily Mail* and *Daily Express* because they had published something that had been released and since cancelled about the presence of British troops in France. The result was that some of the newspaper trains were two hours late away. About 18.00 Col Mount came in full of congratulations and to tell me his son Reggie would make an ideal staff officer for me.'

13 September 1939

Szlumper noted that Biddle rang him at 08.00, 'very disturbed at mess the Board of Trade and Stevedore Company are making of things – says if he could take the work over, the stuff would have been in France by now. Available labour must be shared between military and civil requirements. At present military are talking of bringing military labour to effect the shipment – this will bring the dockers out. Told him to offer to do the whole thing and meantime to report fully to the PSTO, the Embarkation Commandant and me with a view to making it clear there was no fault with the SR.

'Had Finance Committee this morning, about ten there.' Szlumper noted there was very little business at the meeting and that it was decided to have a directors' meeting for general purpose once a fortnight. 'All the directors at the meeting were most complimentary to me and the Southern staff in general.' Amery was amongst the directors but as with most of his diary notes, made no comment on its deliberations, just noting that the Stores Committee was suspended.

14 September 1939

When Szlumper arrived at Deepdene, he noted that everything was going smoothly and that all the previous day's British Expeditionary Force trains had arrived at Southampton well before 15.00 without any mishaps. He took the 11.58 train to Waterloo with W.G. Pape who 'was rather dejected after having seen his damned fool of a son off to China this morning as a missionary – better to go and kill Nazis than save Chinese with a Christianity that does not seem to have produced a very satisfactory result in Europe after nearly 2,000 years.' He proceeded to the REC where he noted there was nothing special but that W.V. Wood seemed to be getting angular, 'probably a reflex of the muddle in which the LMS seems to be.' He returned to Waterloo at 17.00 where he had a long telephone talk with Biddle who was sorry he had taken on the stevedoring and wished he had made them clear up the mess before he took it over.

'Have now received details of the SR evacuation effort. It all went smoothly and punctually and our normal service also ran punctually.' Detailing the movements, he noted there had been a grand estimated total of 675,954 while the actual number of passengers was 280,216 (41.4%) of which 242,067 had entrained at SR stations while 38,149 (13.9%) were transferred by LPTB. He commented that the estimating had been frightful with the resultant waste of engine power.

'Spoke to Greig at midday and told him I was ready to be at the War Office at five minutes' notice but it seemed useless to come until the battle between the War Office and the Ministry of Transport was settled and it was seen what the outcome would be. He said this battle was now being fought in the highest quarters.'

15 September 1939

Szlumper took the 08.50 train from Surbiton to Woking to look at the Divisional Battle Headquarters with the London West Divisional Superintendent, J.E. Sharpe. 'At present inconveniently scattered in station offices as the proper structures are not yet ready, although some of the staff will be moved into them tomorrow. However, everything is working well. The headquarters new building (huts) seems much too tart but Ellson thinks still another hut is necessary for some of the Divisional Engineer's men – this is quite unnecessary as far too much sleeping accommodation has been provided.'

Szlumper subsequently attended the REC meeting. He noted that too much time was taken up with the Road Transport Committee report on petrol for lorries, although F.C.A. Coventry, the GWR Road Transport Superintendent, was there to explain it. 'We all wasted about twenty minutes discussing design of Railway Service badges with a selection of examples before us. Things are getting out of focus and later Wedgwood quite deservedly got testy with W.V. Wood who is very petty.

'Dash to Charing Cross and a sandwich on 13.33 train to Orpington with Missenden and Nunn [London East Division] to see round his Divisional Battle Headquarters. All very well settled-in and working comfortably. Too many there due to more than arranged of the Electrical Engineer. Concerned at the amount of bare timber in the premises. But the worse thing is the bad ventilation everywhere – no windows can be opened but must be made to. Ellson seems to be suffering from a crisis complex. Missenden found out he was keeping no less than sixteen locos in steam at his various repair depots with three sets of men, also guards, although many of them are within easy reach of loco depots. Missenden, of course, immediately put a stop to this. While at Orpington, we had very heavy rain and a thunderstorm, the lighting succeeding in bringing down five barrage balloons across the railway between here and London. It looks like an order is necessary that balloons must be "grounded" on the approach of a thunderstorm. Missenden motored me back to his charming house at Bickley for some welcome tea and I caught the 16.49 to Victoria and taxied to Waterloo to find the chairman fully excited as the Minister of Transport had lost his battle and I am to go the War Office – more handshaking and compliments. Euan Wallace or Browett only gave way on the quite proper understanding that the efficiency of the Southern Railway would not suffer and that my successor on the REC should have equal status with his colleagues. The Chairman therefore proposed that during my absence Missenden should actually be appointed General Manager – I agreed.'

16 September 1939

Szlumper went with Elliot to Deepdene where he rang Greig at the War Office. 'They apparently still have no news of my availability. Before my 10.30 officers' meeting was finished, the chairman burst in and said "Have you told them?" On hearing I had not, he proceeded to. "Very proud, great honour, no one would do it so well, has got SR into such good order, we feel it will go on well without him etc etc." Announced that Missenden would be General Manager during my absence, and Elliot Deputy General Manager. Everyone rather excited at the news. Ellson as oldest and senior in service spoke very nicely of pride at my appointment and how well I would do it and how they would miss me, also how they would carry on under Missenden just as if I was there. Missenden was also very nice – said it would not be the same without me but they would carry on so that when I came back to them – and might it be soon. I replied, thanked them and exhorted continuance of loyal team work as to which I had no doubt. Elliot quite affected and said he had had two years happiness with me and the place could not be the same if I was away even for one day and he knew every member of the SR would say the same.

'Missenden and I by 12.18 Dorking North to Waterloo and to Park Lane Hotel to lunch and on to REC. Spoke to Wedgwood and told him Missenden was going to be General Manager (not Acting) and would be on REC. Would Wedgwood like Walker also to come on as a supernumerary member? He turned his nose up and said it might bring difficulties and thought it better to leave things as they were. I quite understood and cautioned him to take care of himself and conserve his energy. Ashfield [Chairman of LPTB] at REC instead of Pick. Everyone very nice about my appointment and promised full help. At end of meeting Wedgwood called for a glass of sherry all round to drink my health and to wish Missenden luck. Wedgwood said that when the MoT raised the question of whether I could be spared and whether he looked on me as indispensable to the REC, he replied that no one can be indispensable but that I was the only one of the REC who was any good and that he would greatly miss me. 16.45 went to the Devonshire Club to see Walker who had sent me three or four messages, asking if things were fixed up for me or, if there was too much difficulty, should he volunteer to fill the gap? The steward dug him out of the card room and I told him it was all fixed up; also, that in response to the Ministry's request, Missenden was to be given full status and become General Manager and also the SR representative on the REC. He seemed a bit taken back and asked if I did not want him to look after the London end and be SR representative on REC to save Missenden travelling back to and fro. I told him we had considered all that but the Minister and ourselves considered Missenden should do the whole job. He said, "Oh alright." With my tongue in my cheek, I asked him if he would like me to find out from Wedgwood if he would like him as a supplementary member of REC but he turned this down, saying that he was not inclined to take on a lot of work without being well paid for it – he would have to look for something else.

'On to Waterloo for talk to Biddle who congratulated me and wished me luck and told me half his fellows wanted to cry when they heard the news. He says things at Southampton are going better – in fact, very well as far as everything is concerned except heavy motor transport. This is beginning to pile up owing to unsuitable ships being sent for it. Except for too little headroom, some of the ships themselves are not too bad but the gear is the trouble. He tells me that troops are unloading the stuff the other side and they do the gear a great deal of harm. As the train ferries have temporarily finished mine-laying, it would be worthwhile sending the motor transport to Dover and letting them load themselves on the ferry and off the other side.

'Traffic at Waterloo fairly brisk. 18.27 home. Rang Holland-Martin at Overbury [his home in the Cotswolds] at 21.30 and told him about Walker. He was disgusted the fellow is so damned mercenary and on no account wanted him back near the SR to upset my young team who were perfectly capable of carrying on. He had already secured the agreement of the directors who mattered to the arrangements and had written to the others.'

18 September 1939

Szlumper went to Waterloo where he telephoned Greig to remind him that he was now fully available if wanted. 'He seemed very pleased and said he would ring him after the QMG's daily meeting. Connected later and after much needed haircut, met Greig for lunch at Carlton and had good general talk. Back to the War Office with him and saw his suggested scheme of expanded organisation – seems quite good, so far. Glad he has collared Captain Davis, the Marine Superintendent of the LNER at Harwich, for the Docks and Inland Water Transport job, also Ralph Micklem, a retired Royal Engineers officer, for Stores, but not so thrilled he has brought Jumbo Tyrrell back to look after Longmoor as he is too slow and lazy.' He noted that McMullen had gone to be Director-General of Transport in France with the BEF and thought he would do quite well, especially after his experience in Palestine.

Szlumper was then taken up to see his new room which he thought quite satisfactory. 'Discussed question of title and both agree Director-General Transportation & Movements covers the ground. On question of rank and uniform, he suggests I might be Mr Szlumper and be given an honorary rank of Major General so as to see me through difficulties when visiting the other side – seems a good way out. Went in and had good yarn with Riddell-Webster, the Deputy Quartermaster-General who explained plan of communications and bases overseas, also idea of waves of four divisions – when any four have gone, the next four will be collected and completed on the same ground so as to make embarkation moves simply a repetition of the last one. Location of the four divisions sensibly near port of embarkation but do not like disembarkation ports being so far from anywhere and hope they will be able to size up and control the air menace so that much more convenient ports can be used – these will fit into the advanced base which could then become the base proper. While we were talking, General Walter Kirke, Commander-in-Chief of the Home Forces, came in about feeding new units when first line ones make way for them – he had all the facts and figures in his mind and talked sense.'

19 September 1939
'To War Office and with Greig to QMG's meeting at 10.15. Quite businesslike but little concerning transportation. Greig has got lifted the ban on enlistment on certain tradesmen which will help. Getting Stevedore Battalions together – questions raised as to whether they should be armed. I said that as they have not been taught how to use arms, they would be a public menace. QMG agreed.'

A visit to the Ministry of Supply's Adelphi offices followed to see the Director of Transportation Equipment, R.A. Riddles who had been the LMS Mechanical Engineer in Scotland, and Arthur Redman, Deputy Director at the Ministry of Supply, whose responsibility was to provide railway supplies from all sources. Szlumper thought the draft organisation seemed in order. 'As to wagons, Riddles has told REC we may require 10,000 wagons in six months of which 60% should be covered. He thinks it wiser not to bother about French type as no English maker has drawings or is used to making them. Further, there might be difficulty in hauling them over British railways because of the construction gauge and at the end of the show, the British railways should be glad enough to have 15,000 British type wagons or so many as is left of them.'

20 September 1939
Szlumper lunched at the United Services Club with the QMG when they discussed the logistics of stores. Later in the afternoon he went to the Institute of Transport for committee and council meetings. He called at Waterloo to get his papers about the Admiralty collaring train ferries for mine-laying. 'We must get these ferries back for their proper work, especially as they are, I hear, idle at the moment. Told Elliot to find out from Biddle some facts as to their capacity for motor transport including making a temporary roadway right over the train decks. Mount came in with his son Reggie and thought he would make a grand staff captain for me. I said it was too early, I was not ready with an organisation yet.'

21 September 1939
'To Waterloo and on to War Office. Raised at QMG's meeting question of getting train ferries back – he said raise it with my opposite number at Admiralty and if

unsuccessful he would take it to a higher level. Meeting in my room with Riddles, Redman, General Collins and Greig. Collins and I will both want mechanical diggers. We both agree the sensible thing will be to make an independent unit of digger sections complete with diggers to be available to either of us. Diggers to be repaired at base loco repair shops. Greig is already forming four sections and we will both work out and marry a twelve months requirement. Discussed sleepers – plenty of new ones available for home railways and military railways but good second-hand ones likely to be scarce, so decided Ministry of Supply should prohibit sale of them and I would ask REC to conserve use so as to save them against probable requirements.

'Lunch with Missenden who tells me of abortive meeting yesterday with Browett and Hill at Ministry of Transport about compensation on taking over railways. I suggested they should get chairmen to demand meeting with Minister himself and the Treasury. This delay is childish and hampering. Attended afternoon meeting with Director of Movements, Brigadier Holmes – very businesslike man, although new to the job. BoT representative, Webb, very poor and seemed to know nothing – no wonder they are supplying unsuitable ships if this is the type of man doing it. Raised question of train ferries. Admiralty representative, Commander Osborne, said they were now reloading and there was no likelihood of sparing them for at least six weeks and probably more. He said mines were to maintain safe track for train ferries anyway and it would not be prudent to run them until track existed. I am not convinced this is a suitable use. Osborne said he could do no more and so I must fight it at a higher level.'

22 September 1939
'At QMG's meeting, learned more details of Egyptian proposals and it was decided to try and get them to form their own Movements Control group out there. Also, proposals for brigade via Marseilles (stores direct by sea all the way) and the projected use of Le Havre. Greig let McMullen know what Movement Control and Docks men we have available at Longmoor and McMullen to parcel them out as he thinks best. Talk with Micklem prior to his visit overseas and gave him points to put to Director-General of Transportation there. QMG and DQMG came in from War Committee at 13.45 and wanted a memo by 15.30 for Cabinet about getting train ferries back to proper use.'

He noted Manton who at one stage had been Commandant at Longmoor, came to see him. He was fed up doing nothing, his LMS School of Transport at Derby being closed – he had only been appointed Principal that month. 'He is desperately anxious to work with me and for me. Have put him thinking that Derby could be Longmoor No.2 to deal with 2,000 men at a time. He will let me have a report in three days. Meantime, I will do nothing with Stamp or Wood.

Manton wants to be my personal assistant but I tell him I am not ready to consider it yet. Enquiry suggests he is most efficient but tactless and likely to cause friction; and for other reasons, I am against the course. Am impressed with ability and activity of Director of Movements, Brig Holmes, who has only been at the job two months but has it well in hand. Spent some time in Movements dugout. Wilfred Lindsell, Deputy Quartermaster-General Overseas, complains of long Line of Communication to concentration area.'

23 September 1939
'Long meeting in afternoon with Greig, Robert Léguille [Regional Mechanical Engineer of SNCF and Liaison Officer in London] with Mount and Riddles. Settled many questions about ambulance trains, locomotives and wagons.'

24 September 1939
'QMG saw me about notice of appointment. I got S.J. Page of Ministry of Transport [Assistant Secretary] to OK it over the phone.' That evening the War Office announced Szlumper's appointment as Director-General, Transportation & Movements at the War Office in the department of the Quartermaster-General. The Southern Railway also issued a statement – that its directors wished to record their high appreciation of the honour that Szlumper's appointment reflected upon the company.

Chapter Four

ॐ∽ॐ

Szlumper at the War Office, 1939-40

25 September 1939

This was the official date of Szlumper's move to the new post of Director-General of Transportation & Movements in the office of Quartermaster-General at the War Office. Official photographs were taken at Waterloo and the War Office. After attending the QMG's daily meeting, he went to Canada House to investigate raising Railway Survey & Construction Companies. 'They are anxious to help and think Canada will jump at it if we let them know exactly what we want. To Admiralty at 17.30 to see Director of Plans, Captain Danckwerts, about train ferries. Pointed out that they are specialised vessels and would take twelve months to replace. Their use for motor transport will obviate shortage of quay labour troubles and save ships. They can take fifty Army Co-operation lorries or sixty ordinary lorries and we shall want to be shipping locomotives at end of next month and have just heard from DQMG France that he wants us to take over Nissen hutting on them from 14 October. Danckwerts said if weather kept fine, he would hope to let us have SS *Hampton Ferry* and SS *Shepperton Ferry* in three weeks.'

27 September 1939

'Manton had a long sitting to give the result of Longmoor No.2 reconnaissance. Fixed on Derby with its school and available hutting accommodation, and workshops and loco sheds, and the nearby Ashby branch with eight miles of railway to train the men on. Settled preliminaries with Darbyshire [LMS Chief Officer for Labour] and wrote appealingly to Stamp. General Collins came and removed me forcibly to the QMG's room for a series of photos to be taken of the two of us studying a map of the world. In the afternoon, Sir Herbert Creedy [the Permanent Under-Secretary of State for War] came in to give me a really nice welcome to the War Office and seemed very glad to see me there. Lord Radnor [Southern Railway director] also made a call and seemed most pleased at my appointment – he would like to come on my staff.'

28 September 1939

'To War Office, Holland-Martin telling me, en route, the directors yesterday gave Missenden an extra £2,000 per annum whilst acting as General Manager, and Elliot £1,000 – I think this is proper and had recommended it. Told the chairman I thought the time had come when the railway companies should demand an interview with Minister of Transport and/or Treasury on the question of compensation to be paid by the government for control of the railways.

Found Léguille waiting for me at the War Office to settle some details about train ferries, locos and wagons. Amusing chatter at QMG's meeting – Lady Mount Temple [widow of former government minister] most incensed at action at Broadlands of the Director of Quartering – cannot quite make out if he has put the latrines too close to the house or too far away for her to enjoy the sights. Question also of compensation to be paid for taking up the [LNER] Gleneagles Hotel.' Szlumper thought hotels would form part of the government compensation to the railways with no special account to pay but he clearly had no enthusiasm for this hotel as he described it as 'the most vulgar conception in Europe and sybaritic luxury in God's open country.'

29 September 1939

Szlumper noted that the SS *Twickenham Ferry* had done well on her first trip with Army Co-operation Motor Transport. Taking 1hr 40mins to load, all motor transport had been backed on, while the crossing was 3hrs 30mins with 20mins to unload. 'All of which points to necessity of keeping all ferries at their appointed jobs. May well be worth building a simple one deck ferry for MT only – would be useful for motor cars after the war.'

One of the companies that Szlumper had been a director of since 1921 was the International Cold Storage & Ice Company which since its formation in 1903 had had a large warehouse in the docks at Southampton for the storage of butter, meat and other perishables. He was a nominee of the railway which had helped the company in various ways, in the process acquiring a large share interest in the company. This was the first time that he mentioned it but it was only to record that he went to its board meeting at the Charing Cross Hotel.

October 1939

Noting that Szlumper had been seconded to the War Office, the railway's staff magazine carried a message from him. 'During my absence your leadership will be in the capable hands of Missenden. I look forward to getting back into the saddle as soon as we have stamped out the Nazi rule.'

1 October 1939

Szlumper noted France had made a strong protest against having 22-years-old reconditioned 2-8-0 locos sent to it and wanted the new ones intended to replace them on the British railways. The older locomotives had been built in the previous war for the Railway Operating Division which had been a division of the Royal Engineers with responsibility for operating railways in war theatres.

4 October 1939

At a meeting with Riddles and Bulleid as to whether it would be better to send reconditioned 2-8-0 locos overseas as arranged or the new 3-cylinder 2-8-0s as wanted by DQMG, Szlumper noted every argument seemed in favour of the reconditioned engines.

5 October 1939

Amery, still waiting for the call to join the government, was still attending various board meetings including Fanti. Meanwhile, Szlumper was at the QMG's meeting, later having lunch with Alexander McColl who told him he had recently seen Walker looking old and worn, and as if he had something on his mind. McColl, once of the Glasgow & South Western Railway, had been Chairman since 1936 of the Vacuum Oil Company and had just become Chairman of the Lubricating Oil Committee of the Petroleum Board which was co-ordinating the industry during the hostilities.

6 October 1939

'The great question at QMG's meeting was about soldiers on leave proceeding to Eire. They are not to go in uniform for fear of having brickbats thrown at them when they get there. There are 15,000 men from Eire in the army and about 800 may be on ten days leave at any one time. We must therefore establish a depot, probably at Holyhead, where about 100 men a day can drop their uniforms and change into civvies before crossing to Eire. Great discussion on the sartorial problems, seeing that the suits must be well variegated or will themselves be a sort of uniform.'

9 October 1939

'Lunch with Missenden who seems to be going strong. Ellson has apparently gone back on the arrangement to transfer F.E. Campion from London East to London West and send Dean to London East. We both think this is part of a scheme on Ellson's part to have no one in training as a successor so that when he reaches sixty-five, he will say he cannot go as there is no one to succeed him. Missenden has come to the conclusion that Charles Newton is an absolute bloody fool – I believe he is right.'

Szlumper went to the Charing Cross Hotel at 14.30 for the inaugural session of the Institute of Transport and to step down as president and install T.E. Thomas. He returned to the War Office at 15.50 after which Captain R. Davis, Marine Supt of the LNER at Harwich, reported to him for duty. 'A knowledgeable and intelligent chap. We both agree that as to train ferries, the railway companies shall continue to operate them as our agents and on no condition must the Board of Trade Mercantile Marine Department be allowed to have anything to do with them – bang would go all efficiency. Told Davis to get the LNER to span over the deck of one of the Harwich ferries so we could take motor transport on it.'

13 October 1939

'At QMG's meeting we were told that they would like to form more ammunition depots in France but one of the necessities is more Railway Construction Companies – looks like we must get some more from Canada. Glad to hear from Manton that that he will be ready to receive officers for instruction at Derby on Monday – he has moved damned well and is ahead of the military machine. Took Darbyshire to lunch. He is out to help all he can. He wants his man Davis to come to me for personnel work but I form the opinion Davis wants to be too much a cock of the walk. Mentioned to him that H.L. Thornhill wants a job under me but Darbyshire like me has no use on earth for Thornhill who is a bounder and apparently always short of money.' For many years Thornhill had been the LMS Chief Legal Adviser.

17 October 1939

The possibility was discussed of moving most of the QMG's department to the former Hotel Metropole in Northumberland Avenue which was being vacated by the Ministry of Labour. Later Szlumper lunched at the Royal Automobile Club [RAC] with Riddell-Webster whom he described as a great little man. 'We plan to fly to Paris today week for a brass-hat conference on what ports we shall require to look after our needs over the coming months. I asked him to think out what my widow would require in the way of compensation if I should be unlucky enough to stop one as I plan to tour round with McMullen when the conference is over. The trouble with ports is many-sided. First, our enormous demand, of course. Then the fact that the French will not give us a foothold in any place near a port that from an economical shipping point of view looks the sensible spot to ship to; and finally, that the General Staff will not let us use any sensible port because of the potential air menace. The result is that we are most prodigal of shipping by having to use ports in the far north of France – and by using them are saddled with a tremendous long Line of Communication, so long that it will be unworkable when our quantities rise to look after even twenty divisions.'

Szlumper subsequently had a long discussion with Langley about train ferries, Poole being a possibilty as well as Southampton with Le Havre and Cherbourg in France. It was noted the Board of Trade was beginning to be interested in train ferries 'but we must ride them off – a ferry is only a link in the throughout journey of a train and is not a boat. If we build new train ferries, they cannot run from north of the Thames and therefore they will only be of interest to the SR after the war. So they must be interchangeable with the Dover-Dunkirk train ferries. Any new train ferry must have an unencumbered upper deck so that we can get plenty of motor transport on it in addition to trains or MT on the train deck. If SR takes them over after the war, they could either use the upper deck as another motor car deck or could build on it any passenger accommodation they require.'

19 October 1939
At lunch at the Hotel Victoria, Szlumper encountered his road transport friend, the Director of Associated Road Operators, Roger Sewill. 'After the inevitable congratulations, he fell to talking about the road/rail agreement whereby we are arranging in a friendly way for the railways to do the long hauls and the road to do the short ones. Sewill said the arrangement should work perfectly well but "that Hill bids fair to wreck it."

20 October 1939
'W. Cash (Finance) told me he had taken up with the Treasury the question of compensation to my widow if I was killed as a civilian on military duty. Treasury says nothing more can be done for me than for any other civilian – ie pension of £1.12½ a week. If I consent to become Major-General, pension would be £300 pa.'

21 October 1939
'Went to Sir Frederick Bovenschen [Deputy Under-Secretary of State for War] as to whether they want me to open out informal talks with the SNCF as to terms for them to take over locos, wagons etc at the end of the war. Bovenschen very non-committal but will give me some history of the settlements after the last war. Long discussion with him on question of compensation to Jessie if I was killed on duty. It seems so simple to me, my job is a Major-General's job, therefore my widow should receive Major-General's widow's treatment, although for good reasons I have not actually become a Major-General. However this seems to cut across all Treasury principles.'

23 October 1939
'The changing of the Irish soldiers into civvies is getting to smaller dimensions. Civilian clothes are to be offered to commands for use by men serving in this

country, and the only men we need cater specially for are men coming on leave from France and they will proceed to London and change at Chelsea Barracks. Long talk with Riddles about locomotives. His firm idea is that the LNER ought to part with 300 ROD locos without replacement, the other companies helping them out; and that instead of building Gresley's elaborate 3-cylinder type, the railways and/or manufacturers should make for France a much simpler and cheaper type which could start production in about seven months.'

24 October 1939
Szlumper commented on the difficulty of arranging his trip to France. 'But at last I have my passport back stamped with exit permit from the Ambassadre de France, a permit to circulate in the zone of the armies signed by General Lelong of the Mission Francaise and finally a permit to take a few miserable £s and francs out of the country.' He lunched with Walker at the Devonshire Club, noting that he seemed in pretty good form but 'doing nothing of national importance.' In the afternoon, he had a meeting with Goursat, the SNCF Chef de Mouvement, a French embassy official, Livesey (SR) and Greig to discuss terms of payment by the British for French railway services. He went home early to Surbiton to see Brig A.S. Cooper who had been Director of Docks & Inland Waterways in the First World War. 'Various chatty information from him but very little meat. I really wanted to see if he was active enough to use, he having offered.' Szlumper recorded that he was very nice and wanted to help but he felt that at 68 years, he would not hold up to pressure.

25 October 1939
Amery attended the Finance Committee at Waterloo. Szlumper meanwhile was at the QMG's meeting when supplies to France were discussed in some detail. He called at Sir Herbert Creedy to bade goodbye, it being his last day at the War Office. At 13.30 a car took Szlumper and others to Heston Airport and at 14.31 they were in the air in a Lockheed Electra. He noted passing over Woking and Guildford stations and circling over Shoreham Airport to get identification. They went across the Channel 'with a thick bank of heavy cloud ahead so the pilot climbed over the top of it into brilliant sunshine. Looking down on it was like looking at an illimitable field of vivid white foam or soapsuds, very glaring to the eye – bits of cloud in the shadow of other clouds were blue colour and occasionally one got a peep through the clouds to the greenish waters of the Channel.'

The description of the flight is interesting as none of Szlumper's previous journeys by air had been noted in his diaries. At 15.22 'we came lower and circled over Dieppe with plenty of red crosses on the roofs of casino, hotels etc. Suddenly two "pings" on our wing which I thought to be bullets. Actually they were Verey lights which our pilot had fired off to obtain identification, then on over France, weather having turned dull and gloomy. Flying at the regulation height of 800-1000ft, the roads looked everywhere to be empty. At 15.53 we landed at Le Bourget [the main Paris airport] but found no car awaiting us. A fellow passenger on the military mission took two of us and some RAF officers and the other two into Paris. Not a soul at Le Bourget looked at my passport and no formalities of the most elementary sort. Arrived at the Hotel Metropolitan, Rue Cambon, and found McMullen and Major Gordon Main awaiting us. A welcome cup of tea and the gradual arrival of Russell of Movements Control, a very alive chap, Major Jock Macleab, a big cheery kilted Scott on the General Staff, General Lindsell, the QMG of the BEF, Brigadier Rice of Finance, Arthur Redman, Deputy Director at Ministry of Supply and others.'They later had dinner at the celebrated Maxim's.

'All back to the hotel by 21.30. At about 22.00, fourteen of us gathered round in QMG's private sitting room and discussed things until midnight. Deputy QMG Lindsell is very capable, also agreeable. He said the only thing to do was to provide each of the slow-moving infantry tanks with its own rail wagon on which it would live and ready to be moved to the scene of action.'

26 October 1939
At 09.30 Szlumper with Greig and McMullen went by car to the Quatrième Bureau. They were met by Col Louchet and with others discussed charges. 'At 11.00 the French finance fellows left and in came some of the SNCF folks. Had a useful discussion on railway works that we may want to do from time to time and it was agreed that we may carry out any small works where the cost does not exceed 200,000 francs and if they do not incur the requisitioning of land.

'Motored back to our hotel at 13.00 for lunch and at 15.00 to Hôtel des Invalides for big meeting about port requirements with Admiral Jean Fernet in the chair. Various admirals and generals, Col Louchet, Lejoux and Jean Girette of the SNCF and Crescent (Director of Ports & Navigable Waterways); also Major Redman and Major Illingworth (ADC to Lindsell) of the Franco-British Mission. Admiral Fernet made a most admirable chairman, keeping everyone absolutely to the point, permitting no sub-committees and speaking such slow and clear French that every word was intelligible – he also spoke excellent English.'

27 October 1939
'I walked up to the SR office to have a chat with Newbold [SR General Agent in France] and Durrant [Assistant General Agent] and found them in good shape. Back to hotel 10.00. With McMullen, Greig, Col Louchet, Main and Rice to SNCF office for meeting with Le Besnerais, Lejoux, Léguille and others. Again, all very helpful. 13.00 back to hotel for lunch. 14.40 motor again to the Hôtel

des Invalides with Lindsell, Riddell-Webster, Redman, Illingworth for meeting various French ministerial people. General Jamet in chair. General Lindsell gave brief first rate exposé in French of the requirements of the BEF for next twelve months and Jamet expressed the anxiety of the French to render all assistance they could.' Meanwhile in London, Amery was attending a Goodyear meeting.

28 October 1939
Szlumper left Paris by car at 08.20 with McMullen and Greig, eventually reaching Rennes station at 16.00. After a meeting with Le Besnerais, Lejoux and local French officials, Szlumper went at 17.00 with McMullen, Greig and Col Johnston to the outskirts of the town to see the Transportation Stores depot. They were welcomed by Brady and Chester, the Southern's Engineer at Eastleigh who had just been seconded to the QMG's team. It was noted there was a good deal of railway material already and that the arrangements were beginning to get into ship shape.

It was coincidental that this day Amery flew to France on a two-day visit of the British Anglo-French Parliamentary Committee. Amery noted they flew very low to Le Bourget, arriving at 14.30. They were at The Ritz for a few minutes, then two hours at the matinée performance at the Comédie Francaise which was followed by a visit to the French Parliament.

29 October 1939
At 09.00 Szlumper with McMullen, Greig, Johnston and Major Gentry left by car to St Malo. Describing Gentry as a very nice young fellow from the Port of London Authority, Szlumper noted St Malo had excellent quays for which equipment could be provided, although the depth of water was inadequate. After lunch they inspected the places where the St Malo-Rennes canal contacted with the railway. They arrived in Betton in time to see the cutting of the first sod of an ammunition depot.

Meanwhile Amery and his colleagues had gone by train to Nancy from where they were driven fifty miles to the Maginot Line, passing through Metz and along the Moselle valley to Fort-Soestrich where they were met by a General Condé. Amery recorded he was impressed by the French army and could not imagine there was anything on the German side to touch it.

30 October 1939
With McMullen and Greig, Szlumper left at 08.00 to Bruz to see the site of a Base Supply Depot, then to the Supply Depot at Redon. They continued to St Gildas des Bois where railway work for a depot was just starting. At Savenay they walked down a considerable length of track already laid and saw work proceeding for a large depot. Szlumper noted there were several people he knew including an

old friend, E.C. Edwards, the former GWR Docks Manager. They continued to St Nazaire where they viewed the docks. They arrived at 18.00 at Nantes where, after inspecting the facilities, they listened to various complaints of the soldiers.

31 October 1939

Amery left Le Bourget at 10.30 to return to London. Meanwhile Szlumper, after seeing Payne and Linton, both on secondment from the Southern Railway, left the hotel with Greig and McMullen to inspect the Quai des Antilles dock on the island in the river Loire at Nantes. Later they went to Venton Ordance depot, followed by Bottereau to the east of the town. After lunch, they met Knotts and Cobb of the Southern Railway at Carquefou to the north of the town to see where rails, sleepers and other related material were being stacked in a station yard. After further inspections, they reached Rennes at 19.45.

1 November 1939

At 10.15 they went to Rennes airport where awaiting them was a D.H.89 aircraft of which the port engine was only started after ten minutes of propeller winding. They departed at 10.35 but without the heating working. 'We soon ran into low and heavy cloud and after running through it for a spell, the pilot came below it and scared me by some hedge-hopping, nearly topping the tops of trees. Happily he thought it better to go up, although not supposed to fly at over 1,000ft. The second man told me the pilot did not mind smoking despite the prohibited notices and the stink of petrol, so we all smoked cigarettes. Got to the end of the clouds and after a lot of searching, we recognised Trouville on our starboard bow and landed safely on the hilly airport of Dieppe at 11.55 to find the connecting plane had not arrived.'

At 13.40 Szlumper left in another Rapide, which this time was heated, and crossed the Channel. Reporting from the air over Shoreham, it flew east of Hindhead over Aldershot to Farnborough where it landed at 14.45 on the aerodrome which, he noted, was busy with experimental and training machines. He later recorded that neither at Rennes, Dieppe nor Farnborough had anyone asked who he was or if he even possessed a passport.

2 November 1939

At the QMG's meeting, Szlumper learnt there were 180 wagons of ordnance stores under load at Branston in Staffordshire. It was suggested some might be diverted to Burton and Aldershot where they were very much wanted. The Director of Supplies, General Hill, said he would see what could be done 'but he is a dull fellow, bent on spending his time stating his department is free from every blame in every circumstance.'

Later in the morning, the QMG asked Szlumper to attend a meeting with General Douglas Brownrigg, Adjutant-General to the BEF, and the Director of Medical Services about ambulance trains and ports. Meanwhile Amery, back in London, was active on the international front when he saw Deneys Reitz, the South African Minister of Native Affairs, at South Africa House. Reitz and other ministers from the Dominions were in London for meetings with the government.

3 November 1939

Amery recorded that he spoke to the Director of Military Operations at the War Office, General Dewing, later taking the 16.35 train to Oxford. Meanwhile Szlumper attended the QMG's meeting which was amused about the rumour of a battle between the two Leslies – Hore-Belisha and Burgin – with the former saying he could not get delivery of what he had ordered and the latter saying that he could not get the army to take delivery. Szlumper noted his proposed organisation had just been approved except for his assistant which question was reserved.

6 November 1939

In the afternoon Szlumper met with Riddles and Redman, telling them to get busy with 300 2-8-0 locos, 10,000 French type 20-ton wagons, 200 refrigerated wagons and 200 flat wagons for tanks; he also told them to start enquiries about building three train ferry vessels – it was agreed it would be best to go to the experts, Swan Hunter.

7 November 1939

'Miss Sloane, PPS to Secretary of State, came to see me, bringing a photo Hore-Belisha had signed for Biddle. She said she had known me for years on the phone and I had always been so helpful! It was because he knew I would be helpful that Hore-Belisha had pressed for me to come to the War Office.

'Sir James Grigg, the new Permanent Under-Secretary of State for War, asked me to have a word with him – wanted to know if I agree that charges should not be raised on military traffic, thus avoiding a mountain of accountancy work. I said I thoroughly agreed, both to save trouble and avoid wasting man-power. It depends on the terms of government compensation. Would have a word with Milne about it. Grigg was quite alive, used the same language as I and seemed to think that the Ministry of Transport and Treasury were terribly red tape.

'Milne was waiting for me in my room, having come to see me about his son's calling up papers in spite of being registered at Cambridge University for training as an officer – spoke to General Weymss [Director of Mobilisation] who will try to put this right. The railways and MoT are meeting tomorrow to discuss compensation and it looks as if the meeting will be a pretty stormy one. Thank goodness the railways have got their hackles up a bit at last. Milne has strong enough opinion on Hill and thinks him incompetent and below the average intelligence. He likes Missenden but says he talks too much for one who is a newcomer to management. Also says W.V. Wood gets Wedgwood's rag at times, especially on Irish questions.' Meanwhile, Amery was returning to London after attending a Cammell Laird meeting.

8 November 1939
'Out to lunch with Missenden who was in good form. He and the other General Managers had had a meeting with the Ministry of Transport in the morning about compensation payable to the railways.' Szlumper did not think the offer was fair to the railways.

13 November 1939
At his meeting, the QMG expressed concern about railway troops as the Canadians had advised they could no longer supply them. Szlumper told him his department was trying New Zealand and Australia. He also told him all railway needs were laid on except the 300 locos about which there was a hitch which it was hoped to shortly overcome. With regard to tank wagons for bulk petrol, Szlumper said he just received a suggestion which he had passed on to Director of Supplies & Transport, for the laying of a pipeline under the Channel. He thought there were many difficulties but the feeling was that it was worth enquiring into. Szlumper made no more references to this and would not be involved in its eventual development in 1944 as PLUTO (Pipeline Under the Ocean) for the invasion of Europe by the Allies.

Biddle visited Szlumper in the morning and told him that life was not quite the same on the Southern with a lack of personal touch; and he complained there was no one at Deepdene after about 12.00 on Saturday until Monday morning and no one in the evenings. This galled him as he put in long hours. It was when Szlumper took him to lunch that Biddle opened his heart on the main object of his visit – that he wanted a recommendation for an honour. Szlumper tried to persuade him that it was difficult but as he was really desperately anxious, he said he would mention it to Browett.

Szlumper went by appointment to see the Secretary of State, Hore-Belisha. 'He was very nice, said he greatly appreciated me coming to help. Asked me a lot of intelligent questions about transportation difficulties. Told him I saw little difficulty about meeting the huge programmes of the future and everything was in hand to provide the means of meeting them, the only real difficulty being the terrible uneconomic use of shipping and the terrible long Line of

Communication caused by the ports we now have to use. I hoped we would soon size up and control the potential air menace. We would have to before we could use the north of France ports and we would have to use these in order to handle the tonnage a few months ahead. He asked me how we could protect a place like Boulogne. I replied that was a technician's job and my job was transportation but as we were making great use of one port, Southampton, I did not see why it should be impossible to provide such armaments at Boulogne as to make it safe from German bombers. Told him that many billets I saw in France were very bad, the better ones having been collared by French refugees. He asked if anything could be done to improve them. Told him I thought not but everyone was alive to it but as soon as the front area needs are satisfied, it was the intention to provide hutting in the base areas. He asked me what I thought of the way the WO had catered for the transportation requirements. Told him I could best summarise it by saying that having read the official history of 1914-18 and other books, I was satisfied that the War Office had learned all the lessons of the last war and had adopted all the recommendations. The consequence was that we had started off rather better this time than we were when we finished in 1918. As to the personnel, I was thrilled with the ability and "aliveness" of all the officers at the War Office as well as overseas. He said I had not told him enough! Come again and make a pen picture of the transportation side. We parted after renewed thanks by him to me for having come to the WO. Saw Pennant this afternoon who was with Inland Waterways Transport (IWT) on canal work in the last war. He is modest and not very inspiring but there is no doubt he knows his job, so I agreed to him being made Captain on three months' probation and being sent to McMullen to look after canal work.'

15 November 1939
'The SS *Twickenham Ferry* has been handed back to the French but they are not using her commercially as she is held under twelve hours notice to be ready to evacuate Belgians and Dutch. The SS *Shepperton Ferry* is at Portsmouth Dockyard but nothing is being done to put her right for commercial use as no one has given any orders. Told Holmes to do this and have her train deck sparred over to take motor transport. She can then be used for Italian traffic, subject to three days' notice for military use and subject to definite use for the Cavalry Brigade horses to Egypt via France. The Senior King's Messenger came in to see me and said that although the SR boat between Folkestone and Boulogne always ran, the French one (SAGA) sometimes refused to and preferred to stay in safety at Boulogne. I said it was difficult to order a captain to sail but I would write to Masset of SAGA to ask him if there was anything he could do. The King's Messenger said that it was a rotten journey – the boat goes straight across to Cap Gris Nez and

then creeps along inside the minefield – they always see four or five loose floating mines – it would be dangerous in the dark or in rough seas when the mines could not be seen. Greig brought in for approval as Deputy Assistant Director Docks yet another Davis, from the PLA. Seems a first rate chap of fifty with good engineering experience – will start as a major.'

17 November 1939

Szlumper called at John Patteson, the European Manager of Canadian Pacific Railways, to ask if he could help in getting railway survey and construction units. 'He is sure Edward Beatty [the long-time President of Canadian Pacific Railway] will be keen on it and many Canadian railwaymen are just busting to come over. He is great pals with Brigadier Crerar [the senior officer at the Canadian Military in London] and the High Commissioner and also the Canadian Prime Minister, so I will let him know the types of men we want and he will try to help.'

18 November 1939

'Question again of these blasted Irish soldiers going on leave to Ireland – if they take service respirators [gas masks] with them, it would give away fact they are in the army, so they are to change them when changing their clothes for civilian pattern ones. Holmes says he does not think any respirators are issued in Ireland, so even the possession of a civilian one would give the game away but the QMG decided he would not take the responsibility of sending the men on leave without any.

'Sir Warren Fisher [the North West Regional Commissioner for Civil Defence] rang me to say I was a killjoy. He thought I was chairman of the REC and as such had said no special trains could be provided for the Haydock Race meeting [near Wigan] on 1 and 2 December. Fisher said "they must have the damned trains even if they had to push the bloody things themselves." Struck me as being queer language for the former Permanent Secretary at the Treasury.'

20 November 1939

Szlumper went direct to the Metropole into which his staff were in the process of moving. He noted his room was nearly ready but it was not nearly such a 'palatial' apartment as he had vacated at the War Office but was quite good and with the added advantage of being in the middle of some of his staff.

21 November 1939

At the War Office, Szlumper saw Collins who had become Deputy Quartermaster-General in the BEF. Collins wanted him to try to arrange barge services of cement from Rochester through to the Lille area to cater for the requirements of the Maginot Line but Szlumper did not think the Thames barges would go up the French canals, and he did not think the French canal barges were man enough to cross the Channel. 'So we may have to tranship at Calais but we will see what we can do. It all arose because the Secretary of State, just back from a visit to France, suggested we might put up our own cement factory there; but this would take many months to do and we would be burdened with taking all the raw material to it.'

22 November 1939

Szlumper was at the QMG's meeting at the War Office when Riddell-Webster asked him to forge ahead with Cross-Channel and Inland Waterways Transport barge schemes, particularly to deal with ammunition and RE Stores. Later he discussed this at length with Greig and Davis, deciding to investigate if any Port Discharge and Access canal barges could be found, also to reconnoitre Richborough. At the meeting, the Director-General of Supplies reported there was a project afoot for constructing aerodromes all over France by next March. It would take 2,500 men but it was doubtful if they could be produced in time.

He noted Riddles was back from France, reporting that the SNCF had definitely agreed to wait for main line locos until June and then would be content with only twenty instead of forty a month from February. Szlumper thought the proper thing to do was not to bother the British railways but to build new 2-8-0s as they could be produced in time but the news about wagons was not so good. The SNCF had asked if a wagon 9'2½" wide could go on British railways. Riddles had replied that 9'2" could just be taken. 'It transpires the French thought their standard wagon could be reduced to this by removing the doors but the cornices and bogies would still be foul of gauge.'

23 November 1939

'Greig and I attended a meeting at the Ministry of Transport. Hill in chair, Mount, Wedgwood and Barrington-Ward and Gresley for the railways with Riddles for the Ministry of Supply about the locos I want for France. I have asked for forty 2-8-0 locos per month from next February but Riddles has it in black and white in minutes approved by Le Besnerais that he now modifies his demand to twenty a month from June. Long discussion on the "non-sparability" of LNER engines without replacement at the same time by new locos. Then a still worse discussion on the type of loco that should replace them. Riddles wants to replace them by a somewhat similar 2-8-0. Gresley who was also Chairman of the REC's Mechanical & Electrical Engineer's Committee, wants them replaced by a 3-cylinder loco that will be more expensive and of a type unsuited to overseas. So I said all I wanted was locomotives and not to be embroiled in an argument between technicians.' Szlumper then suggested a strategy which was accepted, bringing the meeting to an end.

24 November 1939

The former First World War port of Richborough in Kent was the destination of Szlumper, Greig and Davis. They were shown round the complex by Fotheringham of Pearson, Dorman Long which owned the site. It was noted that many of the buildings were still in good condition including offices, stores, workshops and some of the barracks which were occupied by German Jewish refugees. The long quay, nearly half a mile long where barges were loaded, was in quite good condition. There were three temporary cranes in use. The former train ferry berth was in reasonable condition while the gantry and gear for the lifting span was still there and was thought to be re-usable. Szlumper thought it would take very little time and labour to get into working order again, although whether it would be better to spend the money necessary to get it right and set up an organisation and produce the necessary tugs and barges in such a vulnerable place was another matter. The great advantage, he noted, was that so long as barges could be used and as long as Britain's armies were on canal routes, the barges could deliver goods at the door. On the other hand, a good type of coastal steamer, usable anywhere and all the year round, could probably be provided in almost as short a time and at cheaper cost in numbers to take the 25,000 tons a week that the barges had reached at maximum in 1918. The only drawback would be their inability to percolate into the French canals.

27 November 1939

Szlumper recorded that Robert Léguille came to see him. He was happy at not having any locos until June and then only twenty a month as the French had plenty of locos as long as the 0-6-0 shunting engines were fitted with Westinghouse and speed recorders so that they could go on the running lines in emergency. As to the wagons, he was still trying to see if a standard French covered wagon could get more-or-less inside the British loading gauge or rather inside the structure gauge near enough to run from the manufacturers' works to port of embarkation. He noted Léguille had kindly brought with him a track model with signalling and some instructional signalling and Westinghouse brake film, but it had been detained by Customs at Heston Airport.

28 November 1939

'Discussion about Lord Warden Hotel at Dover, not now being used, being required to house about seventy officers a night for eighteen nights a month when leave starts. It was suggested it be requisitioned and the NAAFI run it for 5p a night for a bed (no sheets) and 7½p for breakfast, all curtains, carpets and furniture to be cleared out – this would be a poor show for an officer's last night before going back to France and I hope to persuade Brigadier Greenslade to see if Frederick's cannot put a reasonable proposition to run it in a more comfortable way at moderate cost.' Frederick Hotels managed this and other railway hotels by contract with the Southern Railway.

1 December 1939

Szlumper telephoned Wedgwood at the REC and asked him to consider setting up an organisation to look after the provision of comforts for railway troops as had been done in the previous last war. Amery had still not received the call but he was still very active, that day attending a meeting of the Privy Council.

4 December 1939

Szlumper lunched with Missenden who told him the railways were going to turn down the offer of compensation and ask for the question to be submitted to arbitration.

8 December 1939

Szlumper took the 08.48 train to Southampton where he toured the docks with Biddle. 'Everything seems to be in smooth working order there. Saw the plans for a train ferry terminal – they have now produced a satisfactory scheme for berthing the ferry vessel alongside the quay west of the King George V graving dock. Biddle very disturbed that things move slowly at Deepdene. He cannot get Missenden to order the seven new cranes for the new docks, although he has been pressing for six weeks.'

13 December 1939

It was reported 8,350 Canadians were due to arrive Sunday or Monday and would require twenty-one trains from Glasgow to Aldershot. They would all be landed by tender at the "Tail of the Bank" and their train journey would take twenty-one hours. They would need two hot meals on the train but Szlumper noted the government was only prepared to allow 15p per head, although it wished to give them a good first impression of England. As the LMS breakfast alone was 17½p, Szlumper telephoned W.V. Wood to tell him the standard breakfast of about five things was not wanted and asked him to do his best to put up a good show for 15p. In the evening Szlumper and Langley took the 19.55 train to Newport to visit the ports in South Wales.

14 December 1939

Over the following two days, they inspected the dock facilities at Barry, Penarth, Cardiff, Swansea and Port Talbot. Szlumper subseqently wrote that he had been very impressed with the Great Western staff he had met, and also most of the naval and military officers who seemed to pull well together. They returned to

London on the 16.15 train from Cardiff on the second day when he learnt that QMG BEF estimated that 220,000 labour would be wanted in France by the end of 1940, to be supplied at rate of 15,000 a month. Only about a third could be obtained in the UK and it was suggested Chinese be imported as they were unlimited in quantity.

18 December 1939
'At QMG's meeting learned that it is proposed to collect 10,000 Italians now in France for labour. They are anti-fascists and call themselves Garibaldians. Also to collect 8,000 prestateurs – Germans, Austrians and Spaniards. As to Chinese, it is hoped to make a start by producing the first lot in April and to bring 4,000 a month after that. They require a ten minutes stop for tea in every hour but work like the devil for the other fifty minutes. The first of the Canadians, 8,500, have arrived safely at Glasgow and twenty-one trains of them are now en route or are in the Aldershot area.

'At 17.45 went to Victoria to see the first leave train arrive from France. Masses of photographers there in the charge of the WO public relations people. Arrangements quite good. Taxi to Waterloo with Dawes who tells me he is leaving Movements branch and going back to the General Staff.'

19 December 1939
Szlumper was at Euston for board meetings of Carter Patterson and Pickfords. By 12.50 he was at the Metropole after which he took Greig and McMullen, who were back on leave from France, to the Carlton grill for lunch. It was noted that everything on the Transportation side in France seemed to have settled down into a steady stride while the SNCF people had been most helpful.

20 December 1939
It was noted Butlin, the holiday camp pioneer, wanted to build a holiday camp at Filey and let it to the army on some re-purchase basis. It would cost him £175 per head to provide accommodation but Szlumper considered he could get hutting done at £120 per head, although Butlin had greater amenities. Butlin wanted to do the work at War Office cost and to agree to take it over at the end of the war at two thirds of the cost, although Szlumper pointed out he might go bust or something else could happen to stop him meeting his obligations. 'QMG rightly decides Butlin to erect the camp at his cost and WO will pay on a monthly basis of rent.

'Another 7,000 to 8,000 tons special ammunition to go during January from Newhaven to Fécamp. Lord Haw-Haw of Hamburg apparently knows all about this or at any rate announced that we were sending ammunition through Newhaven about the day after we started doing so. I am told he has announced comparatively accurate details of every port we are using. How the devil is such information got across to Hamburg so speedily?' That day Amery attended a Finance Committee and board meeting at Waterloo.

27 December 1939

DQMG told Szlumper that it had been decided that although there was a risk in using Richborough for barge services, it was a risk that was worthwhile taking and so the exploratory work could proceed. Riddell-Webster and Szlumper had a talk with Grigg and Bovenschen about the Canadian Survey & Construction units. It was reported the Chancellor of the Exchequer, Sir John Simon, had 'gone up in a cloud of smoke at the suggestion the British pay for them. Grigg was very lurid in his language about the Canadians and their methods of milking the mother country cow.' Szlumper followed this up later by meeting the Director of Recruiting & Organisation, Bovenschen and his Director of Finance, Austin Earl, whom he described as an Etonian-tied ass. The meeting decided to try to jockey the Canadians into providing two survey companies at their expense. If they would not nibble this, he would suggest they bear their pay, allowances and pensions as they had in the last war, leaving Britain to equip and maintain them. 'Grigg is thoroughly human and quick and speaks the same language as I do; but Bovenschen has cold and slighty brackish water running in his veins and spends his time trying to avoid saying anything that will commit him.'

29 December 1939

'Director of Supplies & Transport's officer who went with the first men returning from leave, reports that everything at the Lord Warden Hotel was very satisfactory – the officers were given an excellent meal for 12½p and much appreciated beds with blankets and sheets. Things also pretty good at Commercial Buildings [Dover] for the men but Director of Supplies & Transport very worried about fire risks with so many men sleeping in a room.'

1 January 1940

Szlumper had a long talk in the afternoon with Conrad Gribble and Beare, both from the Southern Railway, Major Davis and Major Philipe [Transportation & Movements] about train ferry terminals. Szlumper said he considered it highly improbable that a sleeping car service would ever operate from Southampton – it would be too unattractive for a journey of six and a half or seven hours and could not form the basis of any new through sleeping car service to any point abroad.

He noted that at last there was a definite ruling on the question of what compensation his widow would get if he was killed on military service. The answer was that the Treasury could not depart from the Civil Compensation Act which gave £1.12½ a week and even the Treasury suggested the only thing was to give a military rank as the lesser of two evils. 'Military Secretary and DQMG agree it is fantastic and ludicrous but if I wish, they will gazette me as Major-General – so much for the Treasury's intelligent outlook.'

3 January 1940

'Having received the file on my compensation, I went and had talk with QMG and told him I had discussed with Greig the pros and cons of a military rank for myself. So far as I could see the advantages greatly outweigh the snags – easier to get about, especially in the forward areas in France which I wanted to do thoroughly and soon in order to size up the forward transport situation; and easier to get about in docks and depots at home. More appropriate than civilian clothes when visiting Derby or Longmoor. So I cast the die and he will push it forward. I now have about 7,000 transportation troops in France and another 4,000 in preparation to go between now and the end of March.'

4 January 1940

Szlumper and Manton who had just become Commandant at Derby, took the 17.30 train from St Pancras to the city from where they motored to the latter's house at Melbourne. The following day they inspected a house that had been requisitioned to accommodate forty men. They returned to the station and with Harold Rudgard, the LMS Assistant Divisional Superintendent of Operation, and W. Clay, LMS Estate Manager, went by special train over the line to Ashby-de-la-Zouch. Szlumper recorded that it was a 'heaven-sent piece of line, ideal for training.'

They arrived back in Derby at midday when Szlumper was shown a drill hall which had just been taken over for conversion into a holding depot for 300 men. This was followed by the Carnegie Library which Derby had just given up for a Quartermaster's Stores. They saw some drill in a council school but it was noted the men were short of equipment while there were no gas masks. 'Arrived at the LMS school at 13.00 and Manton gave me a full shot of his troubles. It seems to me that some of them have not been cured because he kept them to himself. He has no tools whatever but these have now been authorised and he is sending someone down to Didcot this weekend to collect them.

'Manton has had to get rid of Lawson Billinton who has grown very lazy and unimaginative. He can only think of somewhat old-fashioned mainline steam loco practice and when asked to produce a training scheme for military railway purposes, was only able after a long interval to put about ¾ sheet of paper with no tangible suggestions. I told Manton that if Billinton had been any use, he would have been on the Southern after amalgamation in 1923.' This was the former locomotive engineer that Szlumper had commented on in 1936 when a successor to Maunsell was being sought.

'Inspected the school after lunch and saw the operating people being trained on the model railway. Saw the very nice and very complete set of model French signals that Léguille brought over. Manton ran me to the station and put me on the 15.56 to London, telling me I had made a world of difference to him and that he felt a new man.'

6 January 1940

'Richborough is under consideration again and I gather it is to be used as a gathering ground for the Auxiliary Military Pioneer Corps [AMP] – I reiterated my claim and said I would not want a man on dry land for about four months.

'Great excitement everywhere today on a bare announcement that Hore-Belisha has resigned and will not accept another government post. Oliver Stanley is to become Secretary of State and Andrew Duncan President of the Board of Trade. No inkling of what the trouble is but the War Office is losing a damned good man – quick on the uptake, full of intelligence and with great energy. His lust for publicity is rather annoying but true to a politician's form. Anyway, the army and the country have a very great deal to thank him for. Oliver Stanley [former SR director] is a poor choice. He is a scholar but has been unsuccessful at every ministerial job he has tried. He is not liked by those who have served under him, being overbearing. From my knowledge of him, I give less than three months here – before which period has elapsed, he will have got everyone at sixes and sevens and with each other. Andy Duncan will be a success at the Board of Trade if he can stomach the civil servant and the burden of a parliamentary job.' Duncan, a leading industrialist and a director of the Bank of England, had just been brought into government service.

8 January 1940

He recorded that QMG was very anxious to speed up the completion of the depots in France and for Szlumper to press forward with Transportation Units. Szlumper said he had been doing that for some time but it was uphill work as the difficulties with the Canadian Survey Units had shown, while the process of getting men out of non-technical units never seemed to materialise. Szlumper also noted that one of the railway's ships in government service as a troop carrier, SS *Maid of Orleans*, had had a collision with the quay at Dover the previous day and would be out of commission for six weeks. The QMG expressed concern about this and reported the Naval authorities were saying they must have bow-rudder ships on this route. Szlumper told the meeting that that was tripe and explained the bow-rudder argument to them.

In the afternoon he went to the War Office to say goodbye to Hore-Belisha and told him he was very sorry he was leaving whereupon the Minister asked him if he thought he had done the right thing. Szlumper replied that he did not know what he had done wrong as he only had the information in the newspapers. Hore-Belisha said he had done nothing, the whole thing being a bombshell to him and he had simply been told there was a prejudice against him and he felt right in taking the view that no junior position such as President of the Board of Trade, would be acceptable to him. Szlumper insisted there was no prejudice against him in the War Office and that everyone to whom he had spoken, thought he had done a difficult job very well and he felt sure everyone was sorry he was finishing. He reassured him and reminded him he had served within his ambit for some years and thought he had done each job 'damned well' but he did not feel so happy about his successor, Oliver Stanley. Hore-Belisha said his successor was an able man and as to himself, he said he did not know if the war was being run for the benefit of the nation or of personalities.

9 January 1940
'Director of Movements referred again to use of vessels with bow-rudders at Dover. I again said it was tripe. Apart from the ahead and astern position, a boat going in astern was easier able to screw her stern into the berth and then bring her bow in with headropes, whereas if she came in bow first, her bow was very apt to "fall away" or get blown away from the quay. I understood the New Zealand government has said it will send a Headquarters Railway Group, one Survey Company and one Railway Construction Company to France by April. Also, Australians are getting busy to see what they can send.

   'Settled with Major R. Davis many detailed questions about the new ferries – he is thoroughly capable and a very nice chap. There is a number one-sized row working up between me and the Ministry of Shipping over question of train ferries, their construction and working, also barge operation. I have warned my people I am not going to brook any interference from the Ministry of Shipping and am not going to or recognise or countenance the totally unnecessary number of naval officers they flood the ports with. All I am going to do with the Ministry of Shipping is to have them allocate the shipbuilding facilities I require.'

10 January 1940
Szlumper noted that the main question at the QMG's meeting was how to find labour for railway construction work at depots and for the aerodromes. He lunched at the REC with Wedgwood, Cole-Deacon and John Elliot. He recorded that Wedgwood seemed to have the greatest antipathy to Milne who was always trying to gain an advantage for the GWR without any regard to the adverse effect on other companies and was quite offensive in his methods and remarks. He found Pick most annoying at times but sometimes helpful. Wood was often difficult,

particularly on small matters, and was always inarticulate. Wedgwood did not mention Newton but Cole-Deacon said he was an absolute bloody fool and no help at all. They both liked Missenden and Elliot who, they said, knew their jobs and were fully helpful but quite firm on the rights of the Southern Railway.

12 January 1940

Szlumper with Philipe and Greig motored to Longmoor for a day of inspection. He noted it did not seem in better organised state than Derby despite the fact that it had a complete ready-made organisation; and there was a big shortage of officers on the training side with no one appearing to be making any effort to get them. He gained the impression that the people at Longmoor spent the better part of their day sparring with Derby on every conceivable point but seemed unable to answer any question about Longmoor organisation. They proceeded to Bordon to inspect No. 3 Docks Group which was due to go to France the following day. After lunch at the RE mess at Longmoor, they saw some of the recruits on the square, observing they were progressing well under a good instructor, a "brought-back" infantry major. A tour of the workshops and running shed followed. Finally, they saw instruction at the signalling school.

18 January 1940

Szlumper noted that he had made no diary entries since 13 January as he had had a very short break which represented his summer holiday. He had spent it in Ferndown near Bournemouth and it had included one day shooting in bitter weather. On his return, he attended a meeting about train ferries, noting that the shipping people were far more helpful than he had expected. He explained the arguments for train ferries and gave them full details of the vessels and the work they could do. He recorded that George Duggan, the Director of Shipbuilding at the Ministry of Shipping, felt that the comparatively high speed of 16½ knots would cost money and it would take time to provide the machinery. Szlumper replied that it would increase their saleability after the war and was desirable on a long run like Southampton to Le Havre. He noted that the meeting was of the view that it would probably be more economic to build train ferries than cargo boats to carry the same tonnage, especially having regard to the awkward locos, wagons, motor transport, tanks etc that would have to be sent to France, some of them requiring special vessels.

22 January 1940

Szlumper recorded that Sherrington, Secretary of the Railway Research Service, called – his organisation was then working for the government. The subject of discussion was sabotage on the German railways. 'We have been doing very well lately with sand in the axle boxes while the number of helpers is increasing. This a useful form of getting movements bottled up. Sherrington is now trying to work up a scheme for changing over the labels on wagons, so getting consignments thoroughly muddled up. Also, to try and monkey with Frohlich brakes at Hamm marshalling yard – if anything can be done to tie up Hamm, it means grave difficulties over the whole Ruhr area as this yard controls traffic to it. I will try to bring to London one of the German wagons (ferry type) now held in this country so that the brake etc can be carefully examined by experts. The brake flexibles at the ends of the wagons are particularly vulnerable; and being of rubber, they would be difficult to replace on a large scale in Germany at the moment.'

24 January 1940

Szlumper interviewed LMS Superintendent of Operation, F.A. Pope, with a view to appointing him Director of Railways Overseas. 'I think he knows his job and is a level-headed unexcitable sort of chap but I wish he would look me in the eye when talking or listening to me – also, wish his shirt cuffs were cleaner. However, his experience and the verbal testimonial Ashton Davies [LMS Vice President] gave, justify giving him a try out and I arranged we will do so. He is very wishful to leave the LMS and no one seems happy there.'

29 January 1940

'Not only has the three inches of snow that fell early yesterday morning rested on the ground but another three or four inches have been added to it this morning, making travel conditions awful. About 1,000 people were waiting for a train at Surbiton. Travelled at about 09.30 on the footplate of an engine that was pulling an electric train that had left Farnham at 07.30. Did not envy the driver his job of keeping under control a heavy train with about 1,000 people in it – and only with brakes on his engine, the Westinghouse brakes on the train being inoperative. However, he fetched up to Waterloo in about forty minutes. Cole-Deacon rang to say the railways are in an awful state as a result of the snow and blizzard with practically nothing moving north of Leeds. Wanted to borrow soldiers to help clear it away. I went to see Deputy Quartermaster-General and with him to see the Assistant Chief of the General Staff who sent an instruction out at once that every available man in all commands was to be spared for this duty. Cole-Deacon said the effect was immediate and thousands of soldiers were forthcoming. Late afternoon Cole-Deacon again rang – so many telephone and telegraph lines were down that the LMS was totally out of touch with North Wales while the GWR was only able to make contact with two out of their thirteen divisions – could I do anything? I got in touch with Brigadier Rawson who rose to the occasion splendidly and got immediate instructions to the Signals School at Prestatyn, to Eastern Command Signals at Canterbury and to Headquarters AA Command at

Stanmore to render every help. I got the railways in touch with each of them and they started at once to make arrangements.'

7 February 1940

'QMG greeted me with "Why are you not a general? I want a general and I thought you were going to become one." I told him the Military Secretary's Department had apparently one gear, a very slow one, and they apparently kept on losing the papers. So QMG told de Pass [his Military Assistant] to do something about it. Apparently his effort, coupled with Philipe's persistency, moved something somewhere as later in the day Philipe told me that someone in the Military Secretary's office had rung and said the King had agreed and it was now an accomplished fact; and that I was now a Major-General and the War Office would announce it in due course.'

15 February 1940

'Director of Quartering says he has now completed arrangements with Waley Cohen for taking over Richborough – he wants me to give him a close forecast of my requirements there. Col Burns of the Canadian HQ came to see me about the Canadian Railway units I require – he says the High Commissioner has cabled over to Canada about them but Burns would like to send a cable from the military point of view, pointing out the urgency.'

16 February 1940

In the afternoon, Szlumper gave his first background talk on Transportation & Movements to the press at the War Office. With Major-General Beith, Director of Public Relations in the chair, it took thirty-five minutes. He began by explaining that Transportation was the provision of the means whereby Movement could take place such as the building of railways and docks. Movement was the actual details and translation of men or material from place to place, the detailed timing out of it and the carrying into effect the general terms of movement. He thought it went well and that Beith was pleased. He noted there were about fifty press people present but only three or four questions were asked. His talk was reported in the following day's *Times* but without attribution – the theme was that the railways were required to carry approx the same weight of supplies of all sorts as in the previous war; and that they were working well on both sides of the Channel.

19 February 1940

'Great excitement today as is it my first appearance in Major-General's uniform. The station staff did not believe it was me. Those gathered for QMG's meeting gave what almost might be described as a cheer but were very nice and seemed genuinely glad I had succumbed to it at last, most of them giving me a handshake on the strength of it. Long talk after meeting on the wretched Norway scheme and the provision of a proper Movements Control and Transportation organisation for it.'

29 February 1940
'Philipe and I by 09.48 to Southampton for a long day with Biddle. Brigadier Edward Hodgson, the new Embarkation Commandant, is a very capable and agreeable fellow, and a good disciplinarian but I wonder how some seventy Embarkation Staff Officers and others are able to fill in their time – one or two of them first rate fellows. Biddle had Short, Hodgson, Lt Col Jones, Admiral Tillard, Captain Hughes and Hulbert (RAF) to lunch. Biddle tells me some of our vessels have been having a hell of a time, especially the SS *Isle of Jersey* which has been running round with the fleet in the North of Scotland as a floating hospital, hardly touching shore since 4 September, tobacco and beer running short at times, no baths for the men for six weeks, clean laundry taking six weeks to deliver from Kirkwall owing to infrequency of calls and so on. The crew are quite understandably fed up and want to leave the job – the ship was not built for this sort of life.'

29 March 1940
'Went to Euston to see Lord Stamp to try get Hussey out of him. Pope thought he had made all arrangements before he left, for Hussey to follow him but when Greig asked for Hussey, the LMS said he could not be spared but Pope wants him badly. Old Darbyshire is the nigger in the woodpile and is not being as helpful as he should in sparing men to the technical units of the army. He has evidently been priming Stamp that Hussey is necessary for ARP purposes, although I feel his duties are pretty well ended, and although Stamp was as nice as ever, he said he really could not let Hussey go unless he was convinced the work he was going to do in France was as important as the work he was doing here.' Hussey's position at Euston had been Outdoor Assistant, New Works. 'Reading through McMullen's February report, I see that bulk petrol is going by coasters from Douges [near Nantes] to Honfleur [near Le Havre], also that each aerodrome now being constructed in France will require 1,000 tons of ballast a day during construction – seems a hell of a figure.'

2 April 1940
'Crerar rang to say our bluff with Canada has been at least partly successful – the Canadian government had cabled saying they would collect sixty surveyors from the CPR and CNR and send them here at their expense so that they could be enlisted in the British army on arrival.'

5 April 1940

'A variety of Cabinet changes announced yesterday seem generally to have given satisfaction. I am most glad they have moved Herbert Morrison from Ministry of Food and replaced him by Lord Woolton who seems an excellent mover. I am sorry they have moved Kingsley Wood from Air and put Sir Samuel Hoare there – I have never been able to get enthusiastic about Hoare but will judge him by results.

'At QMG's meeting, the Director of Quartering told us he is reckoning that one third of the men in France are in billets, one third in the trenches and that the remaining third require hutting – we have sent 11,800 Nissen huts out and are sending them at the rate of 600/700 a week.'

6 April 1940

'Riddles tells me he now finds the standard GWR locos of which he hopes to have sixty either built or borrowed, will not run in France because the connecting rod will foul the gauge. He is seeing if the GWR will build LMS-pattern 2-8-0s for us instead.'

10 April 1940

'Our Avonmouth and Stratforce schemes will be ready to go tomorrow, some now on the move. They will take fourteen days supplies with them and thirty days more will be landed. To enable pack transport to be resorted to, QMG has ordered pack mule saddlery to go, and if necessary the mules will be sent from France. Roads are pretty few and far between in Norway.' Avonmouth was the plan to land Allied troops in Narvik while Stratforce was for British troops to land at Bergen, Stavanger and Trondheim.

19 April 1940

'QMG asked what were the chances of producing locos and rolling stock for Norway if wanted? I told him the chances were bad – their gradients are heavy and require specially powerful locos and their braking system was specially suited for heavy grade work – and we know nothing of its operation. My own view of the situation is that the railways in a mountainous and broken country like Norway must be plentifully provided with bridges and I anticipated the Hun would blow up so many of these that we would be many months repairing them. We have sent Richard Clutterbuck there as Assistant Director Transportation and will follow him shortly with Waghorn.

22 April 1940

'Things seems to be going pretty well in Norway, we have landed at a number of points including Andalsnes and are pressing eastwards with rapidity.

'Meeting of London & Home Counties Traffic Advisory Committee in afternoon, mostly for the purpose of saying goodbye to Frank Pick who was eulogised to the skies by everyone including myself. Reason for his retirement is said to be ill health but I have never seen him looking better. I was told later in the day this was nonsense – reason is a split between him and Lord Ashfield, the LPTB chairman. Pick is increasing the bus and tube fares to keep pace with 10% increase on the main line railways but Ashfield is totally opposed to it on purely political grounds – he is a leading light in the Conservative Party and does not want to embarrass the government. They say Pick is not to be replaced. Ashfield will run the whole show – a damned silly attempt for such an old man.'

27 April 1940

'Two large containers of Canadian sleepers and timbers have arrived at Brest and St.Nazaire. During March, McMullen's people laid thirty-one miles of track [in France] but he complains of a difficulty getting ballast. In all since September, he has laid 103 miles of track and 406 turnouts. He is handling an average of 11,560 tons a week for the new aerodromes and has fifteen barges at work on the canals and taking forward about 4,000 tons a week of gravel and sand.'

29 April 1940

'QMG says Narvik is to be captured and held. I assume it will be turned into a sort of military and naval base – we may have eventually 20,000 or 30,000 out there and are to send over some railway people to get the railway going again. The 8th Company are arriving at Longmoor today to get ready to go and do this. We have been having a rough time in Norway, especially from air bombardment at Namsos and Andalsnes and the operations therefrom. It looks at the moment like being forced to withdraw and evacuate from these places.

'After dinner at the club, to Broadcasting House to speak at 21.20 on BBC Home Service, "Troop Trains, the Story of an Army on the Move." I tried it out first at 20.45 and got the OK from the BBC people and so shot with confidence at 21.20 for thirteen minutes. It is a bit dull talking continuously for this time into an inanimate microphone. You have to clear your throat as you go and cannot do it while people are laughing at a joke in making a speech to an audience. However, the BBC people seemed to like it well and expressed the strong hope I would come again and give another one. They pressed into my hand an unasked cheque for £12.60. On the way home, a nice very young gunner got into my carriage and after the usual courtesies, asked was I by chance Major General Szlumper who had just been broadcasting. He said he enjoyed it immensely, heard every word and thought it most interesting.'

30 April 1940

'To lunch with Manton who seems to feel think things are getting into better shape at Derby. He told me about young Glynne Roberts – he had been warned to be ready to embark at six hours notice and to treat this as secret. He goes straight off and tells his wife and either he or she tells Glynne Roberts senior that the boy cannot come and spend the weekend as he is under embarkation notice. Pa Roberts seems to have some kind of garbled message and gets one of his clerks to ring up the Derby School to ask if it was correct. He was given an evasive answer and the matter was reported – result, young Glynne Roberts under arrest awaiting court-martial. Serves him and his nasty father damned well right.' The senior Glynne Roberts was the LMS Secretary.

3 May 1940

'Yesterday it was officially announced that we had evacuated Andalsnes without losing a man and this morning QMG announced Namsos had also been evacuated. Cole-Deacon tells me that Ashfield is being appointed to the REC. I am sure this is a mistake and will lead to trouble. There should only be officers there, not chairmen, especially when they are highly politically motivated.'

7 May 1940

'The Forces Mail traffic to France is growing, although still of modest dimensions – we are taking about 26,000 bags of mail and 19,000 parcels across to France per week. Full dress meeting in House of Commons today to hear the government put up its excuses for the failure of the Norwegian show – Chamberlain seems to have put a good story across and to have put the facts in proper perspective. He also announced that arch-muddler, Winston Churchill, is to be able to dictate the general policy to the Chiefs of Staffs Committee – that means he will try to run each of the fighting departments in detail and we shall have a crash of some sort.'

The subsequent discussion, otherwise known as the Norway Debate, would ultimately lead to the fall of the government after the contribution of Amery. The beginning of the withdrawal by the Allies from Norway had, not surprisingly, earned the government a lot of criticism. It was a lengthy debate with attacks not just from the opposition MPs. Amery was called to speak just after 20.00 hours and it was just before 20.45 that he delivered his coup. Quoting from Cromwell in 1653, he told the Prime Minister to resign. Szlumper, however, did not comment on Amery's speech which in effect mortally wounded Chamberlain.

8 May 1940

'Meeting in afternoon with Waley Cohen, who is trying to hang on as long as possible to Kitchener Camp at Richborough for his German Jewish refugees. Told him quite definitely we should require him to vacate by end of next August. He would like the refugees of whom about sixty will be left by end of next August, to act as cooks and housemaids to us as they have been doing to the AMP Corps but pointed out to him that we were going to train stevedore and docker units and as these have to go out self-contained, it was necessary their cooks and handmaids should train with them. Later a visit from F.Strauss and someone from MI6 about sending some young railwaymen to mid-Europe to do a bit of "finding out" and also to grease any necessary palms to expedite British traffic and delay that destined for Germany. I think we should be able to find some levers of adventure – they would go out either as representatives of *Modern Transport* or of some commercial firm.'

The Norway debate lasted two days and it was on the second day that another Southern director spoke. Sir George Courthope, however, was not one of the critics and he attempted to defend the government. Szlumper made no comment on the second day which concluded with a division of 281 Yes, 200 No votes and an estimated 60 abstentions.

10 May 1940
Szlumper noted that Germany had invaded Holland, Belgium and Luxembourg. He had a long talk with McMullen about French ports. That day the Prime Minister, Neville Chamberlain, resigned, his position being taken by Winston Churchill.

11 May 1940
Szlumper asked the QMG to get Hurcomb to get back every barge and tug from Holland. He later visited the War Room where the new Secretary of State (Anthony Eden) was 'being put in the picture.'

13 May 1940
With the change of Prime Minister, Amery was told that he was destined for the India Office which was not the position he was seeking – he had hoped to be economic overlord or Churchill's deputy on defence. That evening it was announced that the King had approved of the appointment of four new ministers in Churchill's government, one being Amery who would be Secretary of State for both India and Burma.

15 May 1940
At lunchtime, Szlumper encountered Euan Wallace on the steps of the Metropole. Wallace told him he was leaving the Ministry of Transport and would be succeeded by Reith. Szlumper's response was that it was a pity that a more normal person was not following him but Wallace said Reith had a lot of brains and had questioned him hard for four hours that morning.

18 May 1940

Szlumper noted that the Train Ferry which had been 'bottled up' at Calais had been able to get out and would start in service that day; but Brussels and Antwerp had been evacuated.

21 May 1940

Szlumper noted that Le Havre had been mined and was out of action and that the enemy had reached Amiens. Perhaps not surprisingly, Amery was not that day at the annual meeting of Marks & Spencer. The Chairman, Simon Marks, stated that Amery had been invited to join the government and having accepted, had resigned his directorship.

22 May 1940

It was the turn of the Southern Railway to announce that Amery had been appointed Secretary of State for India and consequently had been obliged to relinquish his directorship. Oliver Stanley who had been Secretary of State for War but had not been taken into the new government, would take his seat. Until 1931, Stanley had been a Southern director.

25 May 1940

Szlumper recorded that the French situation was too complicated to write about. He made a similar entry two days later which was the first full day of the Dunkirk Evacuation.

29 May 1940

'Owing to Belgian situation, the Northern portion of the Western Front must now close down and it is a question of getting away as many men as we can. So far, up to this morning, we have evacuated 44,000 of the BEF from there under conditions of greatest difficulty.

Long meeting this morning with QMG in the chair and representatives from each command and Home Forces on the setting up of supply, petrol and ammunition depots at various places. They all seem to think you can just select a small station with a couple of sidings and offload from them and either carry or take by motor transport to the nearest field several hundred tons of stuff, irrespective of whether the station can accept it or not and irrespective of the part that half a dozen lorries over a field in wet weather will make its further use impossible. QMG says they cannot wait for sidings to be laid in to serve the depots. However, I pressed that the depots should be chosen with a view to possible siding provision at the earliest date. Langley is endeavouring to reconnoitre sites in conjunction with Commands to ensure that this aspect is taken care of.'

30 May 1940

'Up to this morning we have evacuated 85,000 BEF from Northern France but with very heavy shipping losses from bombing and gunfire – the crews of some of these boats going to save our lads have refused to sail and have had to be replaced by naval ratings. Capt Woodhouse [Deputy Director-General, Transportation BEF], rang to say the Admiralty are keeping two Train Ferries at Harwich to use as blockships if necessary, despite my strong protests at using specialised vessels for this purpose – vessels which we wanted urgently at Southampton to load rolling stock for France. Woodhouse said the matter would have to go to the Board of Admiralty for decision. Told QMG who telephoned his opposite number at Admiralty, pressing for the ships be despatched to Southampton.'

1 June 1940

'Up to 06.00 today we have evacuated from Northern France 166,000 fit, 11,000 casualties and 29,000 allied troops, an astonishing feat. Yesterday we sent back to France 5,000 French and today hope to send back 16,000, thus easing our burden here. This leaves 35,000 still in Northern France of whom we hope to get some back today. South of the Somme, we have 180,000, many of them Lines of Communication and base units. 151 and 152 Railway Construction Companies are back from France and we want to re-equip them and send them to Derby to be available for Home Forces.' Meanwhile, Amery was following the progress of the evacuation at the War Office.

3 June 1940

Szlumper wrote that the CIGS had circulated a note that there should be no recriminations against the French with anything of that nature being left to the historians. 'The WO is very pleased with the way the SR has handled the job of moving the evacuated BEF, and Snowden-Smith, Director of Supplies & Transport, paid a special tribute to the Station Master at Paddock Wood – he has been indefatigable, twenty-four hours a day.'

He had lunch with McMullen and Greig at the United Services Club. 'Afterwards Greig and I fell in with Mount and Hill. Went with them to Euston to see one of the "gun wagons" of the armoured train. It is fairly practical but I do not think much of the gun itself – a six-pounder tank gun. But what troubles Greig and me are the actual duties to which the train will be put. For patrol work on sections of railway, it has some uses but its movement is much too restricted to deal with parachute troops unless they kindly arrange to drop on or close to the railway. However, now the General Staff have condescended to let the Transportation Directorate into the picture, we will examine it and see what we can make of it.'

5 June 1940

Szlumper described the evacuation as complete, the final figures being 211,000 BEF fit, 13,000 BEF casualties, 110,000 allied fit and 1,500 allied casualties, total 336,425. The movements had taken 670 trains. 'General Lindsell ran into me and handed a big bouquet to the Southern Railway. He thought their performance had been quite astounding.'

6 June 1940

The Times praised the railways for their work during the evacuation which, it asserted, won the admiration and thanks of the whole country. The co-operation of the railways had been excellent. Szlumper filed the article in his diary, with the endorsement that it provided a lesson for all to learn when peace came again and road transport problems arose, concluding that if one wanted efficient railways in time of war, one must make it possible for them to prosper in times of peace.

'Director of Supplies, General Williams, asks if we can do anything to improve conditions at the [Ministry of Supply] ordnance depots at Longtown and Donnington as both suffering bad effects from the railway congestion there. Discussed with Langley who says the whole trouble is that both depots were laid out without any regard to the question of railway facilities – no proper ingress or egress, everything at rail level with no loading platforms and, at Longtown some damned silly arrangements for offloading at each shed about three trucks at a time into Decauville stuff. This Decauville [narrow gauge railway] runs right along inside each huge shed (end doors only) and of course is totally inadequate to deal with any heavy load. It is too late to effect any internal improvements but the WO ought to issue an order that they will shoot anyone who designs a depot without consulting the railway side of the WO.'

17 June 1940

'On the BBC bulletin come the news that the French army has laid down its arms. I am sorry enough for the French – there are many mysteries of major tactical failures yet to be explained. But with French as with us, there seems no reason why everyone who has held a ministerial post from 1919 to 1939, should not be strung up to a lamp post for having failed – either having failed to ascertain the real state of affairs in Germany or having failed to get remedial measures instituted.'

27 June 1940

'Lunch at Waterloo as Missenden had been having an officers' meeting. Short from Southampton was there, saying everyone was well but getting damned tired, having lost sleep for about five nights on end owing to air raid alarms. Saw QMG at his request in the afternoon. He says Finance is getting worried at me having a deputy (Greig) now that I am practically concerned only with Transportation.' The Movements part of Szlumper's work had just been removed. When the QMG asked him to think the position out, Szlumper replied he had been feeling for some days that his job could no longer be justified and he would probably be better occupied back on the railway.

30 June 1940
Szlumper and his wife motored their daughter Cynthia back to the farm at Long Sutton in Somerset where she was engaged on land work. He noted that it was interesting to see blockhouses at strategic points, also old cars that could be dragged across the road and other obstructions; and the anti-aeroplane devices, either of wire stretched overhead between two uprights or a series of concrete drain-pipes upended on the sides of the roads to catch the wing tips and looking like Grecian columns.

2 July 1940
Szlumper went to Waterloo at midday to tell the Chairman that the QMG and he felt that his work had dropped away so much that he was no longer of much service to the Army. 'What about SR having me back on the understanding that if things broadened out again and if the Army wanted me back, I would be allowed to go?' He noted that the Chairman seemed to welcome the idea of his returning, but acknowledged that Missenden would probably feel a bit upset, particularly as he had been doing the job so well. It was left that the Chairman would have an early talk with Missenden. This would be Szlumper's first attempt to return but he did not suspect that it would never happen – he did not know that Missenden, upon moving up to the General Manager post in 1939, had secured a contractual clause that he would never revert to a subordinate position.

5 July 1940
'Talk with Riddell-Webster about returning to the Southern Railway. He agrees that there is not enough here for my services in the present conditions but that there was no need to hurry back to the railway – perhaps, he thought, in two or three months time. In the late afternoon, Holland-Martin came to see me about my return. Said they wanted to have me back and looked forward to that and he was sure that the staff who all loved me, would be glad to see me back but after talking to one or two directors, they thought it would be a mistake to swap horses in mid-stream. Missenden and his officers were thoroughly au fait with all the schemes and arrangements and it would perforce take some time to get into the swing of them and he felt it would be unwise for me to come back and try to pick up the reins at this juncture when we might be invaded. I said there was something in what he said but as the financial people at the War Office were combing every

department in the interest of economy, I felt they might be unwilling to let me stay unless it could be said that my work was essential which it was not.

'In the evening, the QMG sent for me and said he had thought further about me and felt that, useful as I had been in bringing to bear the broad view and in making arrangements for the supply of wagons, locos etc, the work was not here for me to do but that John Reith, the Minister of Transport, had been screaming for me and he, QMG, therefore was going to say he would be prepared to release me. He suggested the best thing I could do would be to go to the REC and replace Wedgwood for whom he seems to have no use.' In his diary, Reith wrote that he wanted the post of Railway Control Officer to be occupied by a railwayman rather than a civil servant; and that he understood that Szlumper's work at the War Office was coming to an end. So he wanted him to come to the Ministry, although he noted the idea was unpopular at first.

10 July 1940
'Browett wants to know if I will take on the duties of Railway Control Officer "for the duration." It seems A.T.V. Robinson is due to retire soon from Deputy Secretary [MoT] and Hill is to succeed him. The change was to be held up on account of the difficulty of replacing Hill but when Browett heard I might be available, he jumped at the chance and said he would feel happier at a man with railway knowledge being Railway Control Officer now the battlefront is in England. I asked him if he had sounded Wedgwood – he had and Wedgwood would welcome me. Browett said he and all his colleagues would be delighted to have me to work with if I would take it on. I said that although Civil Service and Ministers were normally anathema to me, I was out to do anything to help win the war and my answer was therefore yes. I told him I might be able to get the railways to make better use of the Ministry and create a better feeling between them.'

17 July 1940
'Chief of Staff complaining strongly that the multiplicity of motor transport we use and the variety we purchase is bringing difficulties in coping with the spare parts situation. There are 270,000 different spare parts at Chilwell [the Ministry of Supply storage depot near Nottingham] and he longs for some standardisation. But it will take more than a war to make the insular Britisher standardisation-minded. One of the results of people choosing depot sites without consulting the technical transportation people is that four or five sites chosen for the ammunition sub-depots are to be abandoned and new ones found in their stead.'

19 July 1940
'They are still in trouble at Donnington, there being 700 wagons under load awaiting acceptance. This is due partly to the layout of the place and partly that

they are pushing traffic hard at it whilst the contractors are still pushing material there for the completion of the place.' Donnington in Shropshire was the Central Ordnance Depot of the Ministry of Supply to where stores had been transferred from London.

The following day he recorded that the number of wagons under load and awaiting acceptance was growing daily. 'The ordnance people are sending more labour there and I asked if they could work twenty-four hours a day but they cannot as no lighting has been installed yet. The trouble of the place is that, before the building of it is finished, they are pouring into it the evacuated Woolwich Arsenal and the output of the factories that would have gone to Woolwich.'

22 July 1940

'Lunch with Missenden. I told him what was moving about myself and he was delighted and thought it would be a great help to the railways. He also thought it would be good to have me at the Ministry of Transport for the sake of the railways and my own sake when the after-the-war policy was being settled, both he and I being of the opinion that there will always be some kind of government control and regulation embracing railways and road transport. On the other hand, he said he knows he is only keeping my job warm at Waterloo and is perfectly happy to move back from it so that I can resume it.'

23 July 1940

'At his request went for an hour's talk with Minister of Transport, Sir John Reith, who said he was very pleased that I was coming as Railway Control Officer. I corrected him when he said he understood that I did not want to go back to SR until the end of the war. I told him I would far prefer to do so but the Chairman felt it would be unwise to try to get back into the saddle whilst the war was on in this country. I said my sole object was to help win the war in the shortest possible time. I was quite willing to try the Railway Control Officer's job.

'It seems that Milne has been trying to be awkward in getting the Ministry to define precisely the functions, duties and limitations of the REC. Reith feels that the railways are to carry on their day to day working in the usual manner subject to any special requirements he may demand of them through the REC. We both agreed it would be unwise and undesirable to try and lay down what they shall and shall not do but the question is not settled yet. Another outstanding point is the REC Minutes. The Ministry feel they ought to have these so as to see what is going on generally but the REC feels otherwise. Reith said he was entitled to them and could demand them but he felt disposed to say that he would like to have them on the understanding that they would be seen only by himself, the Secretary to the MoT and the Railway Control Officer and that they would not be banded about among juniors or used to let other departments raise all sorts of questions. He does not seem very happy about the constitution of the REC and wishes it were a statutory body on the lines of the BBC with governors who would direct the policy and not concern themselves with the executive side of things but I do not think that would be possible as they must run the railways as one unit and must therefore co-ordinate the working. I rather liked Reith, he is quite human and intelligent – said he would like to see me as often as I would care to go into his room and was most solicitous I should have a week's holiday before taking over my new duties.'

24 July 1940
'With General Williams motored to Donnington. Saw Col de Wolf who outlined his difficulties. By a manful effort, he has unloaded all wagons under load and cleared his congestion. But the place is ill-conceived and the railway layout internally very bad. This can be relieved somewhat but never perfected owing partly to the existence in one corner of the site of a Royal Engineers depot where traffic requirements conflict with those of the Ordnance Depot. Captain Smith, the microscopic ex-LNER Railway Transport Officer [RTO], has done excellent work there in devising order out of chaos in the internal operation of the place and will be much helped when the new marshalling yard and sorting yard at the Trench end of the place is completed sometime in September.'

27 July 1940
'As I am hoping to have three days leave, this should be my last day at the office, so I spent part of the morning in dismantling my room ready for it to be moved two floors lower to the MoT. Saying goodbye, I must say most of them seemed genuinely sorry I am going and sorry I am to leave them, especially Greig who has been a most agreeable chap to work with, showing no sign of resentment at my appearance as well he might have and being entirely patient and helpful.'

Chapter Five

❧

Szlumper at the Ministry of Transport, 1940-41

Szlumper's period of work at the Ministry of Transport as Railway Control Officer should have been a happy and fruitful one, given that he knew so many of the major players in the department and the railways. But he would not enjoy working with the civil servants while his concerns about politicians would be intensified. He would be there for twelve months. His diaries are very interesting for his commentary on the working of the department and on individuals.

1 August 1940

'To the Ministry of Transport. H.W.W. Fisher [Principal Assistant Secretary] inducted me into some of the mysteries. He seems capable and helpful and gave a good first impression. I gather from him that there are plenty of troubles and a little friction with the REC but not amounting to open warfare. I gather from Fisher that the opinion at the Ministry is that the Railway Control Officer should be chairman of the REC. It would certainly have advantages and would keep the MoT in closer touch with the carrying out of ministerial requirements by the railways for which he is responsible. It would also save a mass of correspondence.

'R.H. Hill [the Deputy Secretary and former Railway Control Officer] put his nose round the door to welcome me but was on his way to a meeting – one or two meetings seem to occupy the first eight hours of each day. Lt Col Charles Russell came and had a yarn – a capable chap. He is here to liaise between the Army and MoT and very useful he will be. A day of settling in and reading some of the back stuff with a meeting in afternoon with the railway staff people, the Ministry of Labour and the Army about release of men from the Army. Greig [Director of Transportation] and his wife took Jessie and I, McMullen and Major Philipe to dinner and on to see *Dear Octopus* – a very agreeable outing.' The latter was a comedy at the Adelphi Theatre.

2 August 1940

'Defence (Transport Council) presided over by Browett [Permanent Secretary]. Not so snappy as the Quartermaster-General's meetings but quite useful. Then a variegated day punctuated by loquacious visits from Mount who pretended to be pleased at my arrival. He spent most of the time warning me against the other civil servants and saying how they try to grab bits of jobs from others to make their own more important.'

3 August 1940
'Read through a lot of stuff, especially the various evacuation schemes, civil and governmental. I am against all evacuations of government departments – it would mean chaos and it would not move them to any safer area anyway, nor to so well protected an area as London. But worst of all, it would, I think, shake the morale of the people to the roots to see the government skedaddling when things become sticky.'

5 August 1940
'Spent some time mugging up back history but punctuated by a stream of people poking into the room to discuss things which mostly do not matter. Definitely do not like the way correspondence is dealt with here – all sorts of scribbles on the inwards letters, many quite indecipherable and anonymous until I got to know the initials, and then interleaved with the letters all sorts of scraps of papers similarly scribbled over. Read Pick's reports on the various ports he has visited. Naturally with his lack of port experience, they are not constructive but he makes some good points on what information he has gleamed – he can see the faults when they are pointed out to him but he is not able to suggest the remedies except the obvious ones which are frequently impossible because of labour tendencies or ingrained customs.'

7 August 1940
'Much small stuff about today but the pièce de resistance was a meeting in Hill's room lasting from 15.00 to 19.30 of about twenty people, all smoking different tobacco, to consider the "crash" evacuation – three or four from Ministry of Transport, Ministry of Health and REC and one or more officers from each command. We dealt with every coastal town of any dimensions from Dundee to Bournemouth, tried to settle entraining stations that would not interfere with military moves by road, then regulating stations and reception areas but as no one knew anything about the entraining and regulating stations, the whole talk may have been wasted and anyway it could have been avoided and four and half hours of everyone's time saved by the MoT issuing a note to railway and military saying that crash evacuation was to be catered for and would they both get together and lay down suitable stations and report their locations to here. Definitely the Ministry has a meetings complex and loves to get together a lot of people who do not know anything so that they can interchange their ignorance. The Civil Servant

delights in trying to do the detail of a job instead of farming it out to the man who can do it without having to think about it.'

8 August 1940

To lunch with Mount – I think he is definitely loco-ed and has not got a good word to say of anyone except himself. Then from 15.00 to 17.30 a meeting in the Minister's room with him, Pick, Browett, Tolerton and Sir Brograve Beauchamp (Parliamentary Private Secretary) to go through Pick's report on the ports. Rather tedious. Pick babbling continuously in an undertone and Reith going by fits and starts, sometimes seizing quite quickly on a point and disposing of it, sometimes letting people wonder on and himself dreaming while they did. All the world rather shaken by the announcement that Pick is to go to the ill-starred Ministry of Information as Director-General. He will have his work cut out to hang on to his reputation. I fear he will rise to the baits of sniping criticism and will not be tactful enough in handling them or the Ministry staff.'

12 August 1940

'Took out to lunch Grasemann and Pritchard. The latter is quite likeable but finds his job very strange after his own commercial business.' Pritchard was Joint Managing Director of advertising agent Pritchard Wood & Partners Ltd and had just been seconded to the Ministry.

'Another two and a half hours meeting this afternoon with Tolerton in the chair to consider question of setting up a number of inland sorting depots to which a whole shipload of mixed cargo can be sent "rough" from a port, there to be tallied, sorted, customised and despatched – in order to clear the port and turn round ships quicker. It is an ideal but one I do not think is ever likely to be reached – because a depot will take at least a year to construct, will require much unobtainable steel and will cost, I guess, £500,000; and they are talking about eight.'

14 August 1940

'Talk today about coal situation. It looks as if we shall have to handle 150,000 tons a month over and above all previous figures to the south of England. The Mines Dept has very sparse information and cannot yet tell us the destinations. We here all feel that Mines Department is in a hopeless muddle and will make a muddle of this South of England job and then seek to put the blame on the MoT. We started our coal meeting at 17.00 with Lord Hyndley, the principal attendant for the Mines Dept. Went on until 19.50 with no one much the wiser. Either Hyndley does not know his stuff or is determined not to give it away if he does. He wriggled on every point and, being pressed for destinations for coal for consumption as opposed to coal for government dumps, said the cost would be

Szlumper was still a director of the International Cold Storage & Ice Company when its warehouse at Southampton was largely destroyed by enemy action on 13 August 1940. (*National Railway Museum*)

so high that no one would buy it. I replied that therefore a problem did not seem to exist as no one would be really short. Of course, it will cost more and if the government thinks it prudent for people to stock up, they have got to make some financial adjustment. Anyway, we told Hyndley we must know exactly what the problem is and we will send him a questionnaire tomorrow so that we can become informed.' Hyndley was Commercial Adviser at the Mines Dept but otherwise was Managing Director of coal factor Powell Duffryn.

17 August 1940

'A large bomb fell yesterday on the cutting between Hook and Basingstoke. Failed to explode and this morning all traffic has been stopped past it. The bomb disposal units arrangements are not going smoothly and despite various efforts throughout the day, 18.00 arrived with the bomb still there, although the unit had excavated down to it. I pressed the QMG to have it detonated and we would "tidy" up the railway after. At 22.30 the bomb went off and killed four soldiers whose lives would have been spared if it had been tackled and detonated a few hours after it fell.'

19 August 1940

'This morning Major General King discussed with me the question of unexploded bombs and arranged that the disposal unit should confer with the local Divisional Civil Engineer, should warn him of the probable damage that would follow its detonation and leave it to the Divisional Engineer to say whether he would have detonated it now or wait for it to go off on its own unless it proved to be a dud. In ninety-nine out of a hundred cases, I should think the Divisional Engineer would say "touch it off now." The damage would be the same anyhow and some four days of traffic disorganisation would be saved.'

20 August 1940

'Long talk this morning with Reith about the coal situation. He is intelligent and I rather like him. I find him "leadable" and a bit irresolute and think him more fitted for an artistic career rather than a business one. He asked me what I thought of the Ministry of Transport methods. Told him that he had some very good fellows who did excellent work for which they really had no training – indeed they did or attempted to do a good many things that we would be better done in railway divisional offices. As to methods, well! I was used to doing my own job myself and not collecting committees to consider the matters to be dealt with. Then again I was used to responsibility and to giving definite decisions whereas the whole upbringing and practice of the Civil Service was to avoid giving a decision. Reith told me to do what I liked in the way that suited me best. I thanked him and told him that was precisely what I was doing.'

21 August 1940

'A morning of committees. After the daily Transport (Defence) Council, I had to go, failing anyone else, to the Home Defence Executive which lasted until 13.00 under the chairmanship of Sir Findlater Stewart. A meeting small in numbers, efficiently run with useful things considered.' The committee had been set up in May to organise the defence of the country against invasion. Later Szlumper lunched with McColl who opined that Beaverbrook 'was quite mad and cannot pull with anyone.' The newspaper magnate had been Minister of Aircraft Production since May.

26 August 1940

'Meeting with Hill, Macaulay, Eborrall [Controller of Rates Division at MoT], Hinde and Pritchard in afternoon to consider a possible modification of the Railway Compensation Agreement in view of the possible scream at the proposal to increase fares and rates again by another 6½%, making a total increase of 17% to date. We all agree that the present application must be dealt with and the increase conceded but it looks as if sufficient pressure will be brought to bear politically to make us (MoT) seek agreement with the railways to modify the present compensation terms. The Labour Ministers seem to want to go the whole hog and make a bee line for nationalisation. The Parliamentary Secretary here [Frederick Montague, Labour MP for Islington] seems to want to go as far as any of them on the flimsiest of pretexts – lack of economic management and excessive numbers and remuneration of directors.' Szlumper noted that the total fees of directors of all railways were about £100,000 whereas the increased costs due to wages and rise in increase of materials were £18,000,000.

27 August 1940
'With Montague to meeting of Ministers at Home Office to talk on safety precautions to railway station roofs, and admission of intending passengers to stations during "warning" periods with Ernest Brown MP in the chair. A fairly alive meeting. Malcolm MacDonald [Minister of Health] quite good, Major Tryon [First Commissioner of Works at Home Office] grown into an old woman, Euan Wallace (now Regional Commissioner for London) quite good and very cheery and apparently glad to see me again. Some trouble at Fratton with an unexploded bomb fallen thirty yards from the railway. The bomb disposal officer had inspected and said he dare not "touch it" off but suggests the railway should continue running freight trains past it. The SR was unwilling to do this but I had a talk to Missenden and suggested he put a rake of high-sided wagons loaded with coal on the track nearest the bomb to act as a blanket and to run freight trains on the track furthest from the bomb, telling the train crew to lie down whilst passing the actual spot. He agreed and I was glad to learn later that running had been re-commenced.'

28 August 1940
'We are getting into trouble in South Wales. Thousands of tons of scrap and billets are coming into Swansea and are being discharged and are being railed away far quicker than consignees can accept. Consequently 4,300 wagons are under load en route or at the consignee's works. Ministry of Supply is supposed to have found dumps to relieve the situation but it is steadily deteriorating.'

30 August 1940
'To lunch with Missenden who was in good form. Glad to hear he was appointing A.B. Chester as assistant to Ellson with a view to succeeding him before long. Chester has earned a very good reputation in the Army and is a very capable chap – and Ellson is quite old enough to be packed away. Burgin was at lunch at the Carlton with his girl friend. He came up to me and said, "Well, the railway department at the Ministry is alright now – at last they have someone who knows all about it." I replied, "Yes but what an opportunity you missed when you were the

Minister." Stamp was also there and said "Well, how's my boss?" I said "Alright but take care you do not do anything to upset him.'"

2 September 1940

Reith asked Szlumper what the objections to nationalisation were. His reply was that they were twofold. In every case where a country's railways had been nationalised, it had been a failure with losses and great deterioration in efficiency; and the fear of political interference – the socialist Members of Parliament making the management put three men where two could do the work. Reith said he did not mean nationalisation but public ownership under a board of directors, something like the BBC, PLA or LPTB. Szlumper said he failed to see what advantage would be gained. They discussed the various arguments, Reith spoke about directors, their individual abilities, the extent to which some were any asset to a railway and the nuisance that monthly committees on the technical side must be. He expressed surprise that Szlumper had attended every board committee and reckoned to know in detail what went on in the Southern in normal times.

'He asked particulars of the organisation of each railway and seemed to think best of the LMS organisation. I told him none of the other railways thought anything of it or of the results it produced and that it was an attempt to assuage the internal war due to foolish appointments by the London & North Western Railway, the Lancashire & Yorkshire Railway and the Midland Railway at different times according to the "section" in the ascendant at the moment. He certainly was frank and so was I and he did not let me go until 12.00 when he had to go and keep an appointment. Went to Browett when I left the Minister afterwards to tell the purport of my long meeting. Browett said he was scared stiff at the situation. He had done his best to head Reith away from any mention of public ownership à la BBC but the paper was to be debated at the Cabinet tomorrow and the position was still that Churchill was preoccupied with trying to win the war. Halifax was pre-occupied with Foreign Affairs. Chamberlain who might have been a restraining influence, was away sick; and Atlee and Greenwood were taking advantage of the situation to try to push through something that would stand no chance of going through if non-socialist Ministers could spare the time to watch it properly.'

4 September 1940

'At midday the Minister had me, Browett, Macaulay and Hind for a one and a quarter hour talk on the subject of the Railway Agreement. The Cabinet as the result of discussion yesterday, decided that he should seek to amend the agreement with the companies on the basis that no more rates and fares increases were to be sought over the existing 10% and that he was to try and settle on the basis of a flat £40m with a caveat from the Chancellor that there should be no subsidy. But we told Reith that this just did not make sense and, if increased costs did not come out of the railway users' pocket in fares and rates, it must come out of the taxpayer's pocket in subsidies. I asked why compensation should be a flat figure – were the railway stockholders to have no benefit from a vastly increased traffic? But Reith thought not – armament works and other industries were subject to an excess profits tax and so should the railways be. One good thing was the Prime Minister was against any idea of nationalisation or public ownership. But I warned Reith that if rates and fares were stabilised by some means, the bankrupt condition of the railways at the end of governmental control would necessitate something of the sort or a repetition of what happened last time when rates and fares had to be bumped up 100%.'

5 September 1940
'With Browett and Ball (REC) at Home Office for meeting about coal for London with particular reference to an idea of the Mines Department to dump 100,000 tons in Rotten Row, a small job taking 33,000 lorry loads. William Mabane, Minister for Home Security, took the chair and was very good in requiring answers to his questions. Hurst of Mines Dept [Permanent Under-Secretary] was incompetent and unhelpful and Mabane soon sized him up. Watson of Mines Dept was rather new to the job and did not know his facts – so Mines Dept did not cut a very good figure. They only referred once to transport difficulties but could give no particulars when we tried to tie them down and when Browett asked why they had cancelled seventeen of the special coal trains yesterday, Hurst said it was most unfair to have asked the question.'

8 September 1940
'At 15.00 Fisher and I to Home Office for meeting about evacuation of coast towns from Southend to Shoreham plus Ipswich, Colchester, Ashford and Canterbury. Total numbers are 350,000 but the Home Office and Ministry of Health seem to have no particulars of anything. This war seems to be run by a number of young men with socialite tendencies, raw from Oxford or Cambridge and knowing nothing about anything that matters. Wrote a strong minute, saying that as the Deputy Chief of Staffs committee considers that intensive bombing will preclude any attempt at invasion, the first objectives are likely to be railways. Any scheme for evacuation by rail transport will be probably impossible to carry out.'

9 September 1940
'Fisher and I walked to Home Office for meeting in Mabane's office about coal stocking in London. Mabane was first rate and made the others stick to the point.

Hurst was very annoyed we raised the question of coal stocks for other than London but Browett and I went for him and said that in the three weeks since 21 August when the arrangements were with Hyndley, only 960 tons of coal had come from the North to Bristol Channel ports instead of 9,000 tons. Hurst said the MoT always wanted to interfere with the Mines Dept but I replied, somewhat vehemently, that transport was a vital consideration in coal matters and we were not prepared to suffer inefficient use of transport.

'Hear that at this morning's meeting of Ministers, Ernest Brown in the chair insisted in sending on to the Cabinet the strong part of my minute on evacuation and this caused the Cabinet to come to a decision and to arrange for the issue of posters in Ipswich, Chelmsford, Ashford, Canterbury and the coastal areas, urging the unnecessary mouths to get away. We are to lay on special trains on Wednesday and onwards, to run them to a regulating station, Redhill, thence to Oxfordshire, Wiltshire, Berkshire, Surrey but the thing is full of difficulties, especially in the matter of billeting for arrivals late at night.'

12 September 1940

'Very annoyed in early afternoon to get a message from the Privy Council that Anderson [Home Secretary] had told Reith on the way into a meeting that 2,000 children had been left at Ashford station since 08.00 as there was no train to take them and that they had been bombed. I said I knew it was a lie but would find out the facts. I found out from the REC that the SR had run five trains and shifted 2,700 people and that there had been no bombing. Told the Privy Council office this but the man there said some mistake had been made, it was Hastings, not Ashford. Again, I said I knew it was a lie but would find out the facts. Ascertained that the SR had run nine trains from Hastings to various destinations and had shifted 5,700 people and had expressed willingness to run any more trains required. Told Privy Council, Anderson's secretary, Reith, also the secretary of the Regional Commissioner, Auckland Geddes; and made some strong remarks on my having to waste valuable time on a pack of lies. Then made a strong minute to Minister of Transport giving the facts and saying I could only ascribe it to a fifth columnist in Geddes's office and demanding an enquiry into the source.'

14 September 1940

'Question today of people being allowed to shelter in the Tubes during air raids. Against all arrangements and regulations, it is taking place to a great extent. Ashfield is loath to stop it and the Prime Minister favours it. I am deadly opposed to it. It will greatly interfere with legitimate traffic, and the insanitary conditions will, I am certain, start epidemics of typhus or other sorts. I told Reith it was no function of LPTB to provide refuges.'

16 September 1940

'Meeting with Thompson (Treasury Solicitor), Howland (Mines Department Solicitor) and Robson (Mines Department) which latter I do not like at all. The Mines Department wants to divert coal en route and will not indemnify the railways against actions for misdelivery, nor guarantee payment of freight charges by the new consignee. I do not think the Mines Department is valid. If it was, it might override a contract of carriage, and as the new consignee is to be asked to accept the coal and pay the charges, I would be prepared to ask the railways to accept Mines Department requests. Point to be put to Treasury Counsel to see what he says. The Mines Department think that I am unreasonable but I say if they are sure of their ground, they need have no qualms about giving an indemnity. The trouble could easily be got over by the Mines Department requisitioning the coal and thus becoming the owners, free to send and sell it where they like but this a nettle they will not grasp.'

18 September 1940

'I do not think I have ever seen such a slow acting mechanism as some of the civil servants' brains, especially Hill's. In the afternoon had a message that the Minister might have to take part in a debate in the House of Commons tomorrow on the transport side, so I had to sit down and write the genesis of a speech on the railway side of things.'

19 September 1940

'Reith wanted to see me after his return from the House of Commons. Montague told me that Reith had spoken quite well in an informal manner and had been well received. When I saw Reith, he was in great form and said he had given them my statement practically verbatim and the House had seemed to like it very much – he was certainly pleased with himself.' The debate in which Reith spoke, was about aerial bombardment of the country but took place in secret session.

20 September 1940

'Long talk with Reith who has invited himself to the REC and wants to know what he shall say to them. I made several suggestions – the wagon position, congestion, working in air raids, helpful information to the public and so on. He was greatly obliged. Then he went on to say how isolated he felt. I told him the higher one got, the further one got from the practical side of things and that he could be likened to someone never having been connected with railways, having just been appointed chairman of a railway company. Reith did not seem to feel comfortable that the General Managers were fully competent. I suggested that he should think that the railways had been going for over a hundred years and, until the war, were run efficiently and profitably – so it could be assumed that both the management and "body" of the railways were satisfactory and there was no reason to expect they had changed. This seemed to satisfy him. Reith has no opinion of civil servants, especially Hill here and asked my opinion of them – I told him that, speaking bye and full, there were some quite good brains among them but they could not be expected to switch from pre-war administrative work to wartime semi-executive jobs as they had no executive experience. He asked how I got on with them and I replied "Not too badly, I thought" – none seemed to have resented me and many seemed glad I was in the habit of saying "Yes" or "No" without hesitation. Reith said I was so different from a civil servant, that is why he was so glad I was at the Ministry.'

22 September 1940

'The argument over the use of Tubes as air raid shelters still continues but fortunately Reith and Anderson are both against it. 120,000 slept in them last night. The Aldwych line is to be entirely given up for the purpose but this morning we hear that Ashfield intends to blank off half of it, the northern end, for use of offices by LPTB staff who are to be housed in coaches there – the other half will hold about 7,000.'

28 September 1940

'McColl tells me that it was the Governor of the Bank of England who pressed for Milne to be chairman of the GWR. Duncan thinks nothing of Milne. He also says Oliver Stanley made a big mess of BoT matters – no surprise.'

2 October 1940

'The GWR in difficulty having appointed Milne a director as well as General Manager. The company wants the Minister of Transport to legalise it by issuing an order under the Defence Regulations but the Treasury Solicitor says that the Minister can only issue an order under the Defence Regulations if it is for the purpose of ensuring the more efficient and economical persecution of the war.'

3 October 1940

'Nothing special today except news of ministerial changes – Chamberlain is going, [Sir John] Anderson is to be Lord President. Herbert Morrison is to go from Ministry of Supply to Home Secretary where he may be more of a success. Andrew Duncan to move from Board of Trade to Ministry of Supply, an excellent choice. Reith to go to the Office of Works with a rebuilding addendum – good riddance to him, they have made him a baron. Moore-Brabazon is to be the new Minister of Transport – he used to be wild and bumptious but perhaps he has steadied down now. Anyway he is very road-minded and I doubt if I will get on with him.'

5 October 1940

'The new Minister of Transport asked me to come to have a chat and gave me quite a warm welcome. I wonder if he is tidy-minded as he has already succeeded in making his room damned untidy. But Brabazon was very nice to me and we had half an hour chat on why the SR perpetuated 660 volts electrification to Brighton and Portsmouth.'

21 October 1940

'McColl came to see me about a Transport Officer for the Ministry of Supply. Duncan had asked him to get my views. Recommended Patteson, a man of ability with good railway knowledge as well as Transatlantic knowledge which would be useful; and he has plenty of energy and determination. He thought it a splendid choice and I phoned Patteson to see if he would take a big job without telling him what it was.

'Wedgwood came and had a talk with Hill and me about use of road transport. At long last after three pressings from me, the REC seems to have arrived at the conclusion that the railways are so congested that it might be wise to see if road transport can be called in to help with some of the short-haul stuff. As usual, the GWR is likely to be awkward, although it is in a far worse condition than any other company. It seems incapable of handling any emergency. It does not seem to have efficient officers, staff, communications or methods but will never admit anything is wrong.'

24 October 1940

'Very concerned at the continuing shortage of wagons at the ports and I drafted a strong letter to Wedgwood – that as the REC efforts to cure the position were unproductive, I consider that the time has come to appoint a commission of say three railwaymen not concerned with the railways serving the ports, to thoroughly investigate the position at Glasgow, Liverpool, South Wales and Avonmouth and to suggest any remedial measures. I am sure the REC just passes on to the railway concerned the complaint of a wagon shortage and does nothing to follow it up. The railway in its turn probably says "another damned complaint from the REC about wagon shortage" and that is all that happens to it. Browett liked the draft so much that he wants to show it to the Minister to get him in line with it.'

28 October 1940

'At 04.20 all being in the cellar, we were awakened and alarmed by a fiendish row, a sort of rustling metallic sound which only gave us time to sit bolt upright in bed and for me to try to reach and touch Jessie and say, "My God, it is coming this time" – and come it did in the garden of *Guildown* opposite us. Followed by a sound of falling debris, small bumps being clods of earth thrown up by the explosion and coming down again; and falling glass all around. Saw we were alright and dashed upstairs to see if there was any fire. Dashed all round the house to see windows blown out everywhere but apparently nothing else wrong. When dawn came, I went and surveyed the damage – a ring of broken glass round the house, practically no window frames left and some curtains torn and blowing outside, one or two holes in the outside of the house where splinters had struck it, and some slates loose but so far as I could see, little else. A call to Dorking where I told my troubles to Smart and told him to send men, materials and furniture removers.' This was one of several air raids that had damaged their house and they subsequently decided to move and began packing with a view to putting the furniture into store. At 17.00 Szlumper and his wife motored to Cobham to Alfred Raworth, still the SR Chief Electrical Engineer. The following day was spent supervising blocking up windows and the removal of furniture.

30 October 1940

'Everyone [in the office] very sympathetic. Holland-Martin rang up to ask us to Overbury for a quiet weekend. Spent night at the Dorchester very comfortably but the dinner service very poor.'

31 October 1940

'Talk with Wedgwood on the GWR condition. He agrees to appoint a committee of three to look into things and make any suggestions they can for alleviation – to be Biddle, C.M. Jenkin-Jones [Divisional General Manager of the LNER at York] and S.H. Fisher [Assistant Chief Operating Manager, LMS]. There is plenty they will find wrong but not easy to put right at the stroke of a pen. There is too much drink and not enough energy on the GWR. They have now absolutely isolated themselves in an effort to get hold of the position – no traffic to or from any other company until after the weekend.

Szlumper gave a lunch at the Charing Cross Hotel to give Patteson as Controller General of Transportation at the Ministry of Supply the opportunity to meet and talk with Holmes, Whitworth [Admiralty] and Group Captain Sims [RAF]. 'Very successful and they are all out to help. At places such as Portsmouth where all four of them have an organisation, I think I shall succeed in getting them to club together and work together for the common good.'

5 November 1940

'Packed my bags and left the Dorchester – it is too damned hot there and I cannot get my room temperature below about 75° and I cannot sleep as warm as that. It is not cheap and it is not easy to get back from the Metropole after the guns have started, especially when it is raining. So to the old respectable Charing Cross Hotel.'

Brabazon asked my opinion of the REC and of Wedgwood which I gave him very guardedly and he then asked me point blank if I thought Milne should be superseded. Told him he put me in a very delicate and awkward position but he replied that he wanted my help, so I told him that Milne had considerable ability in some directions but was an angular Irishman with a jealousy complex – jealous of Wedgwood being brought back [from retirement] and made chairman, jealous when I was made Director-General of Transportation & Movements, that I did not think that he was used to playing the sort of cricket I was used to, and that his team was not what I would consider a competent one. But if he were superseded, I foresaw a revolution on the Great Western and would find it difficult to suggest who should take his place.'

8 November 1940
'Browett had a word with me on the eternal Great Western question – their traffic restriction grows no less and I had a heart to heart talk on GWR personalities. Told him the cabal that existed when Pole was General Manager and pointed out that whoever was sent to supersede Milne was likely to find one camp for him and one against him. If a GWR man was to be chosen, I considered Quartermaine the most competent and the man most likely to know those GWR officers who are useless and should be got rid of.' Quartermaine was the Chief Engineer of the railway but since June he had been on secondment to the Ministry of Aircraft Production.

9 November 1940
'Got Wedgwood and Milne to come to the Ministry to talk over GWR congestion. The worst trouble is the blockage of the exchange junctions – too many troop trains passing through them to the exclusion of other traffic. The coal trouble in London and some of the provincial towns is due to the very slow clearance of wagons by firms that have them to the exclusion of coal for firms that have none – this could be altered by a stroke of the pen by the Mines Dept – they should transfer all outstanding wagons to the "have nots."'

13 November 1940
'To House of Commons at midday to hear a debate on railways. I arrived just as the Members were cheering Churchill's statement that the naval air arm had just put paid to about 60% of the filthy Italian navy at Taranto. As Churchill passed me, his eyes were twinkling. He said, "That's little bit of sugar for the bird." He looked most wonderfully fit. The railway debate was opened by Lewis Silkin, Member for Peckham, an extraordinarily dull fellow who wanted the railways nationalised now, or if that could not be done, wanted the control agreement altered so that fares and charges could not again be increased. He was followed by that prize ass

Sir Ralph Glyn who, as far as he was coherent, appeared to welcome the prospect of nationalisation and to welcome the counsels of labour on the boards. I could not believe my ears. Brabazon followed in a most unorthodox style which pleased the very sparse attendance. He did not deal with most of the lesser points but said the railways were doing a fine job of work and would be thanked by all if only people knew the difficulties they had to surmount day by day.' When Szlumper returned from a break for refreshments, Montague was winding up. The Minister asserted he was all for nationalisation but he did not want to do it with bankrupt railways, and the only way to obviate that was to raise rates and fares to keep pace with rising costs or by government subsidy which neither he nor anyone else favoured. Szlumper thought Brabazon and Montague both did well and that the debate ended in the railways' favour.

14 November 1940
'In afternoon, a meeting with the Minister, Browett, Tolerton, Cyril Birtchnell [Assistant Secretary, Road Dept, MoT] and the Minister of Shipping, Ronald Cross, with Hurcomb and Basil Sanderson to discuss clearance of the ports and more rapid turn round of ships. Learned that the War Office is going ahead with making two new ports, with three berths at Gareloch and three at Loch Ryan. We also spoke about the scheme for inland ports, ie the building of huge covered rail-served areas to which a ship's outturn could be sent "rough," there to be checked, customed, sorted and loaded away to destination by rail or road, all to expedite working through the real port. Four depots suggested, to cost £1m each and take a year to build. It would throw a big added load on the railways, creating empty wagon difficulties at the ship's side.'

15 November 1940
'Meeting in afternoon with Waghorn and other War Office officials, Keith Grand – offensive as usual, W.H. Austen, Pike and James Ramsay [Managing Director] of the Shropshire & Montgomery Railway. The War Office wants to take over most of the line to develop from it two big ammunition depots. The line has been worked at an increasing loss for years, and has paid nothing on its debentures since 1932. Arranged to continue government control of it until Waghorn has relaid or strengthened it, and when he is ready to operate it, I will de-control it and the WO will requisition it – and they will have an unenviable job trying to sort out the financial tangle in which it is.

'Browett had a long talk with me on the subject of the REC. He and many others including the Minister are by no way happy about the way it is functioning – they are far too complacent about everything and on the one hand they seem to want to keep the MoT at arm's length and tell them as little as they possibly can, and, on the other hand, their relations with the railways do not seem to be as close and cordial as they might be. Browett said if the Ministry had its time over again, they would doubtless have their own representative on the REC, and that representative would be the Railway Control Officer to see that close touch was maintained and the requirements of the Ministry dealt with speedily. What did I think of the suggestion the Minister should now appoint the Railway Control Officer to be a member of the REC? We discussed the repercussions, the first of which would probably be the retirement of Wedgwood. We both have considerable affection and respect for Wedgwood but there is no doubt he has a conservative outlook on railway matters, that he is very tired through the terrific amount of detailed work he does, and that he is not quite in step with some of the members of the REC, particularly Milne who resents the REC dealing with any matter concerning the Great Western. If I were put on the REC, quite possibly Milne and Wedgwood would cut up rough and there might be a general bust-up. I told Browett, however, that if the MoT was prepared to put up with the consequences, I thought my appointment was really the proper thing and that I would be quite prepared to see it through if that was the decision. Browett, dear chap that he is, doubted if the repercussions might be so violent as I had outlined, placing too much emphasis on my tact and the extraordinary way in which I was able to get on with people. I asked him what had been decided on the very vexed question of the functions of the REC which had been under discussion with the companies for so long. He said it was finished, the Minister had had a meeting with the chairmen this week and had told them that he settled the functions, that he was absolute and had power to do anything he required – and that was that. Thank god for a bit of decisiveness and strength at last. We then spoke of the chairmanship of the REC in the event of Wedgwood resigning, a contingency which we both thought would not really be disadvantageous – we both agreed the next senior, Milne, was quite impossible and could be dismissed without further thought; that W.V. Wood would be equally impossible – indeed, I said that Wood, being an accounting Vice President of the LMS, should never have been put onto the REC which was supposed to have been formed of General Managers. Then Newton was too useless to merit consideration and Missenden too junior. Browett and I agreed that Stamp would be the best choice by far but he would have to look upon it as a whole-time job and would have to disrobe himself of all his other interests – I doubt very much if his vanity would permit him to do this.'

21 November 1940

'Lunch with John Thornycroft, not so garrulous and full of false rumours as usual but in very good form and very friendly. He asked did I not think I should be doing better service by throwing up my Ministry of Transport job, replacing Wedgwood as chairman of the REC and at the same time becoming General Manager of the Southern again. I hedged, having just written to Holland-Martin on the subject of returning to the Southern but told Thornycroft as to the REC chairmanship, this was pretty well a whole-time job and anyway was not vacant. As to the SR, I did not know if I was wanted back. He became quite vehement at this and said of course I was wanted back and the sooner the better. Brabazon questioned me in the afternoon as to the ability of Jenkin-Jones. I told him he was one of the most capable operating men in the country, thoroughly competent, hard-working and trustworthy – a little dull and non-friendly in personality but he got on well with people nevertheless.'

23 November 1940

'Long talk with the Minister who started by wanting the sort of diary of a coal wagon from the time it is put empty into the colliery sidings until it is emptied at the coal merchant's depot. Our talk then developed on general lines with him showing me photos of a complicated model railway layout which he owns. Tells me he was very anxious to be a director of the Southern but was turned down, although he would have been prepared to spend practically the whole time at it. Thinks we, SR, have lost many opportunities, especially in the air – we ought to have had the Continental services. Told him the difficulties but I myself feel we were not bold enough with Imperial Airways – certainly air will be the only means of transit to the Continent for a long time after the war until ports and boats can be rebuilt, an important point item to bear in mind.'

28 November 1940

'Arranged to go to Martin's Bank to lunch with the SR chairman, Holland-Martin. Gore-Browne also there. This was the result of my letter of 16 November suggesting it was time for my own sake that I returned to SR. Holland-Martin started by saying that he and the Deputy and all of them wanted me to feel happy. He then went on to say I was doing a job of great national importance and of great importance to the railways, that I was doing it very well and that it would be a great pity to come back to the railway; and anyway a Continental campaign was necessary to the winning of the war and when this started, he was sure the War Office would want me back again. I replied that I did not consider the Ministry of Transport job of national importance – it had been done by a non-railwayman before. As to the War Office wanting me back in certain eventualities, there was no certainty they would and even if they did, there was no compulsion on me to go there. Holland-Martin said they all knew I did the War Office job so well that no one else could be picked for it, and I was doing the Ministry of Transport so well that it would be against the national and railway interest for me to leave it; but they did not want me to suffer and they would propose to the board that my loss of director's fees should be made up to me as a small help and that my superannuation should be based on a "notional figure" of say £1,000 year more than my present salary – an actual salary increase of £1,000 would yield only small "cash in the hand" increase owing to taxation but a larger superannuation based on a notional increase would be a real advantage. I said I considered this would be less than fair – the director's fees were small. The things that mattered were the potential increases of salary and if I were marooned at the Ministry of Transport for another three and a half years when I reach sixty years, it would be six years since I had a salary increase whereas if I returned to the railway at least my salary would be reconsidered.

'I did not see what was the difficulty of returning to the SR. Holland-Martin replied that the SR's machine was running so well, largely owing to the training I had put in on the staff, that it would be a pity to upset it, especially as I had been at the Ministry such a short time. He wanted me back and everyone wanted me back. I said it did not seem like it – it was only because I had been at the Ministry a short time that I thought it the most opportune time to leave it – before I became bedded in there. I had wanted to return to the SR in August and when Reith had told me he understood that I did not want to go back to SR, I had told him that nothing was further from my thoughts but the possibility of an invasion was a reason for my not going back then – that reason no longer existed. I disliked Civil Service methods, and trying to work with inefficient staff. Holland-Martin said he did not know why Reith thought that I did not want to go back. Frankly I do not believe Holland-Martin. He then said we were sure to have a Continental campaign soon and he was sure the War Office would want me back, so it would be a pity for me to come back to the SR for perhaps a few months only. I said there was no sure about it, we might not be in France until 1942 or 1943.

'Holland-Martin said it will be a tremendous help to the railways if I am at the Ministry when such things as nationalisation or other post-war problems are under discussion, I would be able to guide them into reasonable channels but I replied that it was because of the probability of such questions coming under discussion that I wanted to come back to the SR. It would make me feel very awkward at the Ministry in such circumstances. I should feel like Judas Iscariot, giving the Ministry advice on matters with which I disagreed and which were repugnant to me. Holland-Martin said I must consider my future – look at the wonderful position I would be in the event of some form of nationalisation. I would be the only possible choice to be boss of the whole thing but I replied that I absolutely would not be mixed up with it. It could not be to my financial advantage as the salary would not compare with that of a General Manager but anyway when I was sixty, I had not the slightest intention of spending time slogging to make a thing like that a success with all its tremendous problems. They suggested once or twice that I or they should ascertain from the QMG and from the Minister what they had in mind for the future for me. I said there was no question so far as the Ministry of Transport was concerned – doubtless they were glad to have someone there with railway knowledge doing the job but there was no question of any "future." But suppose the question was put to Brabazon and the QMG, and suppose they said they did not want me – where would I be then? Holland-Martin said that at any rate we would know where we are but I pointed out that we equally well know now, for I do not have to stay at the Ministry and I do not have to go back to the War Office. I told them I considered their ideas were less than fair to me and gave me no feeling of satisfaction. They both said they wanted me to feel perfectly happy and I replied that they had not succeeded and that I felt sore – not happy, and frankly I was puzzled as to why I was not wanted back on the Southern. They said I was wanted back but they considered I was doing much more important national work but agreed I should not lose by it. Having been chatting some forty minutes and apparently not progressing, I said "Well, that's that. I do not see we can get any further at the moment, I must go and consider my position."

2 December 1940
'Studied Jenkin-Jones Committee's report on GWR congestion. It is very helpful and couched in mild terms but pointed out a total lack of vision and ability on the part of the GWR officers for some years past. Hardly anything seems right there including the complacency in which they exist.'

4 December 1940
'Gore-Browne had dinner with me at the hotel and talked my position over. I put before him a memo I had made, starting off, "It is patent that for some reason that is not obvious to me, my return to the SR is not desired." He was ultra-emphatic that this was not the fact and that most definitely he and the chairman and everyone did want me back – it was surely a question of the national interest. I told him it was very clearly in my mind that there was "some funny business," both surrounding my going to the Ministry of Transport and my present wish to return to the SR. I could only assume that those likely to lose financially by my return were determined to prevent it and had so persuaded the chairman who was weak. Told Gore-Browne two courses seemed open for me – (a) just to resign my appointment at the MoT and tell the SR I was available – and then see what happened; or (b) to endeavour to come to financial terms with the SR whereby I would quit their service now and leave any competitors a clear field and no embarrassment to the chairman. Gore-Browne would not for a moment listen to alternative (b) and thought it preposterous from every point of view. He thought that (a) was quite

proper but I should first ask the QMG and the MoT if they wanted me – if they did, then I ought to be adequately compensated. I told him that if the QMG and Minister both said they did not want me, I thought the chairman would be in a hell of a fix and I was too loyal to put him there. So we arranged I would write to Gore-Browne and ask him to find out from Holland-Martin if he would be in a fix if I freed myself.'

14 December 1940

'To QMG and told him I was gradually approaching a state of fed-upness at the Ministry. I did not like most of the personnel there and did not like their methods or anything else about the Civil Service and so might seek to return to the SR. But my chairman had suggested that a Continental campaign might open up again in which case it would not be well for me to be back at the SR for a few months if the WO was likely to want me back there again. Would he say if there was any likelihood of this? The QMG said "Well, old Szlumper, I think the answer is No." He went on to say that I had laid the seeds well and had made many arrangements both with the SNCF and for construction of the necessary rolling stock, cranes etc; and they had all been ticketed and pigeon holed and were ready to be produced again if necessary and he did not therefore foresee there would be any cause for the WO to want me back, especially as McMullen was Director of Transportation and was much more competent and broad-minded than Greig and had had the advantage of being Director-General of Transportation in France. The QMG seemed dubious of the likelihood of a campaign starting from the Channel ports which is a reasonable view having regard to the fact that they must be utterly demolished.' Szlumper subsequently wrote to Gore-Browne to seek an assurance that the door would still be open for his return.

19 December 1940

At Walker's invitation, Szlumper went to lunch at the Charing Cross Hotel. He described Walker as being very friendly, telling him that the board meeting the previous day had had a long talk about him. He thought he would be pleased with what had been decided. As to his return to the railway, he assured him there was no funny business. 'He said that no doubt the War Office will want me back, so it would not be a good thing to bring me back for a few months and push the others down and then have to put them up again when I go to the War Office. I told him the War Office had said they were unlikely to want me. He said he did not realise that but added, "Still, have a talk with the Chairman, I think he will be pleased with what he tells you, and again I assure you there is no funny business."

'Back to the Ministry for a meeting with Browett, Hill and Mount to discuss the Jenkin-Jones report inch by inch. The thing on which I disagreed with Browett was the recommendation that the REC should have on the premises a committee of operating people. Browett was very much all for this and said he thought it was the only way to ensure the railways being worked as one entity. I disagreed and said it would be useless to put underlings there – the superintendents themselves would have to go in order to get anything done but they would have to have a lot of staff with them because, to be useful, they would have to be fully informed of the state of the railway and it would be difficult to do that sitting in a dug-out in Down Street. It would be much more efficient for them to be in the middle of their own work, in constant touch with one another on the end of a telephone and meeting each other as often as necessary to ensure co-operation. Straight on from this meeting which lasted until 17.00, to the Minister's room for a meeting with him and Wedgwood on the £10m works programme put up by the REC. Wedgwood says the congestion, on the LMS in particular, is nearly as bad as on the GWR, largely as a result of embargoes imposed by the GWR, and the LMS is nearly choked. Little argument about the works, only some amplification. Wedgwood said he was unhappy about the REC and the unhelpfulness of some of its members. It certainly does not seem to be functioning properly. Wedgwood told Brabazon that he may have to get him to use the big stick, especially to the GWR in the matter of calling in expert advice from the LMS and LNER on the introduction of "control". The GWR is now putting up a scheme prepared by its own staff who know nothing at all about it. In connection with the big works programme, Wedgwood thought it would be good to have an engineer working direct under the REC to watch the works and ginger up their progress, and we decided to reclaim Quartermaine from the MAP.'

20 December 1940
Holland-Martin wrote to him that day that his issue had been considered at the railway's board meeting. The view was that the national work he was doing was so important; and the board had decided to increase his salary.

27 December 1940
Szlumper returned to London after a Christmas break in Somerset. He was still concerned about his future and the following day wrote to Holland-Martin that the QMG did not think the War Office would require him back. He added that there seemed to be an invisible obstacle to his return to the railway.

7 January 1941
Szlumper went by invitation to lunch with John Charrington [Chairman of coal merchant, Charrington, Gardner & Lockett]. 'Cooper of Rickett, Cockerell & Co also there. They are anxious to bring about a better feeling between coal merchants, the railways and the Ministry of Transport. They flattered me by

saying they thought I was the man to do it. I will have a try but there are some pretty tough guys in their trade, and there is the incompetent Mines Department – headed by Sir Alfred Hurst who is persona non grata with everybody and, in addition, the coal merchants feel that Wedgwood has a considerable antipathy towards them.'

10 January 1941
'Late in the day Browett had a talk with me and told me things are moving on changes at the REC. The Minister has had conversations with Wedgwood who has reluctantly agreed to the addition to the REC of myself and also a Chief Mechanical Engineer, a traffic man and a civil engineer – Stanier, Jenkin-Jones and Quartermaine. These are to be whole-time members and all of us are to be absolutely ordinary members, co-equal in all respects to the existing members.'

22 January 1941
'Browett had a quick word with me about his encounter with the REC yesterday. He said Brabazon led off quite well and said that the necessity had long been felt for more unified working and that at one time the Ministry had thought of abolishing the REC, and having a Director-General of Transportation with one or two assistants but he had dropped this idea after Wedgwood's arguments, and that now they intended to add to the REC me and three technical officers. Milne said three technical men would be an impossible proposition. So Brabazon asked if he would prefer the Director-General idea and Milne replied with a flat yes, doubtless with a mental reservation, "So long as the D-G is Milne." Browett said they all welcomed the abolition of the Railway Control Officer and seemed genuinely pleased at it but their feeling was against the three technical men. However, the scheme was pushed down their throats. Brabazon then proceeded to sound the three men themselves. Jenkin-Jones was not get-able and has yet to be interviewed but the notes of his interview with Quartermaine show that he was a bit apprehensive – he thought he would be better occupied trying to expedite some of the works on the GWR, and wants to discuss it with his General Manager and Chairman. Stanier on the other hand was quite definite as to the advantages and is willing to serve.'

23 January 1941
Szlumper commented on a *Daily Mail* article which he pasted in his diary with the headline, Government to Run Road Service. It reported that Brabazon had announced the previous day that the Ministry of Transport was to invite road hauliers to lease their vehicles to the state for the duration of the war for the use of the Ministry of Supply and the Ministry of Food. The owners would continue to operate with their own drivers but the Ministry would direct what kind of loads

and journeys would be made but would undertake commercial haulage on return. Szlumper described it as a useful development, being the first step in focusing the road operators, which might lead to a growth of cohesiveness in the Road Haulage Consultative Committee, a very dispersed body. He thought they might eventually develop into groups of organised road operators with whom it would be possible for the railways after the war to negotiate some sensible form of agreement for apportioning traffic as between rail and road.

30 January 1941

'The GWR are disagreeing with that part of the Jenkin-Jones report that recommends fully developed Headquarter Train Controls and a committee of experts to examine new control schemes, and also existing schemes to recommend modifications. The Great Western say virtually that they are perfect. In agreement with Browett, I am telling the REC that the GWR must fall into line.'

4 February 1941

With Hill in the chair, Szlumper was at a meeting in the afternoon with Lindsell, Napier, Patteson, Marsden of the Ministry of Food and Fisher of the LMS. Lindsell expressed his fear that the railways were so congested that unless some special steps were taken to clear them, they were unlikely to be able to cope with special troops and ammunition moves in the event of an invasion attempt. This was challenged by Fisher who said he anticipated no such difficulty – the goods yards might be bunged up but the running tracks would be clear for special moves, especially if passenger services were cut. 'Napier, Screen and Patteson voiced their feelings that the railways were in a hopeless jam and could not be un-jammed unless some form of central control were instituted – one man should be running the whole railways show. Patteson suggested it should be me. I said it was no time to try and introduce such an experiment, and that if one man was to do it, he would need to be a man who had forty years experience operating all railways – and that such a man just did not exist. Fisher dealt with the congestion question in great detail and expounded all the difficulties and their causes. He put up a first rate show and, I think, demonstrated to the critics that the difficulties were not due to incompetence but due to circumstances the railways were unable to control such as shortage of manpower, men leaving railways for more remunerative employment, inability of women substitutes to perform a man's work, limited junction exchange capacity, restrictions of working day owing to blackout conditions, slow running during alerts and of course the overload the railways were trying to handle. It was a useful meeting if only because it removed some false ideas on inefficiency held by Napier and the War Office who think that you can learn to run railways from a manual.'

10 February 1941

With his wife, Szlumper had spent the weekend at Sidmouth. On his return, he encountered Missenden who was being seen off by Cox. 'We yarned all the way up. He says that Brabazon was very rude to the chairmen when he had them at the Ministry a little time back to tell them about the enlargement of the REC. He told them he was boss of the railways and could do what he liked with them. All the job that the directors had was to distribute to the shareholders the government compensation when they got it. Missenden says the REC is not very happy – Wedgwood and Milne do not seem able to hit it off together. Missenden welcomes my advent there and says if I were made chairman, the show would go alright because when things became a bit strained "you would get everyone back into a good temper by cracking a joke about some point, whereas Wedgwood deals with it in deadly earnest."

19 February 1941

'Asked Browett how the reorganisation of the REC progressing. He said all agreed about me without any question but no one is agreed about the three technical men – he had no idea there was so much jealously and petty feelings among senior railwaymen.'

4 March 1941

This was the day Szlumper was back as a member at the REC. He thought everyone was genuinely pleased to see him and described it as quite a peaceful meeting.

7 March 1941

'Lunched McColl today and learnt some inner secrets he had culled from Andy Duncan. On Beaverbrook, he said one reason for Churchill's apparent affection for him is because he was or is heavily indebted financially to the little beast. Four of the senior directors of the Ministry of Aircraft Production put in their resignations last Friday, being unable to stand Beaverbrook any longer but nothing has appeared about it yet. The MAP is said to be in chaotic state because Beaverbrook does not believe in organisation. He prefers individualism, consequently production is much below estimates. McColl says the rest of the press do not think much of Beaverbrook and may be unable to restrain their comments much longer. They also do not think much of Frank Pick.'

10 March 1941

'After a quick look into the office, over to Waterloo and joined the 09.30 with a special party – quite like old times to get into the Inspection Saloon with old Rufus to look after us. At Woking we picked up Brabazon and Browett,

Naming of Merchant Navy *Channel Packet* **at Eastleigh, 10 March 1941.**
(*Southampton Local Studies Library*).

Holland-Martin and Missenden and on to Eastleigh Works where Brabazon named the first of the Merchant Navy class locomotives, appropriately enough the *Channel Packet*. Inspection of Home Guard, ARP squads and detachments from the three ports. A poor and halting speech from the chairman who seemed ill at ease, quite a good speech from Brabazon, photos, then a run up to Alresford to try the engine out, and lunch on the way back to Eastleigh. The loco is distinctly ugly, too bluff fore and aft to have the appearance of streamlining. I said it looked more like a cabin trunk than a Channel Packet, and with rough cast steel disc wheels, but a grand tractive effort of 37,500 lbs. The inside of the cab is good and has been thought out to locate the controls conveniently to the men who have to use them. I think it is a fine loco but it is a pity they did not shape it to fall easier on the eye. After a very quick look round the shops, we went on to Southampton and through the docks. The old docks a sorry sight of wreckage but in the new docks the destruction is comparatively slight except at General Motors. We tacked on behind the 15.20 and arrived at Waterloo two minutes before time after a most successful day.'

11 March 1941

'To REC. Unexciting but Frank Pick came and gave a dissertation on the needs of the canals, treading on contentious ground in one or two places. However, with a warning to keep clear of debatable points, he was told the railways would give what help they can in diverting some traffic to the canals. Newton complained to me privately that Missenden is at times sarcastic and that this is much resented.'

13 March 1941

'The railways are in the middle of a £30,000 "prestige publicity" campaign. Milne without seeking the agreement of his colleagues or considering the reaction on the railways' campaign, must needs go and insert in the press a purely Great Western advertisement – and offensively worded at that in as much as it implies that any GWR shortcomings are due to the difficulties of other companies. Wedgwood raised the question of the impropriety of doing this, and all the officers agreed with him. I said the Minister would doubtless consider this the antithesis of unified working and would be bound to be displeased. Milne seemed very uncomfortable when trying to defend his action and said he felt it necessary to maintain the individuality of each company to ensure the continuance of public goodwill – the necessity of this had been suggested to him by his own staff, by the traders and by the press. I told Browett later I thought the Minister ought to write a stiff protest to Milne, and Browett once again returned to the question of suspending Milne as General Manager and asked who could we replace him by – would Grand be any good? I told Browett several reasons why he would be hopeless, and said I really could not suggest a successor.'

25 March 1941

Szlumper was at the Gore-Browne wedding reception which was very much a railway society affair. He recorded that it was suggested that Harry Roberts [LMS] would be suitable to go to America 'to look after the loading of vessels so as to suit rail conveyance when they get here. Stamp and Wood agree, and Roberts came to talk it over with me.'

29 March 1941

'O'Neill sent his beauteous young lady, Miss Richards, to see me with a minute of the Lord President's Committee dated 19 March to say that it had been held up by the Secretary, although endorsed to me. Had I seen it and could I answer it? Told her I had not seen it. The bit that wanted answering was a request to give details of the big works schemes of the railways. But I read the whole minutes and saw that "it was stated" that improvement in railway working was greatly needed and that a new committee was to be set up to operate the railways, that the railways had been dilatory in training men for "higher command" and that the REC was functioning badly. Brabazon had been at the Lord President's meeting and has evidently been telling them a lot of damned nonsense. Later I told O'Neill that presumably being a railwayman, it was not intended I should see the minute. I had heard all sorts of rumours of a super transport council but I had not been consulted, and if they were to unify all forms of transport, good and well. But if they were to operate the railways, then I would put my hat on and walk straight out of the Ministry. I had overheard a conversation with Fleetwood Pritchard and understood the scheme was to be announced on Saturday and the Minister was to broadcast it on Saturday night. In the course of a very pleasant lunch with McColl, I told him a very little of the foregoing in order to draw him – and of course succeeded. He said he did not know much about it but the scheme was going ahead. It had been decided that Stamp was the only man to be chairman – I agreed – and that Andrew Duncan had told the Prime Minister I was the only man suitable for General Manager – we shall see.'

31 March 1941

'McColl phoned me early and again after lunch, and at his suggestion went to see him. Following our lunch on Saturday, he spoke to Andy Duncan about the railway re-organisation, and today Duncan made McColl put off another engagement and come and lunch with him. Duncan is fed up with the way the thing is dithering away. Apparently Brabazon made a lot of wild statements at the Production Executive and was told to produce a scheme to deal with the railway. He later asked Duncan's advice as to who to nominate for the posts in the re-organised railways but Duncan told him he was not going to do any suggesting. It was Brabazon's job to make the scheme and he (Duncan) would not hesitate to criticise anything he considered unwise about it. Duncan is getting very impatient as no scheme has yet been produced. He told McColl that the idea is for Stamp to be chairman but Stamp is by no means popular in some quarters. Some want an outsider put into the job. It is to be a whole-time job and Stamp's idea of a salary has got to be modified – there would be no £20,000 a year about it. Told McColl Stamp was the only man for the job, he has financial ability, great breadth of outlook, and a personality that wins people to work with him. As to the executive head, Duncan said he would not look at Milne, Newton, Wood or Lemon – in his opinion, I was the only man and he was going to plump for me. I told McColl I was not in any way seeking to be appointed General Manager, all I wanted to do was to prevent the government doing some unwise things or making some foolish appointment which would make my position at the Ministry of Transport impossible. McColl said Duncan wanted to see me as soon as he could make an appointment. I said I would wait until Duncan asked me, that I was seeking nothing for myself and only trying to prevent something stupid being done.'

1 April 1941
'After the RCE meeting, stayed on to lunch, asked Cole-Deacon alone how much he knew about the unification of railways plan. He seems to know very little except that Stamp did not much want to be chairman because Montagu Norman is retiring from the Bank of England at the end of the year and Stamp had always coveted this job. Cole-Deacon also discussed the question of who was going to be General Manager. He was sure that Milne – the only suitable one, in his opinion – would not be selected as no one seemed to like him from the Prime Minister downwards.'

5 April 1941
'The evening papers announce the formation of the War Transport Council, a rather mixed body to ensure the full and efficient occupation of all transport. It should do some useful work.' Szlumper wrote that he doubted if the composition of the committee would produce the desired result. 'In the first place, there is not a railwayman on it – with great respect to Stamp; and I cannot think why they have put on it a damned old woman like Griffith-Boscawen. However, by their deeds they shall be judged. I prophecy they will peter out in a couple of months.' The other members were W.P. Allen, General Secretary of ASLEF, Arthur Deakin, Acting General Secretary of the Transport & General Workers Union, Heaton of Tilling, the accountant Maxwell-Hicks, William Prescott of the Lee Conservatory Board, and J.D. Ritchie, General Manager of the Port of London Authority.

7 April 1941
'Cynthia came up for a few hours today en route between Halesworth and Watnall. She seems very well but, unhappily, without any inclination to rise above the ranks of the WAAF. We went and had a good lunch at the Hungaria but unfortunately I could not see her to St. Pancras as I was suddenly hauled off to the Admiralty to attend a meeting with Admiral Moore, Deputy Chief of Naval Staff, about works on the GWR to ease the Severn Tunnel route. When I got back, I hustled Mount and Woodhouse who is always first rate, to get Treasury sanction tomorrow for the

Newport-Severn Tunnel scheme so that Brabazon can tell the Prime Minister on Wednesday that it has been authorised.'

17 April 1941

Szlumper recorded being awakened in the night by a terrific screech and thud with a violent explosion which shook the whole Charing Cross Hotel like a jelly, and was followed by a tremendous clatter of falling masonry and glass. He assumed it was a high explosive and close by. He immediately got up and, pulling his trousers and jacket and overcoat on, went to investigate. He found the shelter fully occupied – by this time it was 01.40. There was nothing he could do but he noted the view outside was grim with several nearby fires. From time to time heavy explosions nearby were heard; and there was a blast that came through the boilerhouse, bringing with it coal and coke fumes.

'We all became as filthy as sweeps. Goodacre, the manager of the hotel looked as if someone had rolled him in the dirt. Then just before 04.00 they came and told us the roof was alight and there was also an unexploded bomb on no.1 platform nearby, and everyone must get out of the hotel at once. So we all trailed upstairs into the hall where Captain Britten, the Railway Transport Officer, was taking charge of the evacuation and doing excellent work. He got all women and children out first and took them to the old RTO's office, the men being told to go to the annexe. But Biddle, Marsden and I decided to make for the Ministry of Transport basement at the first lull, so we waded over firehoses and water ankle deep and out on to the station concourse – the end of the station was a complete mass of flame, the wooden platforms and a couple of trains being ablaze. The hotel was in the dead centre of a ring of fires and so formed an alternative target – and a place to get away from, so out we go into the equivalent of pink daylight, the whole place being lit by the reflections of many fires; but when we got as far as Northumberland Avenue, we saw flames coming out of the windows of the Royal Empire Society opposite the Metropole and decided it would be too unhealthy there and made for the RAC. On in our slippers, through a sea of broken glass. Seeing some fires in the RAC direction, we dived into a public shelter in the P & O offices and waited for the all clear which went at 04.57. We managed to get into the hotel despite prohibitions on account of the mine and the fire. Bits of burning roof were falling into the hall and the whole place was aflood with water. Biddle could not get to his room as it was blocked by debris but I managed to get to mine without difficulty and found it little the worse. We collected armfuls of clothes and treasures and carried them with suitcases to the Constitutional Club which was unharmed. Dawn was breaking and weird it looked – pale greenish blue over the top of a cloud of smoke which was illuminated underneath by the glow of the fires. Shaved, bathed and fitted ourselves with an assortment of clothes. Back to the Metropole where no one was allowed in because of the mine on Charing Cross station – we were instructed to go to Horseferry House. However, I bounced the policeman and dashed up to my room to get some papers, not spending any unnecessary time doing it, and out again, to be told that Horseferry House could not be used because of unexploded bombs. We were to go instead to Romney House. Biddle and I trudged all the way there but no one knew what to do with us when we got there. Heard that Stamp's house had received a direct hit but one of the maids was alive and they were at work removing the debris in the hope of finding the others alive.

'Taxi to REC, traffic in tremendous tangle everywhere. W.V. Wood brought us the shocking news that Lord Stamp, Lady Stamp and their eldest son were all killed – they had recovered the bodies. A foul end to a magnificent man, most brilliant and clear-headed, and very farseeing, but above everything, genial and religious without any narrow-mindedness. I have never seen him ruffled or testy. A great man and a great loss to the nation, and to everyone who knew him.'

18 April 1941

'To Paddington at Milne's invitation to lunch. Naturally we opened out after lunch and he unloosed his feelings about Wedgwood. His great argument with him is Wedgwood's political ambitions. Milne thinks he governs most things from a political viewpoint and this, coupled with the LNER's known bias towards nationalisation, makes it dangerous for Wedgwood to be where he is now. But Milne also said that the show was not working because Wedgwood is so secretive. He deals with many things without the knowledge of other members of the REC, and most of the views sent forward to the Ministry are the views of Wedgwood and not of the REC. I asked Milne why, as a member of the REC, he did not protest and demand a show down. He replied that the only reason was that he wanted to do nothing that would impair the existing very friendly relations between the companies themselves. He said that one of the troubles is that Wedgwood tried to represent the companies on matters outside his ken such as on South Wales coal, at the Lord President's committee; and I am bound to say that I have always thought it unwise of Wedgwood not to take Milne with him to this committee – it would have saved some of the muddles that everyone has got into because of incorrect statements made. Milne thinks Wedgwood out of date in railway practice and as insular as the old North Eastern Railway had the reputation of being. When Milne agreed to the appointment of Wedgwood as chairman [of the REC] in peacetime, he thought it would enable much detail to be cleared up without bothering the General Managers but he never anticipated Wedgwood's appointment would go into wartime. Milne feels sure an alteration would have to be made, and suggested I should be chairman, saying quite categorically that he would be perfectly happy if I was appointed. You could have knocked me down with a feather – and I told him so but he was quite genuine in the matter. I said I had no aspirations in that direction and did not think it would be agreeable to Wood, although one now requires to see what position on the LMS Wood will hold.

'We talked of the proposed appointment of three technical officers to be full members of the REC and we both agreed it was a damned silly and unworkable idea. Milne said Wedgwood's whole object in suggesting it was to do the right thing by Jenkin-Jones, he having tried hard to get Jenkin-Jones made General Manager of the LNER in succession to himself. The LNER directors would not do this and appointed Newton without reference to Wedgwood who now wanted to turn the tables by making Jenkin-Jones a member of the REC, adding a CME and a civil engineer to make the thing look right. Milne also said Wedgwood wanted to be a director of the LNER but the directors would not do it. As to himself and the question of a directorship of the GWR, Milne said he could be Deputy Chairman or even Chairman tomorrow if he wished, but he had done nothing to invite an offer of a seat on the GWR board – but he much preferred to remain an executive officer. Like everyone else, he complained of Wedgwood's long windedness, reading every sub-committee minute at length and so on. He also told me that the unification of railways is dead as Brabazon brought up his suggestions to a cabinet committee which was presided over by Beaverbrook in the absence of the Prime Minister. Beaverbrook told Brabazon to put the scheme away and forget it until the end of the war. I wonder if this is so.'

19 April 1941
Szlumper asked Browett when there would be a new Railway Agreement and how the negotiations were progressing? Browett replied that the Treasury 'had been sitting on their round fat bottoms for three months without doing a thing about it but he was just trying to ginger it up.' After some discussion, Browett asked Szlumper as to whether the REC would be a success so long as Wedgwood was its chairman. 'I replied that if one took a sheet of foolscap – three sheets and folded them down the middle and put the pros one side and the cons the other side, and added them all up, I was afraid the answer would be "No."

'Went to lunch with McColl and we wondered who is to replace Stamp on the LMS. We both feel that Wood will be made General Manager. McColl said that Andrew Duncan is still very perturbed by the railways and wants a talk with me. Told McColl I felt in an exceedingly difficult position. All sides were giving me their confidences and my brain was trying to digest them. At dinner at the REC, only the Cole-Deacons and I there. The general question of the REC came up.

He feels some alteration in chairmanship is inevitable but says no one can come near Wedgwood in ability and I agreed. He asked if I would be prepared to take it on. Replied that if it was everyone's wish, I would, fully realising my shortcomings – and he, diplomatically, said he doubted if I could do it – I had nothing of Wedgwood's ability to write memoranda. Again I agreed sincerely but pointed out that the REC had access to their experts who could prepare memoranda and that in my opinion the prime function of a committee chairman is to ascertain and amalgamate the collective knowledge of his members and to keep the machine running. Cole-Deacon doubted if Milne would accept me as chairman so I had perforce to tell him what Milne had said at lunch yesterday which he said eased the problem a lot. But neither of us knew what Wood would do. He suggested that as a way out, Wedgwood might be given a barony and might replace Stamp on the War Transport Council, this being a reason for him to retire from the REC but I doubt if it would be easy to achieve this.'

23 April 1941

'To Westminster Abbey to memorial service for poor Stamp. A nice service but the clergy in their full robes looked more like a circus turn than persons in charge of welfare of souls. Was greatly shocked at Granet's appearance, a broken-down worn-out old man.' Sir Guy Granet, a former General Manager of the Midland Railway, had been LMS Deputy Chairman in the 1920s.

25 April 1941

'LMS Board yesterday appointed Sir Thomas Royden to be chairman. Seems a great pity they could not find someone younger and more alive. He is seventy and had never fully recovered from the motor smash he had in Paris a couple of years ago. Moreover, he was always lazy, although quite charming and very clever.'

27 April 1941

'Nothing noteworthy yesterday or today save Browett and I had a long chat about LMS. The Minister has written and congratulated Royden on his appointment as chairman and told him he is highly interested in appointments to the executive side. Browett and I assume Wood will be made either President of the Executive or General Manager but have great fears as to how he could run the job. He is a most able accountant but not a leader. We both hope Lemon will not be suggested – he is quite impossible from nearly every point of view and things have gone a good deal less smoothly on the LMS since he returned from the Ministry of Aircraft Production. The only man I would consider for the job is W.K. Wallace, the LMS Chief Civil Engineer, a very good type, able and straightforward. As to the LNER, I told Browett that in my opinion the proper way of filling the Chief Mechanical Engineer's job is to appoint Stanier to be CME of both LMS and

LNER. He is very sound and could make many economies but at sixty-four his age is against him and of course it would savour a good deal of unification.'

1 May 1941

'This afternoon I suddenly learned that places had been provided on the Clipper at 02.30 next Monday from Lisbon for Roberts and Nicholson. The Foreign Office had this news not through the usual channels. Woodley of the United State Lines which apparently looks after these Pan American Airways passengers this end, knew nothing of it but is cabling Washington to find out. Meantime, I got hold of the Air Ministry here to book passages to get the two from London to Lisbon before 02.30 Monday. Now owing to the wonderful co-ordination between government departments, the Foreign Office had never heard of the Air Ministry or v.v. So there is no relationship between the two sections of the journey. Anyway, the fact is that despite every pressure, the Air Ministry says there is no chance of getting two envoys to Lisbon before 20 May. So I have had to cancel the arrangements and hope the Foreign Office will be able to reinstate them about 21 May.

'While in O'Neill's room fixing or rather unfixing the foregoing arrangements, his phone rang. I do not know who his communicant was but the conversation concerned the unification of railways and I learned the scheme was discussed two days ago by the Lord President's Committee and is to be discussed again tomorrow whence it will go to the War Cabinet for consideration and decision.'

2 May 1941

'Startling news on 07.00 BBC of various cabinet or ministerial changes. Beaverbrook is to be Minister of State, Brabazon to succeed him as Minister of Aircraft Production – and, thank goodness, is to take that fatuous old socialist Montague with him as Parliamentary Secretary. Ronald Cross is to leave Shipping and is to become High Commissioner for Australia. Shipping and Transport to be combined and Fred Leathers is to preside over them as Minister of Wartime Communications; and he is to be made a baron. As to Beaverbrook, it turns my blood cold to see that filthy little newspaper man appointed virtually Deputy Prime Minister – presumably he will relieve Winston of a lot of the detail "at home" and will enable Winston to still further dabble in strategy and so the war will continue to be a series of withdrawals. I am glad we are rid of Brabazon. He was simply a bundle of flatulence, accustomed to talk before he started to think.

'Leathers, is fully alive and alert. I think he should be first rate. I rang him at his flat at 07.50 to wish him joy. He seemed pleased and said "Gilbert, it is good of you to wish me luck, I did not know a thing about this until the day before yesterday and I am in a whirl. I told the Prime Minister I could not face the full blast of Parliament and to avoid this he has made me a baron. You, Gilbert, have been much in my mind these last two days."

4 May 1941

'We and the REC have been considering various alternative ways of reducing passenger travel to enable a cut to be made in passenger train services. The REC concludes the most efficient way of doing this is by imposing a 100% tax on the cost of tickets for journeys over say thirty miles – this would freeze out a lot of the travel and would not bring the same odium on the railways as an increase in fares would. Being a tax, it would obviously be destined for the government pocket. The War Transport Committee after consideration has decided against it, partly on the grounds that the poorer would suffer while the richer could still afford to travel; but possibly because it would bring odium on the government. The War Transport Committee wants to bring into force a system of limited trains. I spent some time pointing out the difficulties to Hill and Nelson (secretary of the committee and one of the brightest fellows I have ever come across here). I told them of the necessity of special tickets numbered for each train, of season ticket and return ticket holder difficulties, of the difficulties of passengers wishing to join at intermediate stations but Hill thought it ought to be do-able and said the railways used to do it pre-war. I pointed out that it was for trains between stop and start stations only, and that they did not accommodate season and return ticket holders, and that when they had sold one train they put on another to accommodate the overload, whereas the present proposal was to reduce train services and when the train was sold, disappointed passengers would just have to wait for the next which was bad for important businessmen.'

5 May 1941

'Malcolm McAlpine, having tried unsuccessfully to make one or two lunch dates with me, came to see me this morning for the sole purpose of telling me that he considered me of such national importance that I had a duty in coming to the safety of the Dorchester Hotel and could name my own terms as money did not matter to him and his colleagues. I thought it very civil and sincere of him to take the trouble to come personally to persuade me and I shall go there.' McAlpine was of the celebrated civil engineering family business which had built and owned the hotel.

9 May 1941

'At this morning's Defence Council, proceedings started by Browett saying he was leaving us. Hurcomb is appointed Director-General of the new combined Ministry – to be known as Ministry of War Transport [MoWT] and not, as originally intended, Ministry of Wartime Communications; and, as Browett said, there is obviously not room for two kings. So he goes to the Treasury for special duties and is very sad to be parting company with the MoT. All of us were greatly sad to part company with him. He says the combined Ministry is one of Winston's impetuous moves – do the thing first and try to think out after how the hell it is going to be worked, seems to be his idea.'

14 May 1941

'Great annoyance this evening. I have had the greatest trouble in fixing up the journeys of the two railwaymen (Roberts and Nicholson) to America. The Foreign Office has displayed the utmost inefficiency in the matter. They are fixed to leave for Lisbon tomorrow. I have been busy squaring up matters of pay, tickets, confidential papers in the diplomatic bag and many other such things. This evening at 18.00 Biddle [now at the MoWT] comes into my room and says that Basil Sanderson who has been put over Tolerton's head, has just phoned him to say Hurcomb has decided the men are not to go tomorrow – and will Biddle tell me! I immediately rang Sanderson's office to say I was unused to receiving orders from him by devious routes but his secretary replied that Sanderson had that moment gone. Told the secretary he had better let Hurcomb know. Then I went and told O'Neill, then Hill. By that time, the news had got to Hurcomb who wanted to see me. I told Hill that I would not and that theoretically I had left the office and also told him that if the arrangements for these two men's departure were altered, I would entirely wash my hands of the whole affair and would neither discuss nor do one further thing with it. Told him to tell Hurcomb we were not sending them but only arranging their passages. It was the REC which was sending them and he, Hurcomb, had better discuss any alterations with Wedgwood. Hill and Hurcomb had a long harangue on the phone, the upshot of which was that Hurcomb reluctantly agreed to tomorrow's departure standing. I rang Wedgwood to tell him all this but found Hurcomb had just finished a talk with him on the same lines as with Hill. The first fruits of an amalgamated Ministry with the shipping element in the ascendant.'

15 May 1941

'Hurcomb came to the Defence Council to meet us all and see it at work. We had a word afterwards about the visit to America of Roberts and Nicholson. It seems as if Sanderson had misunderstood Hurcomb's wishes. He only wanted time to consider the question and wanted to make sure the men would be attached to Ashley Sparks, now that the ministries are combined and Sparks is the big noise in the USA.' Sparks of Cunard was the Ministry's Director-General of Shipping in the USA.

17 May 1941

'Short chat with Browett and told him I thought the time was at hand for me to pack my bag and go to Waterloo. I had stayed at the Ministry, mostly because I liked him and now he was going, that pretext no longer existed. I had occupied a subordinate position for many months, solely in the hope of improving relationships between the Ministry, the REC and the railways but now failing any word of the organisation of the new Ministry, I felt I would be doing better service by returning to the SR. Browett said we should be hearing early next week on the organisation of the new Ministry but he realised I had sportingly served in a subordinate position and by my nature had improved relationships all round.'

24 May 1941
'Uneventful day relieved only by a very half-hearted message of farewell from Brabazon to the staff. It was circulated in the form of an office circular which also contained other matters. Poor stuff, typical of the man who could not even be bothered to shake hands with a few of the senior staff.'

29 May 1941
'Today we took our Defence (Transport) Council en bloc to Berkeley Square House to attend a massive meeting with our new bedmates from the Ministry of Shipping and sort of be introduced to each other. At the REC meeting later, Hurcomb and Hill brought the new Minister of War Transport, Lord Leathers of Purfleet, to introduce him to the REC. The introductions went well until Leathers saw me when he saved Hurcomb the necessity of an introduction by saying "Hello Gilbert" to the surprise of the others. They stayed over an hour and had a useful and intelligent talk, largely on the difficulties of coal production and transport and also on the question of the amount of munitions work the railways are doing in their workshops. Leathers created a very good impression on the REC who voted him the most intelligent and human minister transport had had since Burgin.'

30 May 1941
'It is announced today that Wood has been appointed President of the Executive of the LMS. He is an able little chap but with only a sketchy knowledge of railway working; and is not an inspiring leader. Nevertheless, I think he will probably make a success of it. Met J.J. Llewellin, Parliamentary Secretary to the Minister of War Transport. Strikes me as capable and quick-brained. Got on well with him.'

11 June 1941
'To Liverpool Street to see the British Railways exhibition coach of wartime photographs. It was well-arranged and very interesting. Newton took me to the hotel for a drink at 11.30 and showed the dimensions of his mind by his pride in the new lavatories, both of which he insisted on me seeing. I have never really heard him talk of other than piffling redecorations – wider railway matters do not

seem to interest him at all.' Charles Newton had been the Chief General Manager of the LNER since 1939 when Wedgwood had retired.

16 June 1941
'Meeting with Selway [Chairman of REC Passenger Superintendents Committee] to start trying to hammer out a scheme for travel permits. The thing will be full of snags at every turn. So far as we can see at first blush, apart from service duty and leave travel, season tickets and bulk travel business, we shall only have about 5,000 long distance travellers a day to play with. This does not give much hope of 30% decrease in train services.'

20 June 1941
'That gasbag Brabazon seems to have been letting himself go at some press luncheon today. I gather he told them he was a damned fine Minister of Transport but it was a job that did not really require anybody very good. He also seems to have said that he had prepared schemes for the reorganisation of the railways and it only wanted someone to press the button to put them into operation.

'Leslie Dawes at lunch today said he recently saw Gore-Browne who still expects to be made the titular head of the unified railways. He told Dawes he was going to have me as his General Manager, although recently Dawes said Missenden told him that Gore-Browne had promised him the job.'

26 June 1941
'Had a look at new rooms at Berkeley Square House today – very simple and straightforward and more up to date in layout than the old Metropole which we vacate on Sunday next.'

30 June 1941
'Andrew Duncan has been moved back to the Board of Trade, and that filthy newspaper man Beaverbrook, has been made Minister of Supply. What a tremendous pity – he will upset the whole applecart there and undo all the sound building-up that Duncan has done. I heard the other day that at the Ministry of Aircraft Production, Beaverbrook had a personal staff of thirty-seven who took the work out of everybody's hands. He also had his personal telephone exchange and used to ring up firms direct – countermand their present order and order them to something entirely different and then fail to tell the staff anything about it.'

5 July 1941
This was the start of a week's holiday in Stratford-upon-Avon for Szlumper but two days later it was interrupted by Sir Andrew Duncan telephoning and wanting him to come to his office to hear some proposals. 'If he had known where I was, he

would have come to me yesterday but as he wanted to see me urgently, I caught the 14.35 up and dined with him in his private room at the Dorchester. He said that the cabinet is in a flat spin over coal which everyone now looks upon as the most important thing there is now. They anticipate a rapid decline in civilian morale if domestic supplies are short in the winter; and any stoppage of production due to shortage of industrial supplies would be looked upon as very grave. The problem was how to get the 234,000,000 tons per annum target figure to the consuming points, and he wanted me to come to him at the Board of Trade to run the whole of the transport side – rail, coastwise, road and canal. Told him I did not purport to know much about the coal world or about the heavy railways but he replied that did not matter and it was an advantage sometimes not to know too much detail. He said he wanted the best for the job and he thought that was me. Told him I did not like the idea of quitting the railways proper but he replied that many of us have to take on jobs we dislike for the national good. Look at him, he had a raw deal if anybody had from that mountebank Beaverbrook but he was so seized with the importance of coal that he had gone back to the Board of Trade to do what he could.

'He referred to Reith as a dreadful fellow, quite incompetent and I fully agreed. He said he wanted someone of prestige and standing to handle the transport, someone who would have the entreé to all three sides, coal, railways and shipping and who would be trusted by them all. I said that I was known to very few of the coal owners. He replied that I personally might be unknown to them but they all knew of the General Manager of the Southern Railway. Told him I did not know how I would get on with Sir Alfred Hurst as I was not particularly fond of him but Duncan said Hurst was first rate and he could guarantee me 100% of his help. My opposite number on the production side would be Hyndley and he knew we were friends and would work well together. He said Hyndley might not be brilliant but he was very able and knew the coal trade inside out. Hyndley was in the BoT, not in the Mines Department. Duncan's idea was that transport was so important that I should also be in the BoT. I asked him, supposing I came, who would there be between me and him. He replied "No one. What you say goes, if I concur." He said the railways were now on trial, and knowing them as I do, would be a valuable asset to them and to me.

'I said the Lord President's Coal Committee seemed to have been a thorn in everyone's side. Where would they come in the picture? He replied that it would cease to exist; he would have none of it. Told him I thought it was going to be difficult to manipulate the transit of coal at times and to arrange diversion of it unless the government assumed ownership of it. He replied that he is quite prepared to assume ownership of any coal once it is raised – he possessed the necessary powers. But he was not prepared to assume ownership while it was still in the ground – there were too many snags in that.

'Asked him what would happen if I came to him, and in a month or two's time he was moved to some other ministry and I found myself landed with some other fellow like Brabazon as a Minister. He replied that I need not fear that, he and Winston Churchill had undertaken to see the war through together and he, Duncan, was staying at the BoT at least until March – and even then he would not move without consulting me and would preserve my return to my present job. He said Brabazon was a lazy fellow. He pretended to know but he did not. I said that if coal was to have absolute priority, I thought he should insist on matters concerning its conveyance coming out of the hands of the civil servants at the Ministry of War Transport and that I should have direct access to the railways or the REC on all such questions. He quite agreed and said he would try to arrange this. I also stipulated that Fisher should not succeed me on the REC on the grounds that it would put the cat among the pigeons. I told him there is no one I would like better to work with than him but I hated the idea of leaving the railway side and the REC where I had felt I had been some good. He replied that the new set up of things would ensure railway co-operation and that I would have full support from Leathers on the railway and coastwise, and again repeated that it would be my job to look after coal from pit to consumer. I told him not to think me ungracious in not jumping at the job – there were many difficulties in it and it was likely to be a very thankless task. I would like to sleep over it. Certainly, he said, and have a talk with Leathers in the morning.

'He said Leathers was much too wise to go for railway unification. As to Beaverbrook whom he called a showman, he said that as a Minister of State, Beaverbrook had started interfering with the Prime Minister's job and duties. The Prime Minister would not have that and wanted to put him back in charge of a department, hence his appointment as Minister of Supply and the change round. But Duncan was very sick about it and seemed to anticipate Beaverbrook soon messing things up and trying to collar all the credit for things that had been initiated months ago. But fortunately Duncan had given the House of Commons in secret session a little while ago a lot of facts and figures that would not enable Beaverbrook to scoop all the kudos.'

8 July 1941
'At 09.00 to Berkeley Square House for talk with Leathers. He said that from a political point of view, some changes had to be made – and soon. The Cabinet felt, some of them strongly, that there was too much of a railway element about, and that it was wrong that the government through the Ministry of War Transport should be represented on the REC by a railwayman. So he had to make some changes on the REC and was going to put on, perhaps over it, a non-railwayman, someone with no railway interests. As this change has to be made, it

provided a chance to give me some heavier work to do, something more in line with my energy and ability. There was a feeling, expressed in high places that I was not being allowed to output my best, that I was not the Gilbert Szlumper I used to be. Some said it was because the REC had not given me the welcome or help they ought to have. Others said it was because I had not been given a free enough hand. I emphatically denied the first suggestion about the REC, and said I had been at the Ministry for eight months before being put on the REC, but since I had been there, I certainly had received full help and welcome and I was quite confident the REC had absolutely no feelings against my appointment. We were all on the most amicable terms and I felt rightly or wrongly that my presence had helped bridge over the gulf that was growing between the REC and the Ministry of War Transport. The whole trouble was that mine was a subordinate job without any scope and was under a lot of civil servants who knew nothing of transport but who wasted a magnitude of time in meetings to discuss points on which they were entirely ignorant and who upset the REC by continuous suspicion and unconstructive criticism. I got on well enough with the civil servants as individuals but theirs was a dead hand on a businessman, and all the time I felt I had no opportunity to pull my weight which was why I was so anxious to get back to my own job on the Southern Railway. Leathers quite understood but said he thought it was not the appropriate moment to go back to the SR. So he had to make changes now. If I dropped out and went back to the SR, people would wonder why. Whereas here was the President of the Board of Trade himself asking me for the most important job there is, and telling the War Cabinet that Gilbert Szlumper is the only man that can do it. That put me in a very strong position and, whatever the inclinations might be, his advice to me was to take the coal transport job on. He and Andrew Duncan knew that my particular flair for getting on with everybody and getting the best out of them would be most valuable.

'Leathers went on to discuss the REC and the poor quality of the General Managers, especially Wood and Newton. I said they should really be a committee of the MoWT and not a sort of separate body. Leathers thought the REC was a statutory body but I corrected him and said it was appointed by Order-in-Council which could be varied at will. Leathers rather thought they should be divorced from their railways and be whole-time officers of the Ministry but I disagreed and said it was not a whole-time job. It was necessary for them to be in touch with their railways. He said could not their deputies look after the railways – but I thought not. The deputies were in some cases not too good. Bell was about to retire and I did not think much of Grand. Leathers said he had a shipping committee composed of various shipping men, whole-time, under Vernon Thomson, and although they generally co-ordinated their work through Hurcomb, they always had direct access to him and he always took the chair of their meetings.' Thomson, head of Union Castle Line, was Controller of Commercial Shipping at the MoWT.

'I suggested that something similar was wanted for the railways. We mentioned Brabazon. Leathers said he had formulated some wild schemes for the railways and he, Leathers, was going to have his work cut out to stop them. If he was going to stop immediate nationalisation, he must make changes at once and introduce a non-railway element – there was a cabinet meeting to talk things over tonight. He said there was much loose criticism of the railways. I told him destructive criticism was always easy and he quite concurred. He said he had told his colleagues and critics what he thought in no uncertain terms but said the railways had got to look at things more from a national point of view than they have been doing. But I pointed out to him that while the present agreement with the government existed, it was difficult for the railways which still had a duty to their shareholders. He quite agreed but said that was being attended at once. It had been left too long as it was. He thought Andrew Duncan had been so badly treated that the government could not make a further move with him for some time; and if, later, he did move and I did not like his successor, then I could always go back to the Southern Railway. I told him I would have a go at the job but as coal was to have priority of transit, I considered I ought to have direct contact with the REC and not to have to transact business with them through a lot of civil servants who knew nothing – he would receive opposition from them on this point but I considered it was necessary. He agreed and promised to try to arrange it and made a note of it.

'At Hurcomb's request, went in to have a word with him. Ministry of War Transport has been formed since 2 May and this is the first time I have been invited into the Director-General's room which shows how the civil servant deals with the "outside businessman." We had a general chat. He said he was opposed to the present form of agreement with the railways. I told him all the General Managers were against it from the word go. I think he feels some of the weaknesses of the chain of command. He said he had always been one to ride people on a loose rein and to let them do their jobs in their own way but some preferred a tidier and more orderly arrangement. He wanted any suggestions from me. My first one was to abolish the title of Railway Control Officer which was a misnomer anyway. He said from a policy point of view, he did not think that could be done. It was rather lack of "control" that was being talked about now. So I advised him to be very careful as to whom he appointed to the office. He asked me what title I would give it and when I suggested Railway Liaison Officer as being more appropriate, he said it was too weak. I wonder why every civil servant wants to control something. I suppose it is a natural desire to "spread themselves" in wartime and exercise a brief authority in wartime that they do not possess in peacetime. Hurcomb asked if the REC had objected to the appointment of a

Railway Control Officer, and I said yes. It had given them an attack of indigestion from which they had never recovered – as was expectable in putting in nominal control of the railways someone without railway knowledge. Hurcomb said he would much like a talk some time with me on future organisation of MoWT. Managed to catch 11.05 Paddington back to Stratford-upon-Avon to resume the broken holiday.'

9 July 1941
With the ending of another episode in his war-time career, Szlumper wrote from Stratford-upon-Avon to Duncan that after a full talk with Lord Leathers, he was confirming that he would be with him on Monday and was looking forward to doing what he could do to solve the problems of coal transport between the pit and consumer. He reminded him that he had agreed that he would come directly under him without the intervention of a chain of civil servants which he was sure would make for speedy decisions.

Chapter Six

❧

The Board of Trade and the Mines Department, 1941–42

14 July 1941

After the week's holiday, Szlumper returned to Berkeley Square House. He saw Fisher who, having learnt of his move, expressed astonishment at the suddenness and secrecy of the change. 'He tried hard to pump me on the contingent changes at the Ministry of War Transport and I had pleasure in giving him no information whatever, only suggesting that some more startling and drastic changes were to follow. I am glad to be rid of him, he has intelligence and energy but spoils everything by his terrible bumptiousness and ambition. He would make a good general foreman to a local builder and is not gentleman enough for anything better.

'Went to the Board of Trade at Millbank to have a look round – like the look of my room there. Then in to see Hyndley. He welcomed me and looks forward to our working together. Then back to Berkeley Square House to pack. To see Hill to say farewell. He was as warm as cold fish can be, expected we would often meet and hoped I might even sometimes attend the Central Transport Committee, to which I replied, "No bloody fear." Back to Millbank. Bumped into Malcolm McCorquodale who is Private Parliamentary Secretary to the President of the BoT, also very warm in his welcome. To dinner at REC with Wedgwood and Cole-Deacon and told them just as much as I thought proper of the conversation I had had with Leathers last week. Wedgwood's main fear is that the REC might be saddled with Gore-Browne as my successor.'

15 July 1941

'To Berkeley Square House to see Leathers and suggest that as soon as he is in a position to do so, he should ask Wedgwood for an informal chat or let me ask them both out to lunch or dinner. Wedgwood would like to see him – but does not like to make the direct approach – to give him any guidance he can and to warn him of any pitfalls. Leathers will do this but his tongue is tied at the moment and therefore it is useless to see Wedgwood now. Brabazon and Sir John Anderson had very largely poisoned the minds of the other ministers and encouraged every anti-railways thought in them. In addition, Brab had put forward a series of wild proposals for nationalisation. These are favoured by some Ministers and, of course, by Bevin and Morrison and all the Labour gang. Leathers agreed with me that Bevin is a dangerous man. I told Leathers that if the government wanted a war within a war, the easiest way to produce it would be by trying to introduce nationalisation now. But he said the cabinet is to consider the whole question this evening and he has some fear as to the result. He thinks that there will be such a divergence of view that the Prime Minister will have to decide. There is no doubt Leathers himself is railway-minded and, like many of us, wonders why there is such an anti-railway feeling but, as I told him, the railways and income tax have always been fair game and every traveller judges the whole of the vast railway organisation by some minor failure or shortcoming at his home station. He said he would have to relieve Wedgwood of his job. Anderson was dead up against Wedgwood because of his tactless attitude. He often used to tell Anderson that a thing could not be done and then go away and have it done. Then again if Anderson asked him any question about railways, Wedgwood would tell him, "Oh, that's a technical question and you would not understand the answer if I gave it you."

'I asked Leathers to make the bump as light as he could, perhaps by putting Wedgwood on some high-sounding committee. Leathers said if he was successful tonight in riding off nationalisation, it would be at a cost and that cost would mean the chairmen of the railways would have to swallow terms they did not like in the new compensation agreement when he discusses it on Friday next. Then went down to REC to say farewell. They too were very warm. Then back to Berkeley Square to say goodbye to Mount, the excellent Colonels Woodhouse [Deputy Director of Transportation] and Birney [Technical Officer]. Spent the rest of the day settling in to my new quarters. Room is first rate on the sixth floor in what is known as the Director's Corridor which has its own private lift.'

16 July 1941

'Still settling in and beginning to digest facts and figures. Meeting in afternoon with Duncan, Hyndley and Hurst to discuss some of the various problems ahead. In view of my volume of work on the Mines Department side, I am to have a room in that department also.'

18 July 1941

'Lunch with Patteson who seems to be going strong with Beaverbrook who apparently consults him on all sorts of general matters far removed from transport. Tells me Leathers has pressed him (Patteson) very hard to succeed me at the MoWT, coming directly under Hurcomb, side-stepping Hill. But Patteson has turned it down definitely and said he is bound to Beaverbrook. Leathers has also pressed Beaverbrook to release Patteson but nothing doing. He tells me Col Screen has great aspirations for the job, also that Barrington-Ward would take it on if offered.'

21 July 1941

'Long talk with Hyndley and others. They seem to have the right ideas but no powers to enforce them. For instance, the District Coal Supplies Officers [CSO] who look after the allocation of output, are paid servants of the coal owners and are loath to enforce the requests of the Mines Department in cases where it would upset the normal trade channels of the collieries – and the Mines Dept cannot force them. Even if they issue a direction, they doubt if it is carried out.'

22 July 1941

'Long talk with Ernest Meadon of Mines Dept on subject of government coal dumps which is his job. He certainly knows all about it and seems a most competent and likeable chap. He thinks less than nothing of the Ministry of War Transport, especially of Fisher. Then a talk with Picknell who was a yardmaster at Willesden. He looks after railway matters in Mines Department. A bit of a blasterer and lacking in education but I daresay he does some useful work. Had a chat with Hyndley. Shortage of labour in the pits and the receiving end is going to be a continuous difficulty but it is not easy to see the army part with many.'

23 July 1941

'Talk to Dr Robson about canals and the department in general. Like everyone in the Mines Dept, he complains strongly against the CSOs who are loath to accept any request from the Mines Dept if these would tend to upset the normal trade channels of the collieries in which they are interested parties. Sir Robert Burrows, the CSO in the Leeds district, is also a colliery director of Manchester Collieries Ltd, and LMS Deputy Chairman. So I should think his divided loyalties must at times put a strain on his conscience.'

24 July 1941

'Attended Lord Hyndley's bi-weekly committee this morning. Welcomed very warmly by everyone there. Certainly a different atmosphere from Ministry of War Transport. A more capable bunch of fellows. Later Duncan sent for me, saying we are going to cut down exports, principally anthracite, so as to put more in the home market. He wanted to know if we could take 100,000 tons a month more out of South Wales by rail. Fortunately the GWR told Ravenshear only this morning that they could do 25,000 tons a week more than they now are carrying.'

28 July 1941

'There are a great many statistics in Mines Dept but apparently none showing areas to which the output of the different pits or even different coalfields goes which is rather fundamental information from a transport point of view. So have asked for some figures to be obtained. Lunch by invitation with John Charrington. Lester Horne [Director of Charrington, Gardner, Locket] also there. They both seem to welcome my appearance on the coal side. The only point on which they expressed misgivings was when I suggested it might facilitate things sometimes if the government became the owners of the coal – they thought this unnecessary and said the widespread machinery of the merchanting organisation should meet any requirements for diverting supplies whereas ownership of any coal by the government would upset all the normal course of trade.'

31 July 1941

'Attended Hyndley's weekly meeting with all the Divisional Coal Officers who seem an intelligent and active lot. Except in some producing areas, they all consider that some system of rationing will be necessary before this winter is through. The Scottish CSO mentioned two cases where consumers wishing to stick to a particular supplier had their coal and coke brought forty to fifty miles by road whereas they could have obtained it from a supplier only three miles away from them.

'Biddle took me to the RAC to dinner where we found ourselves sitting next to Lord and Lady Leathers. He came and had a very informative yarn with me and told me has already arranged for Sir Alan Anderson to become Controller of Railways and chairman of the REC. He said he had taken a lot of pains to tell Wedgwood gradually and gently, although I guess it was a bit of a shock; and that he was going to see Milne tomorrow to make him Deputy Chairman of the REC to look after the technical side of things. I do not somehow feel that this is going to be totally successful. Anderson with no real railway knowledge is bound to be very much in the hands of the four General Managers and the REC sub-committees, and will be hard put to it if he has to arbitrate on any question. Leathers also told me he had seen the chairmen and announced to them what the government were prepared to do in the way of a new Compensation Agreement – he said this had given the chairmen indigestion.

'Biddle unburdened himself at great length on the way Missenden is treating him as if he were an outcast. Not allowed to have access to anyone or information at Dock House [Southampton] which seems very petty to me. He also instanced Missenden's disloyalty to me in various ways and we both grieved at the way Missenden and others take life easy with much time off which they could better devote to getting round the staff at sticky places and giving them words of cheer.'

3 August 1941

'Although the Board of Trade is a city of the dead on Sundays, I went there. Duncan, who has spent the past week touring coalfields, evidently heard I was there and asked me to come and see him, greeting me by saying, "What are you doing on Sunday, Gilbert?" to which I replied I spent most of my time on deck. Duncan is hopeful that the coal output will be stepped up by mid-August to 4½ million tons a week and wanted to know what the chances were of having it carried to destination. I said it could be done at the sacrifice of other facilities until late October when blackout would interfere much with working. I promised to get together an appreciation of the transport situation for a debate the House of Commons is to have on coal on Tuesday.'

6 August 1941

'Yesterday's debate not too good. Everyone slating Board of Trade and Mines Dept for not having foreseen present situation of under-production and preventing loss of men from mining to other industries or to the Army, the Cabinet receiving general blame for not returning them from the Army earlier. Interesting facts emerging from the debate were that in 1940 there were 500,000 men less in the industry than there were in 1914, largely due to the spread of mechanisation, although this should have no adverse effect on output. Over 100,000 men have left the industry since the war started.

'In the course of the morning that dreadful little fellow Gilbert Ponsonby who lectures at the LSE, came in to tell me he was employed at the Mines Department and would be happy to give me the benefit of his views on transport. Like most of the LSE men, he is totally theoretical.'

8 August 1941

'Masses of statistics here but very difficult to find those which are germane to finding exactly what was carried by each form of transport, and what the maximum capacity of each form is. Certainly everything surrounding coal is of great complexity – questions of price, quality, variety and size, and many other similar considerations enter into this picture and have to be solved before action can be taken.

'In afternoon, meeting with Duncan, McCorquodale, Hyndley and others to consider the re-settlement of the 25,000–35,000 men who have registered as miners and who Duncan wants placed within the next ten days or so. We have to be careful on this – Duncan wants them placed in the areas in which they used to work and no doubt this would be quickest and easiest but would result in 8,000 going into South Wales and this would boost the output up beyond the figure the GWR can handle if it all has to come through the Severn Tunnel.'

13 August 1941

'Duncan called a hasty meeting to get reports of progress. He is most hopeful that output will reach 4,300,000 tons before the end of this month but I see no likelihood of it – a good many miners are on holiday and it takes two weeks for them to get into their stride again, then up to the day before yesterday only 7,100 of the registered miners had been sent to the pits for employment, and many of them will not settle or are unsuitable. We are still aiming at an average weekly output of 4,250,000 tons and this is just about the amount all transport can handle if conditions are about the same as last winter. Last winter an output of 3,900,000 tons a week just about filled transport up but since then various works have been put in hand to ease operation, the Central Wagon Control is working well, railways are getting a slight improvement in marshalling yard lighting, speeds during alerts are higher.

'Lunch with the SR board which is very troubled at the terms of the new agreement. The government has said take it or leave it. Gore-Browne wants to tell the government the boards cannot agree as trustees of the stockholders and to suggest to the government that the terms be submitted to the stockholders. I doubt if this will frighten the government into anything better. For all this, they have to thank that flatulent bounder, Brabazon.'

21 August 1941

'I asked Patteson how he rated Beaverbrook's brain and he said the comparative assessment at the Ministry of Supply was that Herbert Morrison, was by dint of hard work and poring over it, able to pick up about 25% of the points. Andrew Duncan, by solid work, was able to pick up about 85% of the points pretty quickly but Beaverbrook was able to get 100% of the points that mattered in a flash and come to correct decisions on them.'

28 August 1941

'Lunch with SR Board. Sat next to Thornycroft who without doubt is the most indiscreet man I have ever met, scattering about in a most prodigal manner information that is very secret – a safeguard is that he frequently has incorrect information.

'Terms of the new agreement of the government with the railways announced this evening, a flat £43m per annum with some trimmings and with war damage left in the air. I reckon this a good £3m per annum less than the railways could justify and is the price of buying off for a time some form of nationalisation or government control of a continuing nature. I consider the price is too high but I suppose the country would have held the railways to be wrong if they had turned this amount down.'

2 September 1941

'Long talk with Hyndley and his deputy, William McGilvray of Mines Dept about gas works, especially in the South West. They are very short of stocks but will not accept supplies we want to send them from Durham, partly on the score of expense. It may cost them up to 50p a ton more than they are now paying but mostly because they want their usual coal from their source of supply. Some of them such as Bath openly defy Mines Dept and say it is no use sending fresh coal they will not accept. So we must try compulsion. Mines Dept will send a couple of trains a week to the West Country and distribute it where wanted, and direct any recalcitrant company to accept it.'

9 September 1941

'Took Leslie Dawes out to lunch. Leslie tells me the mad Beaverbrook who is going to Moscow, is determined to fly though the flak instead of via the reasonably safe route – no doubt to get headlines in his filthy *Daily Express* but to the risk of perfectly good bomber and crew and, no doubt, a large escort of fighters. Called in on REC at 21.00 to find Cole-Deacons entertaining Richard Temple and two others – champagne, liqueurs, cigars and doubtless a repast, regardless of all rationing. This sybaritic method in these times is very revolting and disgusting.

'The return of miners to the mines from other industry is in my opinion a flop. At this afternoon's Coal Production Council, we learned that 106,000 had registered, about 45,000 had been offered to the collieries and just under 16,000 placed at work. The Ministry of Labour man said he thought it highly unlikely that many more than 45,000 would be offered on account of physical unfitness and doing work of national importance. If ultimately we get 25,000 out of the deal, we shall be lucky – and this will just about counter-balance the natural wastage and the sap in output per man-shift. The coal owners present said that despite every appeal, absenteeism had greatly increased, especially since the agreement about the bonus whereby it ceased to be necessary to work every shift in a week to qualify for the bonus. The underlying trouble – or one of them – is that there is so little for the men to spend money on.'

9 October 1941

'Went to Milne for a long talk to get a view of his South Wales position. His troubles are many. On the freight side he is sending out of South Wales every day 1,000 more wagons of general merchandise than he was this time a year ago, largely due to the fact that there are 178 new factories on the GWR in South Wales, most of them government munitions factories, many with a very large output. Growth of imports is troubling him – last month they amounted to 407,000 tons compared with 330,000 tons in September 1940. The GWR is taking 130 freight trains a day out of South Wales into England – one every eleven minutes. On the passenger side, he is very pressed, and Milne showed me figures of his loadings on the London-South Wales services with no train less than 500 passengers and some with over 900. To try and freeze short-distance passengers out of the long-distance trains, he is considering imposing a 50p supplement on everyone travelling by long-distance trains but I expect this is too sensible for the Ministry of War Transport.

'Had Biddle to dinner. He has just returned from a fortnight's tour of the ports on the west side of Scotland and Northern Ireland and says the War Office is getting on very slowly with the port works at Loch Ryan but has completed a giant marshalling yard there. Biddle was enthusiastic on the efficiency of the many Americans in these ports. They bring everything they want with them, loaded tactically so that the first thing out of the ships are the lorries to take away the loads – clever adaptations of Nissen huts ready to put together in large sections, some of them refrigerator huts, some bakery huts etc. The units are entirely self-contained, and fresh milk and meat are about all they buy.'

22 October 1941

'To House of Commons to listen to the debate on the new railway agreement which was expected to develop into a wrangle on all sorts of things including nationalisation. It was poor watery stuff. J.J. Llewellin, Parliamentary Secretary, Ministry of War Transport, was quite good and paid a certain amount of tribute to what the railwaymen and women are doing. As the discussion came up on the motion for an adjournment, it was not possible to discuss anything that would have entailed legislation – and as any nationalisation would be a continuing thing after the war, legislation would be necessary for it as the Defence Regulations die with the war and would not therefore cover the question of nationalisation.'

25 November 1941

'At lunch, McColl said Duncan was very concerned with the way the railways were being run. He – Duncan – has no use whatever for W.V. Wood but had something in mind for Lemon. However, McColl had to tell him that Lemon was drinking heavily again and was unsuited to any big job.

'Had dinner with Gore-Browne who was very depressed about himself. He still says he was definitely going to get the job of Controller of Railways and would have had it if Brabazon had not been whisked away from the Ministry of War Transport – Gore-Browne says this was done by the government whips because they felt Moore-Brabazon was too intent on nationalisation. Gore-Browne then went on to say how he was asked to be boss of the NAAFI, then financial boss of the Home Guard, then was in the running for a Regional Commissioner. I really think his brain is affected by a dose of megalomania.'

29 November 1941

'Long go with Andrew Duncan, Hyndley and Gibson about coal stocking (dumping). John W. Gibson [the department's Technical Adviser and distinguished civil engineer who had loaned himself to the state during the war] is getting on well but striking some difficulties, especially apathy on the part of some of the LNER folk – the chain of command seems tortuous and slow. Duncan asked me how the REC was working under Alan Anderson – is it better than it was? I said no, I did not think they had heard of the declaration of war with Germany, although they had been expecting it for years; that Milne and Wood were two wild Irishmen who banded together to fight the others and when finished, turned round and fought each other.'

3 December 1941

'To Euston to lunch with Lemon who was very affable. I went to learn from him details of his proposed coal silo – the idea is to erect at West Kensington as a start a battery of hopper chutes, eight of them with a capacity of 250 tons each. The wagons to be lifted by an overhead travelling gantry and tipped into the appropriate chute, then to gravitate through a weighing and bagging machine to lorries. It should greatly expedite wagon turn-round and also road delivery as lorries will not have to wait for coal to be hand-weighed and hand-bagged. It will mean local merchants pooling their supplies and resources, which in itself is a desirable thing – and they ought to be willing to do so if they reap some of the financial advantages. Further, if successful, it should enable a number of depots to be closed altogether with a valuable acreage of land released.'

10 December 1941

Szlumper was not desk-bound in his coal work and on occasions visited mines and other locations to sort out problems. Thus on this day he went with Gibson to the electricity station at Coventry which had storage problems. He resolved them when he spotted a disused siding which had not been seen before as it was the other side of a fence. Their next call was the outcrop workings at Orchard Colliery at Dordon. They continued their journey through Chesterfield, reaching Doncaster at 18.00. The following day they drove via Catterick, Bedale, Chester-le-Street and Darlington to Newcastle, reaching the Royal Station Hotel at 11.15.

'At Newcastle we had a meeting with Jenkin-Jones, Paul Gibb and other LNER men, also Hornsby (CSO, Durham) who is quite good and Norval (CSO Northumberland) to settle a lot of outstanding questions about coal dumping. After lunch Gibson and I met the Fifeshire Coal Stocking Committee, headed by the rather formidable-looking Charles Reid [Director and General Manager of the Fife Coal Co Ltd]. We told them we were there to help, not to dictate and that we were not civil servants but merely a couple of outside experts. This got us on good terms at once and they promised to have some definite schemes by next Tuesday.'

12 December 1941

Szlumper had never been down a mine. After telling Clive Cookson of the Cowpen Coal Company, he was taken to Cowpen's Bates pit near Blyth. He noted it was a new pit of eight years, employed 934 men and had a weekly output of 6,564 tons. He described in detail the operation of the pit when he descended in a cage to the Beaumont Main East seam which was about 720 feet down. 'I came away with a vivid impression which I shall retain – of efficiency, cleanliness and working conditions infinitely better than I anticipated; and a first rate relationship between master and men.' They later returned to London.

15 December 1941

Szlumper recorded that they were due to see the Fife Committee the following day when they discovered that Hyndley had been making other arrangements. 'After various arguments, Gibson decided it would be best for us to take his car up with us. At 16.20 I telephoned Barrington-Ward to know if it could be arranged, returning tomorrow night. At 17.00 Gibson had loaded it into a motor car van at King's Cross. We later took the 22.15 sleeping car to Edinburgh.'

16 December 1941

'Arrived at Edinburgh Waverley Station at 08.15. Met by the Station Inspector who conducted us to an advertisement hoarding about twenty yards away from our coach. The inspector swung the hoarding to one side and there was the end of the motor car van with Gibson's car in it. Gibson backed it out within six minutes of our arrival and rightly characterised the whole operation from 16.20 yesterday afternoon as the smartest bit of work he has seen since the beginning of the war. To the hotel to breakfast. Inglis, LNER Divisional General Manager for Scotland, came and talked things over with us.' Szlumper and Gibson left the Scottish capital at 09.30 in Gibson's Rolls Bentley, reaching Glasgow at 10.35 for a meeting of the Central Stocking Committee.

'After introduction we led off with the same formula: "We are not civil servants, we are two alleged experts. We have not come to dictate to you. We have troubled to come here to see if we can be of any assistance to you." We soon got down to business on the subject of dumping or stocking and had a thoroughly satisfactory meeting. Back to Edinburgh. My neighbours entirely agreed with me that if the mines, like the railways, are to avoid nationalisation after the war, they must have ready some scheme of unified working where the rich will carry the poor; and that they will crash into nationalisation if instead they apply themselves to fighting it or fighting to regain pre-war control and individual ownership.

Entirely satisfactory meeting with the two committees followed – we found they had made plans since last Thursday for stocking coal at the pits up to the maximum possible amount, a thing Mines Dept has been unsuccessfully trying for the last nine months to get them to do.'

After a visit to Leith where they saw a site which he described as ideal for a large quantity of coal on some reclaimed land in the docks, they returned to the Scottish capital to dine with Inglis and Sir William Thomson of Scottish Motor Traction, 'a most genial little chap who believes in enjoying life and spreading happiness to others.'

17 December 1941

'Lunched with SR Board and officers. Chairman very affable and said the remarkable spirit and team work on the SR was due to me. He also made some criticisms of MoWT. In reply, I denied the SR spirit was due to me. It was due to the fact that we would not have the wrong sort of people on the SR. I said also I was glad he had said some home truths about the MoWT – now they might be able to realise I had spent twelve months of purgatory there but I had suffered because I felt it be my duty. Chairman said each company had set up a committee of directors and officers to plan the future, and an inter-company committee to consider inter-company working. I begged him neither to fight nationalisation, nor to fight to return to the old individual regime but to apply themselves to having ready at the earliest moment a scheme for unified working and if necessary unified finance and was sure this was the only effective counter-move to nationalisation, and, if drawn up properly, would keep matters within the companies' own control.

'Dined at REC with Cole-Deacon. He says that W.V. Wood seems to have practically gone off his head. He is by far the most awkward member of the REC while Milne is very much improved and more helpful. Cole-Deacon says that Milne and Grand are both on final trial and that they have been told by the Minister if they do not improve they will go.'

15 January 1942

Szlumper's diary entry was a cutting from *The Times* which was the announcement that the Railway Companies'Association had selected Keith Grand, C.K. Bird (LNER), F.A. Pope, F.J. Wymer, T.E. Thomas and H.G. Smith (Assistant to LMS Vice President) to serve on the commission set up under the chairmanship of Sir Ernest Lemon to consider the post-war planning and reconstruction of the railways. He wrote alongside it "Good God."

26 January 1942

'Lunched Roberts and Nicholson who are back from their American and Canadian trip. They seem to have done good work and made many friends. Their chief trouble has been to get any info out of Ministry of Supply over here as to the destination of any despatches from the other side – lack of this information has largely stultified their efforts to get ships loaded intelligently and to the most suitable ports.'

4 February 1942

'Lunch with Patteson to learn more about imminent changes in government. As anticipated, that beastly little press king, Beaverbrook, is to become the first Minister of Production. Patteson says there is a good deal of compromise about the appointments as some of the Ministers are difficult, especially Bevin who does not relish having Beaverbrook as his boss – what a charming pair they will make! Duncan is going back to Ministry of Supply – and damned good of him to do so after the way he has been treated. He is probably the only man who can rectify some of the damage Beaverbrook has been doing there. Patteson does not know his own future – Beaverbrook might want him to go to Production but Patteson has some views about the MoWT. He, like many of us, thinks it is the poorest show in the government and is very concerned that Leathers has come so much under the control of the civil servants. Went in and with great regret said adieu to Duncan, who was very nice. Told him I would not stay at the BoT but he pressed me to stay for a time anyway to see the working into and out of all the dumps in smooth working order but I said I thought I would pack up now. He replied "Do not be in too much of a hurry, you never know what may turn up."

9 February 1942

'After our usual Monday meeting with the President of the Board of Trade, J.J. Llewellin asked me to stay behind for a word. He said Duncan had told him I had done a grand job of work and hoped I would stay on. I told Llewellin that in my opinion the job was nearly at an end. I did not feel that I had done anything special but the coal is certainly much better distributed this year. I outlined the methods by which I had worked through existing staff, the Public Utilities Undertakings Committee etc and said that perhaps my greatest use had been in knowing the individual to go to and in "wangling" things that were difficult to obtain officially.'

14 February 1942

'To chat with Lord Leathers in morning, having written a week ago to Holland-Martin to tell him my work at the Board of Trade was coming to a close and I wanted to return to the Southern Railway. Leathers very friendly and made my mission easy by welcoming me with the words, "Well, Gilbert, what's your position now? I knew you went to the BoT at Duncan's special request and wondered if his departure would make any difference to you." Told him I thought

I had pretty well come to the end of my useful work there but he said that was not the general view. However, I told him this winter was pretty well past and it had started with a much better distributed stock of coal. That we had done as much as seemed possible to re-allocate the distribution from mines in such a way as to avoid unnecessarily long or awkward rail hauls and that with a low output and the improved railway facilities, there should be little enough trouble in handling the problem next winter. He agreed about the latter. I told him I had accordingly written to Holland-Martin that I wished to resume as General Manager. Leathers said he appreciated my desire but it would be difficult to go back in the middle of a war, to swap horses when crossing the stream. Once got into "government circles" in these circumstance, one sort of had to keep in them.'

Szlumper replied that he had been away from his proper job for two and a half years and considered he ought to go back to it. His colleagues in the railway and some of the staff had been saying 'Why will they not let Szlumper come back to the railway? Do they think he cannot manage it or what?' Leathers said he knew full well how the staff had affectionate feelings for him and could fully appreciate his wish to be back among them. Szlumper emphasised that he had not a hard day's work to do and that he liked to sweat at his work which he was not doing. Leathers' response was that the railway was in smooth going order and if he was to go back, it would probably cause a certain amount of disruption and re-shuffling of jobs.

'I told him there should be no difficulty, that Missenden was at first appointed Acting General Manager during my absence but at Euan Wallace's suggestion, I readily agreed that the "Acting" should be dropped in order to give Missenden better status with his colleagues but the appointment was made on the quite distinct understanding that he reverted to his former position as Traffic Manager when I returned. I said supposing I did not get back now but waited around until the war ended and supposing it ended in a year's or so time – as I could retire in less than two and a quarter years from now, should I want to go back for one year to grapple with all the terrific problems of peace reconstruction? That led him to talk about post-war and Lemon and his committee. He asked me what I thought of the Post-War Committee and I told him I was not prepared to discuss it – I was not responsible for their appointment. I asked what he thought of Grand and he put up his hands and made a wry face. He said the committee had made an unfortunate start and I said it would have been surprising had anything other happened. He said he should have thought Lemon was the last man to have anything to do with post-war planning, his outlook was too parochial and specialised on the mechanical engineer side. Leathers then went on to say that although Anderson still had some troubles with the REC, things had improved to some extent due largely to a long talk he (Leathers) had had with Milne during a visit to one of the London stations during the blackout in the early days of the winter. He said he had told Milne quite plainly that he was not used to the sort of behaviour Milne was exhibiting and if Milne did not alter his ways, he (Leathers) would have to make some changes. He asked me how I would feel about going to the Ministry of Supply as Controller General of Transportation if Beaverbrook took Patteson away from that job. I turned up my nose and said, "No, I would rather go back to the SR, that is my job." Leathers replied that he quite understood, adding that the Ministry of Supply was a hotbed of intrigue and jealousy. Leathers was very friendly throughout and told me not to pack up at the BoT too soon.'

20 February 1942

'More political changes. Thank heaven Beaverbrook dropped on grounds of ill-health – mental, I should say. There can be nothing but good from his going, a nasty, pushful muddler, upsetting every decent man and torpedoing every programme for the sake of making a theatrical splash. It is said he is going to America to help co-ordinate the American effort with ours – I hope America likes him!'

21 February 1942

'Jessie and I went to the wedding of Margaret McColl and the splendid and enjoyable reception at the Dorchester. McColl tells me Duncan made it a condition of his return to Ministry of Supply that Beaverbrook should be pushed out of the government. He told Jessie that I had been doing a magnificent job at the BoT and must not now desert it. But I told him his successor Llewellin had made a poor start and put up a pitiful show at the Coal Production Council and I anticipated he would leave things to the Mines Dept in which case Gibson and I would be starved of work as Mines Dept could not be expected to relish our interference.'

23 February 1942

'A further list of government changes announced this morning. Reith is succeeded at Ministry of Works by Lord Portal. Portal should do quite well, a practical man of the world. That ass Brabazon also goes, his place at Ministry of Aircraft Production is taken by Llewellin who has been at BoT just eighteen days. Let us hope he will do better at MAP than he showed signs of doing here. His place at BoT has been taken by Dr Hugh Dalton, lately Minister of Economic Warfare. Said to be somewhat of a blusterer, no one seems able to say how good he is but he suffers a handicap of having been a professor of economics. Lord Wolmer, succeeds him. Quite good, I think. The prize move is at the War Office. The Secretary of State, David Margesson, goes out and is replaced by Sir James Grigg who until today was the Permanent Under-Secretary. Certainly the most unorthodox of civil servants, using the vernacular freely and with a terrific reputation for ruthless efficiency.'

26 February 1942

'Gibson is in trouble – the new President of the BoT, Hugh Dalton, wants his room for someone else. So Gibson intends to clear out altogether. A great pity as he is most alive and capable and has got the government dumps going in a manner no one else would have.'

27 February 1942

'Bad reports of Dalton's rudeness to everyone. He sleeps in the office and is turning various people out of their offices to make bedrooms for his entourage. This afternoon my secretary came to tell me she had been asked to ascertain my reactions to a suggestion she should work in my room so as to release her room for use as a bedroom for the President's Personal Secretary. Told her my reactions were unfavourable and asked her to tell them to hold their hand as I should probably be clearing out very soon.'

3 March 1942

Szlumper met Leathers who advised him his services could not be used by the government. Later he lunched with Holland-Martin at Martins Bank after which they retired to the latter's room. Szlumper explained his situation at the BoT – that he no longer had enough to do there and the new president did not seem to be taking the interest in coal which Duncan had had. With changes at the Mines Department he did not see a future there and in any case would not work under Hurst. He explained that he had spoken to the Minister and that he could not see any way he could be used in government circles. At this stage in their discussion, Gore-Browne came into the room. Holland-Martin said the directors had discussed his case at the last board and had come to the conclusion that the Southern machine was running so well that they did not want to disturb it. Moreover, they could not have him back immediately in view of the critical months ahead with the possibility of an invasion. Szlumper challenged the invasion suggestion as a card too thumb-worn to play any more and said he could see no reason to stop him from resuming his place on the railway. They said they wanted him back as did everyone but it was very difficult to arrange then or in the immediate future.

'There were many plans and schemes in existence and it would take me some little time to master them but I replied it should not take me very long. They said that surely a man of my organising ability and capacity must be wanted in some government department. I asked them where as I knew of nowhere. They said that surely Andrew Duncan wanted me but I told them that Patteson had been there eighteen months and had organised a Transportation Department and was running it well. So there was no vacancy there. They said surely there was some other suitable post but I told them I knew of none – transportation was my line of country and I was not prepared to tackle anything else. They sympathised on my bad luck that things had turned out as they had. If the war had gone as expected, I would still be at the War Office doing a great job. I replied that a lot of things had been upset by the collapse of France and that my mistake was in going from the War Office to a subordinate post at the Ministry of Transport. I ought at the time to have pressed to come back to the SR and it was only the possibility of early invasion that had held me back from doing this as invasion was a possibility in August/September 1940.

'They again said that they had talked it over at the last board and had come to the conclusion that it was impossible for me to return at once. I asked them how soon they anticipated I could return but they were unable to say. I said "Is this the position then, that I do not come back to the SR so long as the war continues, and if it goes on for two years and six weeks, it would mean that I retire and wave goodbye to the railway from a distance?" They seemed to think this possible and again said it was very bad luck things turning out as they had. I replied that luck did not come into it. It was not luck. It was desperately unfair to me. They told me that they had heard from everyone that I had done my various jobs very well, and no one had suggested that I could be spared to come back to the SR.

'I said my answer is that I definitely have not enough work to do to occupy me and this did not suit me. I could foresee the new President of the Board of Trade wanting my room for one of his entourage if Mines Dept is divorced from the BoT. This might mean me walking the streets for two years with nothing to do. They said they must ask Andrew Duncan and the Minister of War Transport if there was not some government place in which I could pull my weight. I had the unhappiest twelve months of my life at the MoWT. I had been shuffled into it. Holland-Martin asked "Who by?" Said I did not know but Reith could not have been aware I was likely to leave the War Office unless someone had told him and that when he (Reith) said to me that he understood that I did not want to go back to the SR, I had made it clear to him that nothing was further from my thoughts and wishes. Once more, Holland-Martin said the railway is running so well that they could not risk disturbing it – due to the fact that Walker and I had trained the staff so well and had a "replace" for everyone doing a job of importance. I said that apparently I had trained them too well, so well they could do without me. I said it seemed to me that if the team had been working so well for two and a half years, I might as well be told that they could go on doing so for another two and a half years by which time I should be eligible to retire. Would they like to consider the suggestion I had put to Gore-Browne fifteen months ago that we should come to terms for my retirement now. Gore-Browne pointed out that there was no reason for the railway to "pay me out" and all I could expect would be the pension to which I would be entitled to at age fifty-eight (note, I am entitled to no pension before age sixty save on the grounds of ill-health.)

'Holland-Martin said it would be difficult for the railway to ask for me back, especially as Missenden took such a leading part at the REC and as the Minister got on so well with "The Team" – and besides neither Duncan, nor Leathers had said they were ready to release me and he (Holland-Martin) doubted if they would. I replied that I did not think there would be any difficulty if I asked them. Both Gore-Browne and Holland-Martin expressed frequent sorrow at the position at which I found myself. I said it was a most extraordinary position and most unfair to me. At the end of thirty-five minutes, I said it did not seem we could get much further today. In coming away they expressed warm sympathy for me but I said it was an extraordinary poor reward for forty years loyal and devoted service to the railway. They said I must not look at it that way but I said I could see no other way of looking at it. On the parting handshake, they said you must know that we have the most sympathetic feelings for you to which I replied "Words count so little, I believe in the motto *Spectemur Agendo*. [Let us be judged by our acts.]"

4 March 1942

By appointment Szlumper saw Duncan to update him on his position. Duncan told him the departmental changes had not evolved as he expected but he thought Dalton would be taking much interest in coal and that he was pleased to have the support of Szlumper. If he did not do as he expected, he had other things in mind. Szlumper replied that he did not see that there would be enough work for him but Duncan did not agree.

Szlumper opened out when he said he felt there was some "dirty work" somewhere – not on the part of the directors but on the part of those who advise them and who would be likely to suffer by his return, although it had been clearly laid down that the contingent promotions on his secondment had been purely temporary and that the beneficiaries would automatically step back on his return. He said the reason for his visit was to ask him if he is approached by Holland-Martin to say that I could be released. Duncan said he thought it would be a mistake to go back and that the government was very lucky to have a man of his ability and experience at its disposal. Moreover, if he did go back, he could be pulled back again within three months. Szlumper, jokingly, said he was not being a bit helpful to his cause. He pressed him to see what government changes there would be. 'If it did not fan out alright, he had something else in mind for him.'

6 March 1942

'To Berkeley Square House to have a talk with Leathers. He said he had been giving much thought to me. He said he was still quite sure it would not be in my own interest to quit government circles and return to the railway in the middle of the war. He could well understand his feeling but in times like these one had to leave sentiment out of it – he instanced his own case where he would very much like to go back to his own firm which would like him back desperately as it was manned by two old men who were staying on to try to keep things together. But he did not feel justified in quitting the government and returning to his civil occupation. He said the war would not continue for less than two years, so I remarked that that would see me to the age of sixty when I could retire. Leathers replied that he was more fortunate in that he would have to go back to his firm to help get it onto its feet again and he had no superannuation whereas Szlumper would take up a comfortable pension without any sentiment about retiring and leaving his successors to deal with the after-war problems. Leathers said he had rang Duncan who had impressed on him the urgency of the coal problem and its importance and his view that Szlumper was the best person to handle it. Duncan also said he would speak to Dalton who Szlumper understood was a very curious type of fellow, pompous and irascible, and gather not liked by anyone. On Missenden, Szlumper said there was no question about his ability, that he liked him very much and wished him to be given all the credit that was due him. As for himself, he did not care a hoot where he worked or how hard he worked so long as he knew it was, from the war point, a worthwhile job but he was not working hard enough at that moment.'

Szlumper returned to his anxiety about the forces blocking his return when he said he had doubts about the kind of cricket that was being played at Waterloo. 'Those who might suffer by my return might openly or insidiously fight against it, although I always considered there could be no question about it and if I thought there was any plot to prevent my return, I would fight like a tiger against it. Leathers said he could see no sign of any plot but he rather felt that Missenden had made a point of giving due credit to me for many things and when Leathers recently spent a day with Missenden, the latter said many nice things about me and my efforts for the Southern Railway. However, now I had mentioned the possibility of underhand work, he would be on the lookout for it. Again, Leathers said he had been giving much thought to me but at the moment he could not see any more useful sphere of work. There were very few jobs in the Ministry which had autonomous conditions. One such job was Regional Port Director and he had been considering appointing one for London and the South Coast but it would seem rather a retrograde step for me to go back to port management. Duncan seemed sure that there was enough at the BoT to keep me busy until the end of next winter and is very sure I should be wiser to stick to government jobs.

'Leathers commented a little on Holland-Martin. He did not think he was very bright and had noticed at meetings that he had an imperfect idea of what he had come to talk about and did not seem readily to absorb the purport of what took place at the meeting. Leathers had noticed that the other chairmen had shown some impatience at this. I said he was sketchily interested in art, archaeology and architecture. Leathers replied that perhaps that accounted for his idea to subordinate all post-war railway planning to the architectural aspect.'

11 March 1942
'Hurst has gone. The new President of the Board of Trade never even saw him but sent him some abrupt message saying he was being transferred to some remote part of the Paymaster General's office on post-war matters. Lunch with Norman Hulbert at the House of Commons where we ran into Brabazon who greeted me effusively. He has been put on the board of EMI but I believe is very sore being turned out of government. I learnt that America refuses to have Beaverbrook there at any price – they seem to have him properly assessed.'

'Met Dalton for first time at the Coal Production Council. He is somewhat unprepossessing and forbidding at first sight but not so bad as I had expected. He was very patient and attentive for two and three quarter hours, the trade union leaders using a good deal of his time to let off a lot of steam. At some of the lighter remarks, a twinkle came into his eyes as if he had an embryo sense of humour – so I may find him not so black as he is painted. His strident voice is like a foghorn. He informed the meeting that the War Office now agrees in principle to release miners from non-mobilised units. Numbers were expected to be 13,000 but are now found to be much less. We went through an excellent memo on manpower prepared by Wilson, the statistical man in Mines Department.' This was the young Harold Wilson who had left academia at Oxford for the Civil Service and was destined to become a Labour Member of Parliament.

23 March 1942
Szlumper had a meeting with the Principal of the University of King's College, Dr Halliday, about the ongoing squabble between the headmaster and his staff at King's College School – Szlumper had been a governor of his old school since 1936. When Halliday mentioned that Beveridge had gone to the BoT to try to devise a scheme of fuel rationing, Szlumper gave vent to his feelings about economists. Halliday agreed, adding that Beveridge had reduced the LSE to a state of chaos during his rule until 1937 and that it was only beginning to recover.

25 March 1942
Szlumper's anxieties about Dalton were realised when he received a letter from James Helmore, the Private Secretary to the President of the Board of Trade, who was also the Establishment Officer. Dalton had very considerably increased his

personal staff and wanted them near him. Helmore asked Szlumper if he would agree to move to room 627. He inspected the room to find it was small and ordinary with windows looking only out into the lightwell of the building. Three days later Gibson called at Szlumper to tell him that while he had been away, a letter had been received from Helmore asking him to transfer to his room as his was wanted. Gibson said that on no condition would he consent to occupying his room. 'While we were chatting, Skinner (Helmore's Assistant) came into my room to ask Gibson for his reply. Gibson told him that under no circumstances would he move into my room and if his room was wanted, he was quite ready to turn out of it and out of the building – never to come back as he was fed up with the BoT. I told Skinner that it would be more sensible for Dalton to hire some bedrooms in Marsham Court than to turn good offices into bedrooms. Skinner retired for a time but soon came back to tell Gibson that it would not be necessary to move him for the present. Skinner then said to me he had instructions to move me this morning to room 631. Told him he was free to move my personal belongings into that or any other room and I would be obliged if he would let them remain there a few days until I could get the railway to collect them as I had no intention of using the room. Skinner was very sorry but said he had no option in carrying out his instructions. Gibson gave vent to his feelings in no uncertain manner but I told my secretary I was going out and I put my hat and coat on and walked out of the place. My room, I gather, is wanted for some young pup of a civil servant, Gaitskell, who until recently was Private Secretary to Dalton and who now is a sort of dog's body to shadow his master everywhere and keep track of everything – hence the necessity for him to be near at hand.' Hugh Gaitskell would become a Member of Parliament in 1945.

'It makes me very angry to think that the Establishment Officer (Helmore) could not deliver the ultimatum to me himself and to send his assistant (Skinner) to do it. If Dalton was anything approaching a gentleman, he would of course have come to me himself and put his difficulty himself and asked me to help by moving to a back room which probably I should have agreed to but he has the reputation of being mannerless and rude in the extreme.' Szlumper also recorded it had been announced that Brabazon was being made a baron, 'a high price for incompetence.'

30 March 1942

This was Szlumper's last day at Millbank and after clearing his desk he went to Waterloo. 'I hear' through my intelligence department that Missenden put pressure on the SR board to make his appointment as General Manager for the "duration" but I doubt the truth of this.' Seemingly this was the nearest Szlumper ever got to discovering the circumstances blocking his return to Waterloo. The same day Holland-Martin wrote to Szlumper. It was not the kind of letter he wanted. The railway's chairman stressed that the door at Waterloo was not necessarily open on the day he left government service. Holland-Martin wrote him another letter when he returned to Waterloo that day. He acknowledged that the Minister had treated him badly and stupidly about his room, but he thought he had acted too precipitately in resigning.

2 April 1942

'Went to Martins Bank for talk with Holland-Martin and Gore-Browne. Started by saying we had all known each other too long to let there be any misunderstandings and I handed him a short note on a microscopic letter he had written me a couple of days earlier dealing with the point as to whether I had irrevocably left the BoT; and also challenging his statement that the action I had taken was not "worthy" of me. Holland-Martin read my note aloud and both of them clicked their tongues as if to suggest "damn this pernickety fellow Szlumper. Here he is making a nuisance of himself again." They both said they thought it petty of me to have succumbed to a pinprick, annoying though it was. Holland-Martin and Gore-Browne then asked me had I resigned or not. Said my view was that I had but if I had to eat humble pie, I felt I could still go back and say I would re-start in any room they chose to give me. The real trouble is that under the present regime there is not any work for me to do and I would just sit there manicuring my nails. The Chairman said I must really make up my mind and the Deputy Chairman said I had already caused three flutters in the dovecote because the cards had worked out very badly for me. I corrected him and said "only two" as on the first occasion that I had wanted to return to the SR when I left the War Office, I had readily agreed that at the moment with the possibility of an invasion, it was imprudent to do so. Said the second occasion was not of my making but because of changes at the Ministry of War Transport – I was not persona grata there because I was a practical man who only wished at efficiency and would not be swayed by political considerations. They wanted someone who would bow to political expediency and I could not be so.

'Holland-Martin said that it would take some time to re-shuffle on SR so as to make my place available for me again, perhaps six months and that if I retired at sixty, that would give only eighteen months of railway work and would upset the team which was working so well together. They could not make the change now owing to the months of intensive warfare ahead and all the emergency plans that it would take me some time to pick up – did I not therefore think it would be better to return to the BoT? Replied that I would be prepared to work hard anywhere but the work simply did not exist at the BoT. Holland-Martin said he had seen Duncan who had high praise for the work I had done but who did not agree that there was no work still to be done at the BoT. Told

Holland-Martin I knew that was Duncan's view but it did not seem to be Dalton's and that, although I would work anywhere so long as it was hard work and work of a suitable and important character, I would far rather work on the SR. As I would be fifty-eight in a few days, how would I feel about resigning from SR now with suitable compensation? Replied this was one of the alternatives I put up to Gore-Browne eighteen months ago and that I would be quite prepared to consider it. The Chairman said the idea would be to give me my pension plus a cash payment clear of income tax. No doubt I should get some directorships. He had no idea what the cash sum would be – would be for discussion between us. Told him I would be quite prepared to consider it. It would be a bitter blow but it might be the solution to the present difficulty. Said I did not want to start talking terms now and had nothing unreasonable in mind but I did want to remind him that until my sixtieth birthday, I was heavily committed with life insurances – this had been my method of saving.

'Gore-Browne said another idea had occurred to him but it had to be treated absolutely secret as he and the chairman had mentioned it to no one – the Post-War Planning Committee which had had a very unhappy start but they had it in mind to discuss at the Railway Companies' Association – how would I like to be associated with Lemon on it? Perhaps Lemon and I working full time with Gore-Browne as a neutral chairman. Replied that the idea would appeal tremendously, I had some idea on post-war planning – Holland-Martin and Gore-Browne said they knew my Institute of Transport paper on it and it was a herculean task I would be glad to take a part in. Chairman said it was an enormous thing covering not only railways but road and air transport. They wanted a scheme prepared so as to have it ready as a counterblast to nationalisation proposals which they expected the government to put forward. I reminded them I had frequently told them that this was the proper tactic. The chairman said that the MoWT would not agree to having two General Managers on the SR, one of them seconded to the post-war transport committee and I replied that that seemed to fit in, if it could be arranged. It would form a perfectly logical reason for me leaving the government service and retiring from the railway. We all seemed to agree that it would be a good idea but they said they would have to talk it over with the other chairmen.

'They asked me what I had to do to resign from government service and I said that I had never had a formal appointment so that no formal resignation seemed to be called for but I would go and see Duncan and take his advice. I asked if it would suit them better that I should continue to work for the government and they rather thought that I ought to. Said I would definitely prefer the post-war planning job to anything the government could employ me at. Gore-Browne said they wanted to get finality in the steps I should take and after some further talk, we agreed that these should be:

I would not return to the BoT.

I would see Duncan and if he says "Stay in government work," I would stay if he is able to find a job of sufficient importance and satisfactory to me.

If Duncan says no, or there is no suitable job, I then leave the government service.

I then say to the SR, I am free, do you want me back on the SR or do you want me to retire?

If they say "retire", we discuss terms and when agreed, I retire.

If possible, work at the Post-War Planning Committee to be arranged, and to be linked with the reason for my retirement.'

7 April 1942

'Went to see Duncan and started by apologising for being a nuisance to him but he would not hear of apologies. Told him briefly circumstances of my departure and showed him copy of letter to Dalton. He quite agreed I took the only proper course and was exceedingly annoyed with Dalton and very grieved that I should have suffered such treatment. He recapitulated his conviction of the importance of coal and its movement and the necessity of having a heavyweight railwayman to look after the railway side. Told him had broken the news to Holland-Martin who before considering the question of my return to SR, had asked me to see him (Duncan) to make sure there was no other suitable and responsible government work I should undertake. I said could think of none myself but thought I had to put the question to him to satisfy Holland-Martin. Duncan said things had turned out differently to what he expected – he had fully anticipated that a Ministry of Fuel would be formed with a certain person (Hyndley) as Minister, and that Gibson and I would come into our own and have really big positions in it because he considered it necessary to have a heavyweight railwayman to take care of all transport matters and an engineer of Gibson's capacity to look after all the dumping questions – however, the idea of a Ministry of Fuel has been abandoned. He could think of no other appropriate job and it would be absurd for me to take on a secondary job – a job could be made for me but I would be ill-advised to take on such a makeshift and instead, I ought to be back managing the Southern. He said he had spoken to Leathers about his position and they both agreed I should receive proper treatment – they would not have any hanky panky about the SR. He asked how old was Missenden and I said I thought he was a few months younger than me (I found out later that he was just two years younger). He then asked what the retiring age was. Replied that it was sixty with extension to sixty-five at the pleasure of directors. He then said it was true the SR was still running but my place was back there and Missenden and others must step back.

I mentioned nothing about the chairman's suggestion that I should retire. I told Duncan that for Hyndley or him or any normal person, I would work my fingers down to the bone and did not care a hoot where I worked – in a WC if necessary but I was not prepared to be sent there by an Assistant Establishment Officer; and there had to be enough work and sufficiently important to make me feel I was really helping the national effort. He said "Quite right, Gilbert, quite right. Otherwise you are far better back on your own job as General Manager."

'He thanked me warmly for what I had done at the BoT for him and said I ought to take a little holiday before starting other work. We parted on very friendly terms. I then wrote to Holland-Martin telling him I had taken the first three steps and was ready to go ahead with the others.' Following the meeting, Szlumper wrote to his chairman that he had talked to Duncan and had written a letter of resignation to Dalton. He emphasised that he still wished to return to the railway but if the board thought it best for him to retire, he would.

8 to 16 April 1942
Szlumper made no entries. Consequently he did not mention attending the Company of Shipwrights on 16 April when he was elected to its Audit Committee. In effect, another chapter of Szlumper's life was closing while the beginning of the next chapter was starting to evolve.

Chapter Seven

৵৹৶

Post-War Planning, 1942

17 April 1942

Szlumper and his wife moved to Cranmer Court near Sloane Avenue in Chelsea to become flat-dwellers for the first time in their lives. 'We had hardly got our nose inside the front door when the phone rang – Holland-Martin to say the Railway Companies' Association at its meeting yesterday agreed to the Post-War Committee, Gore-Browne as chairman and me as Technical Adviser. So that seems a propitious start to our new mode of life. Gore-Browne then rang to give the same news and to fix for me to come to lunch to talk things over.' The lunch was that day and he noted that Sir Robert Burrows was also there, describing him as very alive and forthright and one of the most intelligent railway directors he had met for a long time. 'The committee does not seem to be decided on in all aspects yet but as good as. Met Walker who referred to my case as a tragedy but do not know how much he did to prevent it happening.'

Below the entry, Szlumper wrote that the next few entries were written after a big interval of time and were in skeleton form only.

26 April 1942

'Gore-Browne came to dinner to discuss detail, the birth of the committee now having been decided on. We drafted a letter for him to send to the chairmen to set the ball rolling. Jessie gave Gore-Browne a bad quarter of an hour on the subject of the ingratitude of the railway.'

28 April 1942

'Had a long talk with Holland-Martin and Gore-Browne at former's office about terms of my departure from the railway. Holland-Martin was very agreeable and most obliged to me for being so amenable and we had no difficulty in arriving at terms.'

29 April 1942

'As arranged yesterday, I resigned. I wrote to Holland-Martin setting out the things as I understood them and saying I was prepared to accept them. He afterwards told Dawes it was quite the nicest letter he had ever received. He sent me by hand today a reply that I had been cruelly unlucky.'

30 April 1942

Szlumper recorded that Holland-Martin telephoned him that the board had agreed the terms; and that he reiterated his gratitude for what he had done for the railway and for the way he had fallen in with the arrangements. The railway issued a press release that Szlumper had been released from government service and at the same time had resigned as General Manager.

There was an undated note in his diary following the 30 April entry that what followed covered five months. No longer being employed on war work, he wrote, he ceased to write up the diary. 'I applied myself solidly to the work of the Post-War Committee, collected a mass of details and information and tried to guide the members in the direction on which I thought they should go. Gore-Browne and Burrows were with me 100% from the start in thinking that a public corporation to control all forms of transport is the proper thing with complete fusion of all interests and limitation of dividends. Sir Murrough Wilson [LNER Deputy Chairman], a very nice chap with ability, favours only a financial pool of the railways to start with but a pool of all receipts and expenditure which is about the shortest route I know to gross extravagance and inefficiency; and the idea of leaving the road haulage interests alone until the railways have settled down into a new stride is just too damned silly to consider – I never had any use for helping at your own execution. The fourth member of the committee, Sir Edward Cadogan, is somewhat of a character study, somewhat woolly about mundane matters, too. He is what I would call a true politician, not knowing what he wants and afraid to voice any definite opinions for fear of the voting going against him. He favours as far as I can gauge a pool of gross receipts less an allowance for working expenses, the companies retaining their individuality. Indeed, I suspect he harbours some hope that the railways may return to their pre-war status and isolation or should it be insularity? I also would favour this if someone will convince me there will be no road transport and no air competition after the war – not otherwise.'

It was on 22 September that Missenden made a presentation of a silver salver to Szlumper at the Charing Cross Hotel before an audience of nearly fifty officers. According to the *Railway Gazette*, Missenden heaped praise on him, describing him as always a very approachable General Manager, always susceptible to new ideas and always with that human understanding which gave him that happy knack of getting the best out of staff.

Szlumper noted that it took about six months of pleasantly hard work to complete 'a watered-down report but one giving enough data to enable railway directors to decide on the general line of policy to adopt.' Otherwise he made few comments on his work with the Post-War Committee which had a small office in Victoria Street. The report was completed in October 1942 and outlined three basic principles – private ownership, the necessity of combining road and rail interests and the value of a central board and executive, suggesting these could be secured by either a pool of the finances and resources of the four main line railways and road undertakings, or an outright merger of the two modes of transport. Although the report was a compromise by its members who had conflicting views, it has been described as an exceptionally positive approach to the problem of post-war organisation. In the event, it was still-born and the companies soon made it clear that they preferred to retain their separate identities after the war. The committee, including Szlumper initially, continued to meet and produce reports.

At an unrecorded date, Szlumper noted that it had been decided that Patteson was to go to Canada as representative of the Ministry of Supply and that he had tackled him twice about taking on the job he was vacating. Twice Szlumper had given a very definite no. He also recorded that at a dinner with Alex McColl at another unrecorded date, he was 'half-tackled' about the post. McColl said that Duncan was very concerned about the way the invading armies would be rail-served on the Continent. It would be necessary, he stressed, to plan the rehabilitation of the railways and ports on the Continent so that they could look after the phase immediately following a landing and advance, ready later for the bigger problem of salvaging what was left of the Continental populations and getting food to them. This was the context of Szlumper's decision to resume his diary.

29 October 1942

Szlumper noted that Gore-Browne had rung him to say that he had been approached – but could not say by whom – to ask if he, Szlumper, could be spared if wanted at the Ministry of Supply and that Andrew Duncan would be ringing him to make an appointment. Gore-Browne had said that, although it was much against the grain, they would have to spare him if demanded and if he agreed to go. Szlumper was quite firm, however, and told him that he definitely did not wish to go. Gore-Browne said that ultimately it was his decision. In the evening, Rutherford Tippetts, the Principal Private Secretary to the Minister of Supply, telephoned Szlumper that Duncan wanted to see him the following day.

30 October 1942

Tippetts rang Szlumper again to say that Duncan would like him to come to lunch with him and Alex McColl. A few minutes later McColl rang him to ask if he had heard about the lunch appointment and asked him if he knew what it meant. 'I said I could guess but was it connected with the wider matter he had mentioned on Friday evening? He said it was. I went to Duncan's office at 12.45 and found him most friendly. "I will come straight to the point. You know Patteson is going to Canada – I want you to come and take his work over."'

Szlumper replied that he would not, asserting that he had finished with government work but Duncan said he had got to come and that he had intended that he should have come when he left the BoT but it had taken some time to arrange. 'He had wanted to send Patteson to Canada but first he had to reduce the swelling that Beaverbrook had caused in Patteson's head before he would be acceptable in Canada and this had taken time. Patteson had had a difficult job but had done it splendidly, he had built up a good organisation but perhaps there were too many in it – it was best to get plenty in at the outset and then weed them out a bit and this would fall to me to do and "You are the man I want to do it, so you will say Yes."

Szlumper replied that he was making it difficult for him and that if anyone else had put it to him, he would have refused an interview. A lunch followed at the American Club together with Alex McColl when Szlumper expressed his frustration with civil servants but Duncan said his main contact at the Ministry of Supply would be Sir William Douglas, the Permanent Secretary, who was first rate and totally unlike a civil servant, a man he would find more after his own heart. Szlumper would still not commit himself and suggested there were others. Duncan asked him what he thought of Pope. He replied that he was very capable but possibly inclined to be a little lazy. Szlumper then suggested Walker, a man of the greatest ability, but Duncan said he would not have him, even if he was thirty years younger and that he could not mix in the way required, McColl adding that he would require too high a salary. Szlumper mentioned Barrington-Ward who he described as a very able and younger man but Duncan said he would not have him as a gift because he had such an unfortunate manner. Duncan said he had mentioned the job to W.V. Wood who had replied that "Gilbert Szlumper is your man surely." When he spoke to Milne, the reply was, "Gilbert is the only man for the job."

2 November 1942
Szlumper attended the Ministry of Supply, telling Duncan that he was still not committing himself. A meeting with Sir William Douglas and Patteson followed when he asserted he would not do any business with Hill which prompted Duncan to comment on Hurcomb, 'not about his ability but his manner, lack of tact and good fellowship.' According to the diary, he and Douglas formed a mutual liking. 'The whole place seems to have a happy atmosphere. How different from the Ministry of War Transport.'

'To tea with Gore-Browne and discuss the situation with him. He seems genuinely sorry to part with me and rather fears our little organisation will close down as he quite realises he himself is without the necessary technical knowledge to keep it going. I suggested a small technical committee should carry it on and promised to put my ideas on paper for him. We then fell to talking about people. First he told me that Hambro is going to vacate the GWR chairmanship as he is so fully occupied at the Ministry of Economic Warfare; and Milne is to become Chairman and General Manager. Then, that Alan Anderson is going to vacate the chairmanship of the Railway Executive Committee and he is desperately anxious to replace him – he begged me to do anything I can to help him achieve this. He had a good deal to say about Missenden who apparently is very tender-skinned and very jealous of the rights of general managers; and Gore-Browne seems to feel very strongly about it. He also told me the SR may be losing Elliot – Leathers is concerned the LPTB has no leader since Pick went, and wants to appoint Elliot. In some ways, not bad advice but one drawback is that Elliot is not a "transport-trained" man. Still, I think he would grow into the job. Gore-Browne's idea would be to bring Biddle back to SR but I do not know in what precise position.'

4 November 1942

'Told Foreman and Miss May – my sole staff at Victoria Street on the Post-War Committee – that they were going to lose me. Both seemed very sorry. Foreman said "You are the finest chief I have ever had. I am trying to aspire to the head of perfection you have reached but I shall never succeed." Miss May said her time at Victoria Street was the happiest she ever had. I borrowed both these young people from the GWR. They have both been first rate and I am sorry to lose touch with them.'

Chapter Eight

❧

Szlumper at the Ministry of Supply, 1942-45

Szlumper continued his diary at the Ministry of Supply. It was interesting as he would still be much involved with transport and he would not lose contact with his former colleagues and the railway industry; and he would be happy. The department had been formed in the spring of 1939 with responsibility for the administration of the Royal Ordnance Factories and for the design, inspection, research and experimental work in the supply of munitions, clothing and other stores to the War Office and Air Ministry. It had several other functions including the control of the acquisition, manufacture and prices of raw materials. By this time, it was a very big and important department and had become the sole importer of all raw materials, machine tools, munitions components and finished munitions. It had also become an important customer of the railways and it owned over 4,000 road vehicles.

5 November 1942
The press reported that Szlumper had accepted appointment on a honorary basis as Director-General of Supply Services at the Ministry of Supply. Szlumper recorded that he met a great number of his new staff, most of whom he thought were 'alive.' Sir William Douglas, the Permanent Secretary, took him to lunch with Graham Cunningham, the Chief Executive of Munitions Production, who was on secondment from the Triplex Safety Glass Company.

10 November 1942
'Had long talk with Muir Wilson. He seems determined to return to his own business. Seems to have been a thorn in Patteson's side who says he is ambitious and ever wanting to spread. Do not object to him and should think he is very capable and energetic.' Muir Wilson, a director of a Scottish carpet manufacturer, was a Deputy Director-General at the Ministry of Supply.

16 November 1942
This was the official start of Szlumper's work at the Ministry and he noted that Douglas came to welcome him. He had a long talk with the Deputy

Director-General of Supply Services, Forbes-Smith who was on secondment from the LNER, describing him as a bit suet-puddingy, quite able but desperately serious and somewhat impressed with his own importance. 'Very anxious to maintain his autonomy and not to be too much interfered with by me. Am sure he will be quite loyal and when he sees I have no axe to grind or position to make for myself, I think he will open out and share his sorrows with me to the full. The only trouble in the Ministry is the apparently universal duck shoving that goes on, everyone trying to grab a bit of someone else's business or trying to spike someone else's guns – seems funny when it is only a war-time set up and so many of them have perfectly good civilian jobs to return to when the war is over.'

18 November 1942
'Lunched Biddle to give him his periodically requisite dose of cheering-up. Gather some kind of minor earth quake at MoWT. Tolerton is to become Assistant Director-General and to have under his charge rail, ports, canals and highways but apparently Hill will still deal with railway policy and finance. However, Tolerton is very much more broad-minded and tolerant than Hill, and this will be some improvement. That dreadful uncouth fellow, H.W.W. Fisher, is being transferred to the Ship Repairs Department – he knows as much about ship repairs as railways.

'In afternoon went with Frank and Oliver Lucas to inspect the garage and our "pool" of Mechanised Transport Corps [MTC] headquarters there. Seems to be efficiently and economically run but in general the MTC is a bit of a nuisance, although they do their work very well. There was a lot of snobbishness about it at one time and the natural corollary is that the Ministry of Labour, who cannot stand any decently spoken or properly educated person, is doing its best to bring about the disbandment of the Corps. In London, in the regions and at some of the Royal Ordnance Factories [ROF], we have about 400 of them and want about 250 more but it is a tough struggle in face of the restrictions that the Ministry of Labour endeavours to impose.' The MTC had been formed at the beginning of 1939 as a voluntary organisation to provide women drivers for government departments and other organisations but by this time they were paid.

19 November 1942
'Beginning to glean some idea of the dimensions of the job – for instance our traffic sent by rail amounts to about 1½m tons a week excluding coal. It represents 60% of the total railway traffics, 90% being raw materials. Our conveyance charges amount to over £60m a year, divided as to railway £1,700,000 a month, road about £100,000 a month and shipping £3,500,000. We convey about 250,000 workers a day to and from the Royal Ordnance Factories in 480 trains and 6,200 buses – and have 2,700 buses of our own to distribute them inside the ROFs.'

20 November 1942

'Long talk with Muir Wilson who has decided that he could work with me, although his firm want him back. Told him would be glad to have his assistance. He seems to have found Patteson bombastic and untactful and indeed there seems to be a general feeling here that somehow he has managed to get the staff at sixes and sevens with each other. A great pity as Patteson is a perfectly good chap at heart. I am sure the main problem is due to speculation and false ideas acquired under the Beaverbrook regime. Probably too, some lack of knowledge of English transport methods and details caused him to use a certain amount of bluff – and Canadian bluff is pretty tough.'

21 November 1942

'Capt L.G. Burleigh, the Controller of Factory Transportation [on secondment from ICI], came in and had a yarn – seems first-rate chap. Asked me if I would like to meet the Factory Transport Officers when they are all here on Tuesday and I said, yes, I would like to show them I am a human being. He replied, "I think they will feel themselves damned lucky with their new chief."

24 November 1942

'Lunched with Mount. He is making a post-war railway memorandum and is most anxious to find out the contents of the one I have been preparing this last few months but I did not do much to enlighten him. Anyway, he is more on the physical side and is recommending the provision by the government of very large sums of money which the railways can spend after the war on new stations, good sheds etc. Took 23.45 train to Liverpool. Comfortable journey. Forbes-Smith came with me.' The journey was for Szlumper's first inspection.

25 November 1942

'Left train at Liverpool at 07.30 and walked to hotel for breakfast. Looked around the docks, not a busy day and a lack of "pep" everywhere. The docks are very untidy and slovenly and I always think this has a psychological effect on the workers.'

26 November 1942

'Another 09.30 start by car to our offices in Fountain Street – and very good offices they are but the Ministry of Works & Planning is trying to dispossess us so they can expand. To the Regional Controller, North West, Admiral Laurence Turner who was very friendly and wishful to be helpful. Then on to Sir William Chamberlain, the Regional Traffic Commissioner who spent some time telling me what a wonderful chap he is and then got down to discussing the many traffic problems in the area. He is busy trying to cut out cross-haulage of work people and endeavouring to get them re-allocated to ROFs near their homes. Back to our own offices to meet Kinghorn, the Port Transportation Officer who speaks six languages, a capable fellow without enough work to occupy him but we are trying to cure that by bringing him to London. Went all round the offices and met all the staff. They seem to be an efficient bunch and, although they are very cramped and working with the poverty-stricken furniture of the government, they all seem very happy.'

9 December 1942
'See from War Cabinet statistical digest that Ministry of Supply imports about 1,200,000 tons a month, largely raw materials. Long chat with Maundslay, Superintendent of Pontrilas Explosives Store [Herefordshire]. Very nice chap, one time Deputy General Manager of Egyptian State Railways. His depot is in course of being doubled in size and when it is finished and full, it will contain £11m worth of explosives.'

10 December 1942
This was the start of another inspection which took Szlumper and Muir Wilson to Manchester. They visited a new plant at Capenhurst in the Wirral Peninsula where shells were received, re-painted and stored. The following day they were at Chorley to see another stores and the ROF factory.

23 December 1942
'Gathered my clansmen around me at Charing Cross Hotel today and stood them lunch, thirteen of us. A very pleasant little party which I hope will get them closer to each other and help to stop some of the petty jealousy which seems to thrive among them. Today had my cheque £15,000 from SR in accordance with terms arranged. I am feeling opulent and now only have to try to live until 1 January to produce £1,200 a year reversion of my pension to Jessie.'

30 December 1942
'Went to see Malcolm McCorquodale [the Parliamentary Secretary to the Minister of Labour & National Service] to enlist his aid in fighting the cause of the Mechanised Transport Corps. Told him that so far as I could see, his department has its knife into the MTC, mainly because they speak decent English – they do their work most efficiently and conscientiously and if they are bled to death or get disheartened and quit, I shall be faced with the very difficult task of suddenly having to find 400 trained drivers. McCorquodale said he thought the difficulty was in the question of uniform – the War Office hated the MTC because they wore a khaki uniform but I pointed out that so did many organisations; and anyway the MTC wore distinguishing blue armlets.'

31 December 1942

'Political changes announced today. I am sorry we are losing Parliamentary Secretary, Ralph Assheton, who goes to Treasury, a very likeable chap, quick, intelligent, helpful, quite unlike a politician. Duncan Sandys (the Prime Minister's son-in-law) started today in place of Assheton. Started throwing his weight about. Wants a big car and soldier-driver. When explained that no big cars at Ministry of Supply, he was quite agreeable.'

1 January 1943

Szlumper was gazetted with the honorary rank of Major-General on his retirement from the Territorial Army. He did not comment on this in his diary but he did make stringent comments on the Honours List. Describing it as an insult to the railways which received just three MBEs, he noted that 'the regular civil servant had as usual looked after himself, in doing so removed practically every railway name from the list.'

5 January 1943

Assheton said goodbye to Szlumper who regretted his departure. He was not enthusiastic about his successor, Duncan Sandys, whom he described as a bumptious young man. He added that the Prime Minister's other son-in-law and radio comedian, Vic Oliver, would have been better.

15 January 1943

Szlumper noted that Sir William Rootes would be leaving the Ministry of Supply and returning to civilian life, having finished his task. He wrote, RIP to another Beaverbrook product, describing him as just a high pressure salesman.

9 February 1943

He noted that Duncan Sandys was continuing to be a nuisance. In particular, he was using his car for social purposes and after drinking one evening had been rude and abusive to his lady driver.

23 February 1943

In the evening he went with his wife to dinner with Gore-Browne who was despondent about the post-war railway situation as the LNER and the GWR would not shift from the idea of a reversion to the pre-war status plus pooling of railway investments only and therefore excluding road. Szlumper thought it was madness to think of such a policy succeeding but he could not see how the companies would see the daylight. A little mischievously, he told Gore-Browne that he had received an invitation to become a railway director? 'His eyes bulged more than usual until I told him it was only the Shropshire & Montgomery Railway.'

7 May 1943

'To lunch with Sir Ronald Matthews [LNER Chairman]. When inviting me, he said he wanted to clear up one or two points about the post-war transport problem. I find he is firmly fixed on a pool of net revenue. I warned him of its pitfalls and objections but do not think I shook him at all. He said each company had different ideas. The GWR felt there ought to be no difficulty in the railways reverting to their pre-war status. The LMS was 100% for a complete financial fusion and was going soon to put forward its own scheme if the other companies failed to make a move or come to a decision. The Southern had turned down the special committee's scheme but he did not know what they had in mind. I told him the end of it would be that the government would produce – and push down the companies' throats – a scheme which had been hatched by the Ministry of War Transport.'

11 May 1943

'Went to see Gore-Browne. He is very concerned at the inactivity of the railways about post-war and especially of the SR. He is angry at the chairman's laissez-faire attitude to anything that really matters and says some of the younger directors have strong feelings that the chairman should move out.'

15 July 1943

Szlumper did not mention that he lunched at the Worshipful Company of Shipwrights together with shipbuilder Wigham Richardson, Leathers and Ebbisham. But he did record that later Gore-Browne came to dinner, 'mournful and pathetic as ever' and that he was very despondent about the progress of post-war railway plans with no agreement amongst the railways. He told Szlumper that Ronald Matthews had had an interview with Leathers the previous day. Leathers had told him that he would prefer the principle of private ownership maintained if possible but he foresaw the probability of transport being sacrificed on the altar of appeasement to the socialist demand. He thought the railways should be preparing a scheme on the lines of a public corporation, run on a regional basis. If they did not get something ready, he thought they ran a risk of being swept away in a scheme of nationalisation.

12 November 1943

Szlumper attended an Institute of Transport luncheon meeting when Noel Baker, the Parliamentary Secretary at the Ministry of War Transport, was the speaker. Szlumper must have been pleased to hear the Minister's words – that the railways were carrying 50% more freight traffic and 50% more passenger traffic than before the war; in addition, they had run since the beginning of the war 150,000 special trains for troops and were now running 1,000 workers' special to the factories every day. Traffic moreover was still growing; and he believed that everyone was now agreed that something must be done in the future about the competition between rail and road and water. Szlumper recorded he had the 'doubtful pleasure of sitting next to Hurcomb who was much improved and now human.'

19 November 1943

'Took old Will Bishop to lunch with Leslie Dawes who has just flown back from USA. Bishop is obviously going downhill, getting quite deaf and woolly in the brain. Dawes on the other hand is just the same and just as ebullient. Today Forbes-Smith and his staff start to move to Bush House. Bound to react on efficiency with the department split in two but the daily visible swelling of government departments throws a continuous strain on accommodation.'

23 November 1943

Szlumper attended a symposium at the Institute of Civil Engineers on post-war transport. He spoke for twenty minutes in which he advanced the ideas of the Gore-Browne Committee. He noted that no one disagreed but there was little constructive discussion.

26 November 1943

Szlumper noted the announcement that T.E. Thomas was to be the General Manager of the LPTB while its engineer V.A.M. Robertson would go to the Southern to succeed Ellson as Chief Engineer at the end of the year. Describing them as two excellent appointments, he wrote that he had great respect for Thomas who had started life humbly and had mounted every advancement by sheer ability and by a helpful and human conduct towards his fellow men. He described Robertson as a first rate chap and a very capable engineer with a most agreeable disposition. 'The Southern Railway and his new colleagues are very fortunate to have secured him, especially after Ellson who has ability and many good points but also many points which have alienated his staff from him, a fiery temper, rudeness to subordinates and sometimes a distorted sense of justice. In addition, he has clung on to his job up to the age of sixty-eight, thus destroying all hopes of promotion to some of his officers; and has stubbornly avoided finding and training a successor from among his staff.'

16 December 1943

Szlumper attended the luncheon of the SR Directors and Officers at the Charing Cross Hotel Hotel. 'As usual, the chairman sat me on his right and was very flattering. He had to leave early and handed over the chair to Gore-Browne who gave one of his usual team-work happy family speeches, stressing the excellent work Missenden had put in. Missenden made a very nice reply and gave credit to all the officers and staff for the part they have played. Walker looked awfully bad, face sunken and ashen and figure bent on a rigid diet and not smoking. The chairman asked me about post-war aviation (in which I foresee a tremendous development). As T.E. Brain who has been Acting Secretary, has had a stroke and is finished, Holland-Martin thought it might be a good idea to try to get Leslie Dawes back from the Army to take up the post again and take under his wing the odds and sods of non-purely railway business such as aviation, hotels etc. I think this would be quite a good idea – Leslie has more energy than he can expend on the job of Secretary and the odds and sods are now rather subordinated to the railway outlook proper. Indeed, I think Missenden has never flown and consequently does not think there is anything in aviation. Holland-Martin asked what I thought of Denis Handover who has just been sacked from British Overseas Airways Corporation by that blustering bounder Critchley for faults which he had not committed. I told Holland-Martin that Handover knew more about air traffic operation than anyone. He has a rather angular manner and used to make a rather liberal use of the bottle but both these faults were correctable if indeed they still exist in him. Holland-Martin said they were thinking of appointing him as Air Adviser to the British Railways.' Handover's appointment was announced a few days later.

22 December 1943
Szlumper was at the luncheon at the Dorchester given by the four railways to celebrate the coming of age of the grouping of the railways. He described the speeches as distinctly good, noting that Holland-Martin told Leathers that they regarded him as trustee of the family estate; and that as trustee they looked to him to return the property at the end of the war.'

A message from the Prime Minister was read – it was that despite the heavy air raids, the railways by grim determination, unwavering courage and the constant resourcefulness of the railwaymen had enabled the results of damage to be overcome very speedily and communications restored without delay. According to a press report, Matthews took the opportunity to remind everyone of the need for a proper balance between the different modes of transport, particularly in their several responsibilities to the public, their charging powers, their rates of pay and hours of labour; and that before the war, there was too much irresponsible and often cut-throat competition which did no good to the transport industry as a whole. It also made it impossible to earn sufficient revenue for re-equipment and in the end would only result in a steadily deteriorating service to the public. But he added that too much planning, co-ordination and centralisation could have a stultifying effect.

25 January 1944

In his official capacity at the Ministry of Supply, Szlumper gave a paper 'The Trend of Transport' at a luncheon of the Engineering Industries Association. According to press reports, he said that in the brave new world to come, transport would be a major factor in the cost and efficiency of all industry and it must not be operated adversely to the national interest. The advantages of each form of transport had to be fully exploited to the good of the nation and the individual user but he believed that it was the duty of industrialists to see that transport in the post-war era would be reborn to suit these requirements. He was totally opposed to nationalisation which he thought would be a disastrous course with a horde of black-coated, stripe-trousered young men, full of theory and playing at trains or lorries when their knowledge of transport was limited to the cost of a season ticket from their home town to Whitehall. He was convinced that needs could not be met unless rail and road transport were married to live in harmony. He explained that his idea was that rail, road – both passenger and goods – canal and internal air services should all be brought under a central control with their expenditures brought into a common account.

26 January 1944

Szlumper noted that much publicity had been given in the press to his talk and with much approbation of his ideas in letters from friends and from people he did not know. But the four railway chairmen put a disclaimer into the press that his remarks were made on his own responsibility – and they did not agree with his ideas.

28 January 1944

'Hear this morning that Holland-Martin died quite suddenly in the night. He was a nice-natured man with good intentions but with not enough strength of character to carry them through. A certain amount of ability of the general knowledge sort which is not necessarily much use in the commercial world. But he was transparently honest and not self-seeking – I liked him.'

2 February 1944

'To Duncan Sandys at his request about my speech as a MP had put down a question in the House of Commons. Sandys said he would do his best to get the matter dealt with quietly but officially he could not support me as a civil servant was debarred from making public pronouncements on politically controversial subjects and must not give the idea he is personally strongly opposed to one policy or the other.' Later that day the question came when Labour MP, Ellis Smith, asked Duncan Sandys if Szlumper's statement had been sanctioned. The reply was to the negative whereupon the Stoke MP asked if it was the practice of civil servants to indulge in political controversy. Sandys agreed that the speech touched on certain matter of a highly controversial nature and was of a kind that should not have been given by a civil servant. He also stated that Szlumper was rendering valuable service to the department. In his diary, Szlumper noted that the Permanent Secretary had written him a nice letter that he had transgressed the rules. 'I went and made peace with him and told him as my remarks concerned post-war planning and as the Ministry of Supply had nothing to with transport, I did not think I had broken any rule but he pointed out that controversial subjects were banned for remarks by civil servants. So I apologised and said I would not do it until next time!'

4 August 1944
Szlumper was still making occasional inspections and during the first two weeks of August was in the North of England and Scotland.

17 October 1944
Duncan introduced Szlumper to John Martin from South Africa who explained that there were some difficulties on South African Railways. He had been commissioned by Smuts, the South African Prime Minister, to find an independent expert to report on the situation and asked Szlumper if he would do it. He would be provided with a private railway coach with a government aircraft at his disposal. He could name his own fee and could take a secretary and anyone else he wanted. Szlumper told him he did not want a fee. He was not wealthy but had stopped working for money and only worked for whom he liked. 'Duncan said Martin was the most influential man in South Africa – involved in mines, newspapers, a confidant of Smuts and a director of the Bank of England.' He immediately rang his wife who agreed to go with him. He later telephoned Martin to tell him he would go – he did not really want to disturb himself at that stage of the war but if it was felt he could be of any use to the Empire or to South Africa or to Smuts for whom he had the greatest admiration, he felt it was his duty to give his services willingly.'

12 November 1944
Szlumper and his wife departed from Birkenhead in a Dutch cargo boat with ten other passengers. They arrived in Cape Town on 3 December. Thereafter and until 25 January, his time was largely divided between Cape Town and Johannesburg. Szlumper's brief was to advise on the reorganisation of the railways and the expansion of the terminus in Johannesburg. He was also to report on the development of the foreshore at Cape Town as the state railway administration and the city council had different views. He left South Africa on 18 March 1945, arriving back in England on 17 April.

19 April 1945

This was Szlumper's first day back at his office when he recorded that nothing startling seemed to have happened. The following day he told Duncan that he would be leaving the Ministry.

14 May 1945

Szlumper was still busy at the Ministry of Supply and visited the Royal Ordnance Filling Factory at Burghfield near Reading. On 28 May, he went to Chilworth near Guildford. On 4 June he was at Chorley and four days later at Greenford and the Everlasting Tile Works at Iver.

25 July 1945

Szlumper had another overseas task when he left from a wharf near Tower Bridge on a cargo ship to Sweden. He arrived in Malmo on 1 August, after which a train was taken to Stockholm. The following day he started work, meeting shipping agents and manufacturers. On 3 August and for the next two days, he was at the town hall of the capital, discussing housing. The diaries do not reveal exactly what his mission was but it was probably related to the importation of prefabricated houses which Britain needed to ease its housing shortage. On 11 August, he returned to England by air.

14 August 1945

He saw Duncan to commiserate with him on his loss of seat in the House of Commons. The following day the war ended in Europe.

29 September 1945

There was no question about their journey to Pitlochry by car. It was for a holiday of just over two weeks together with Rubelia Raworth. It may have been a holiday but Szlumper still managed to 'look in' the following day at the ROF Filling Factory at Thorp Arch, West Yorkshire. Similarly, after leaving Pitlochry on the return on 12 October, he called at the Ministry office in Dundee; and four days later at the Newcastle office.

2 November 1945

This was Szlumper's last day at the Ministry of Supply but he continued focussing on what needed to be done until the very end. Thus he telephoned Sir Percival Robinson, the Permanent Secretary at the Ministry of Works, to tell him all he thought about Forbes-Smith and Lidwell who were both pursuing the same job, 'saying I felt it right in the interests of justice I should do so and in case he should have formed any false impressions due to window dressing on the part of Forbes-Smith. He was greatly obliged and said he would have no hesitation in giving the job to Lidwell.' He had a long chat with the new Minister, John Wilmot, who said he was grateful for what he had done and was sorry he was going, adding that he did not think he would be idle for long. This was followed by goodbyes to a number of his Civil Service colleagues. 'All expressed gratitude for my co-operation and all envied me, shaking the government dust from my feet.'

The customary farewell lunch was arranged when his sixteen deputies, controllers and directors and Sir George Turner of the War Office entertained him at the Hungaria Restaurant. The lunch was chaired by Forbes-Smith and a number of complimentary speeches were made. It was one of the senior officials who stressed that on no occasion had transport failed to meet requirements, no mean achievement. 'He liked my method of getting on with the job, unostentatiously and without bothering anyone – and my stories.' This was Szlumper's final diary entry.

5 November 1945
This was the official date of Szlumper's resignation and release from the Ministry of Supply. The year's end was in effect the close of another chapter in Szlumper's life but he did not know that his services would still be sought, albeit not by railways.

Chapter Nine

∂∞∂

Adieu

Leo Amery lost his seat in the House of Commons at the General Election in July 1945. His interest in politics continued but he never returned to Parliament. Nor did he return to the board of the railway in its last years before nationalisation. He did, however, return to some companies including Goodyear, Marks & Spencer, Trust & Loan of Canada and Gloucester Railway Carriage & Wagon. Without doubt, he had made a valuable good contribution to the working of the Southern Railway in the 1930s. Leo died peacefully in his sleep on 16 September 1955.

The end of 1945 was not the end of Szlumper's transport activities. It was not surprising that on the last day of 1947, he was at the dinner at the Charing Cross Hotel to mark the end of the Southern Railway. Many of his former colleagues were there including the man who had blocked his return to the railway, Eustace Missenden who in 1944 had been knighted. Former directors were also there including Gore-Browne who was the last chairman of the railway. In October 1948 Gilbert was at the first reunion dinner of the new Southern Railway Association.

Szlumper continued to serve the Worshipful Company of Shipwrights and in April 1947 was installed as Prime Warden. He also continued to support the Institute of Transport and, as chairman of its Premises Committee, was present at the opening in 1948 of its new home in Portland Place. In 1949 he became the London representative of the North British Locomotive Company of Glasgow. The same year he became a member of the new Air Transport Advisory Council. His support of the Territorial Army was undiminished and he often attended the annual dinners of the Engineer & Railway Staff Corps.

He never became involved in the affairs of the nationalised railway system but he did become chairman of the Atlantic Steam Navigation Company after the war, when freight services were started between England and Northern Ireland with converted tank landing ships. Upon the purchase of the company in 1954 by the British Transport Commission which controlled the railways, London Transport, bus companies and some road hauliers, Szlumper and other directors resigned.

His final railway action was on 30 October 1968 when he presided at the annual luncheon of the Southern Railway Association at the Charing Cross Hotel. Gilbert died peacefully at his home on 19 July 1969. It is not intended as an epitaph but the comments of one of his senior officers are not inappropriate.

In his autobiography, Sir John Elliot wrote that Szlumper handled his work with energy, combined with affability and good humour to all except those he generally described as bloody fools; and he was of a shining integrity with a loyalty to the principles of behaviour to the board he served and to a splendid team of officers. But Szlumper never obtained his potential as a General Manager for the reasons which his diary has revealed.

This focus on the diaries of a Southern Railway general manager and a director has been an attempt to provide an insight into the mindset of an outstanding railway manager and of a distinguished director of a great railway. It has also been an attempt to provide a new insight into various aspects of the inner working of the Southern Railway from 1932 and of certain government departments during the Second World War.

Bibliography

Primary Sources

BBC Written Archives, Caversham: Reith Diaries

Imperial War Museum, Lambeth: Szlumper Diaries

London Metropolitan Archives: Worshipful Company of Shipwrights

National Archives, Kew: Railway records

National Railway Museum, York: Szlumper photograph album

Southampton Local Studies & Maritime Library: Szlumper photograph album

Books

Amery, L.S., *My Political Life, Volume 3: The Unforgiving Years, 1929–1940* (Hutchinson, 1953).

Barnes, John (ed.) and Nicholson, David (ed.), *The Empire at Bay: The Leo Amery Diaries, 1929–1945* (Hutchinson, 1988).

Bonavia, Michael, *The History of the Southern Railway* (Unwin Hyman, 1987).

Day-Lewis, Sean, *Bulleid: Last Giant of Steam* (Allen & Unwin, 1964).

Oxford Dictionary of National Biography (Oxford University Press, 2004).

Elliot, Sir John, *On and Off the Rails* (Allen & Unwin, 1982).

Faber, David, *Speaking for England: Leo, Julian and John Amery. The Tragedy of a Political Family* (Simon & Schuster, 2005).

Jackson, Alan, 'Allhallows, or Incautious Southern Optimism Deflated.' (*Journal of Railway & Canal Historical Society*, July 1991).

Klapper, Charles, *Sir Herbert Walker's Southern Railway* (Ian Allan, 1973).

McIntyre, Ian, *The Expense of Glory: A Life of John Reith* (Harpercollins, 1995).

Periodicals

Modern Transport Magazine. Various issues

Railway Gazette. Various issues

Southern Railway Magazine. Various issues

Index